Power and the Self

Power and the Self deals with an important but neglected topic: the ways in which power is experienced by people, both as agents and as objects of the exercise of power. Each contributor presents a case study drawn from a variety of cultural contexts, including analyses of the appeal of Japanese superhero toys for American children; the conditions that lead to dehumanising treatment of patients in an American nursing home; the experiences of a Turkish immigrant woman in the Netherlands; the relation between the capacity to commit genocidal violence and "everyday forms of violence", and the psychological effects of colonialism in New Guinea and Samoa. The introduction provides a readable historical review and synthesis of the theoretical ideas that provide the context for the work presented in the book.

JEANNETTE MARIE MAGEO is Associate Professor of Anthropology at Washington State University. She has lived and done extensive fieldwork in the Pacific, and she writes about self, power, transvestitism, spirit possession, moral discourse and cultural history.

Publications of the Society for Psychological Anthropology

Publications of the Society for Psychological Anthropology is a joint initiative
of Cambridge University Press and the Society for Psychological Anthropology, a unit of the American Anthropological Association. The series has been
established to publish books in psychological anthropology and related fields
of cognitive anthropology, ethnopsychology, and cultural psychology. It includes works of original theory, empirical research, and edited collections that
address current issues. The creation of this series reflects a renewed interest
among culture theorists in ideas about the self, mind–body interaction, social
cognition, mental models, processes of cultural acquisition, motivation and
agency, gender and emotion.

1. Roy G. Dandrade and Claudia Strauss (eds.): *Human motives and cultural
   models*
2. Nancy Rosenberg (ed.): *Japanese sense of self*
3. Theodore Schwartz, Geoffrey M. White and Catherine A. Lutz (eds.):
   New directions in psychological anthropology
4. Barbara Diane Miller (ed.): *Sex and gender hierarchies*
5. Peter G. Stromberg: *Language and self-transformation*
6. Eleanor Hollengerg Chasdi (ed.): *Culture and human development*
7. Robert L. Winzeler: *Latah in Southeast Asia: the history and ethnography
   of a culture-bound syndrome*
8. John M. Ingham: *Psychological anthropology reconsidered*
9. Claudia Strauss and Naomi Quinn: *A cognitive theory of cultural meaning*
10. Alexander Laban Hinton: *Biocultural approaches to the emotions*
11. Antonius Robben and Marcelo Suarez-Orozc: *Cultures under siege: Col-
    lective violence and trauma in interdisciplinary perspectives*

Power and the Self

Edited by

Jeannette Marie Mageo

Washington State University

PUBLISHED BY THE PRESS SYNDICATE OF THE UNIVERSITY OF CAMBRIDGE
The Pitt Building, Trumpington Street, Cambridge, United Kingdom

CAMBRIDGE UNIVERSITY PRESS
The Edinburgh Building, Cambridge CB2 2RU, UK
40 West 20th Street, New York, NY 10011-4211, USA
477 Williamstown Road, Port Melbourne, VIC 3207, Australia
Ruiz de Alarcón 13, 28014 Madrid, Spain
Dock House, The Waterfront, Cape Town 8001, South Africa

http://www.cambridge.org

First published 2002

Printed in the United Kingdom at the University Press, Cambridge

Typeface Times 10/12 pt.   *System* LATEX 2$_\varepsilon$ [TB]

A catalogue record for this book is available from the British Library

Library of Congress Cataloguing in Publication data
Power and the self / edited by Jeannette Marie Mageo.
    p.   cm. – (Publications of the Society for Psychological Anthropology ; 12)
Includes bibliographical references and index.
ISBN 0 521 80839 1 – ISBN 0 521 00460 8 (pbk.)
1. Ethnopsychology.   2. Power (Social sciences) – Cross-cultural studies.
3. Self–Cross-cutural studies.   I. Mageo, Jeannette Marie.   II. Series.
GN502 .P68   2001   155.8 – dc21   2001035587

ISBN 0 521 80839 1 hardback
ISBN 0 521 00460 8 paperback

Contents

Acknowledgments

I thank Professor Naomi Quinn for her unrelenting guidance, encouragement and support of this project and the scholars who reviewed this manuscript for their many insightful suggestions on the overall shape of the volume, on the introduction, and on the chapter contributions.

List of contributors

JEANNETTE MAGEO
Anthropology Department
Washington State University

BRUCE M. KNAUFT
Department of Anthropology
Emory University

NANCY SCHEPER-HUGHES
Department of Anthropology
University of California at Berkeley

WILLIAM S. LACHICOTTE
The Department of Anthropology
The University of North Carolina
at Chapel Hill

ANNE ALLISON
Department of Cultural
Anthropology
Duke University

KATHERINE EWING
Department of Cultural Anthropology
Duke University

DOUGLAS DALTON
Department of Sociology and
Anthropology
Longwood College

HARRIET WHITEHEAD
Department of Cultural Anthropology
Duke University

CATHERINE LUTZ
The Department of Anthropology
The University of North Carolina at
Chapel Hill

GANANATH OBEYESEKERE
Anthropology Department
Princeton University

Foreword

Gananath Obeyesekere

This is a powerful collection of papers on "power and the self," many of them original and inspiring and making decisive contributions to the social construction of selfhood or identity. Power, as we know, has come into deep play in the human sciences largely owing to the work of Foucault but it has almost taken a life of its own analogous to sexuality in the Freudian scheme of things. And, as far as "self" is concerned, despite the bold attempt by Jeannette Mageo and Bruce Knauft in their Introduction to give this term theoretical significance, it seems to me that the term has less than a definitive provenance in our current thinking. Is self coterminous with the Freudian Ego; or with the "I" and "Me" of G. H. Mead or, closer to home, of the self-psychology of Heinz Kohut? Is it integrated in the sense of the Eriksonian ego identity; or is it fragmented, as some antipsychiatrist thinkers like R. D. Laing, or almost all postmodernists and unrepentant Nietzscheans and Buddhists from at least the fifth century BCE, seem to imagine? Can people live with fragmented selves? To complicate matters some ethnographers, following some dubious South Asian scholarship, have posited polarized selves, the permeable "dividual" selves of many non-Western societies and the individual selves of the European world. I am glad that the editors of this volume have not fallen into that trap because I am not sure whether the invention of another globalizing binary opposition on the lines of the West and the Rest enhances our knowledge of being human. This opposition may be another orientalist conception reified as theory. I wonder how many theorists of dividualism have looked into the genealogy of the word "dividual" or at least have gone back to Nietzsche's imaginative appraisal of this notion – not something about the rest but as a critique of the good old Western obsession with the Cartesian "I think, I am" and the reification of the Ego as the fixed point in the swirling ocean of methodological doubt.

What then is the contribution of the present volume? I think it is an indispensable forum for debating the very issues that I have tentatively raised. Hence this should serve as an excellent casebook for discussions in a wide variety of disciplines in the human sciences: history, politics, and cultural studies; and above all to those working in the area of cultural psychology and psychological anthropology. To put it differently, this volume ought to appeal to those of us concerned with issues of subjectivity and power and the creative (and uncreative) inter-play between them. Specifically, the discussions I have suggested could range from: a critique of the hitherto neglected idea of power in cultural psychology and psychological anthropology to the sophisticated theorizing of the self, in Mageo's chapter, to the detailed and finely grained ethnographic analyses that focus for the most part on individuals and the manner in which identities are constructed or "unconstructed" – if one might be permitted that neologism.

Several chapters deal with the "unconstructing" of self or personhood under the aegis of different power constellations. Take the case of Roger in William Lachicotte's chapter, who is pushed from one mode of treatment to another and from one diagnostic statement of his psychiatric condition to another. While we might think that this arbitrary shifting around of Roger's persona could have disastrous prognoses for his "illness," the patient himself weaves a precarious identity out of these conflicting and disturbingly irregular diagnoses of his con-dition. As his sense of personhood gets "unconstructed" he reconstructs it on another level. So is it with Mageo's Samoan women, caught between colonial and older indigenous values on female sexuality; as concepts of the self or no-tions of personhood gets "unconstructed" there is a progressive reconstitution of the self going on. Equally important is Katherine Ewing's sensitive exami-nation of Nergis, the Turkish guest worker in the Netherlands, caught between two or more worlds, the imagined traditional world of her parents and kinfolk and the openings that the modern European nation state provides for her self-development. Here again is an attempt to discard the fragments of a former self and to create new conceptions of selfhood based on her enveloping experience with Netherlands' modernity and finally arriving at a point in which she can be reconciled with her own folk and with herself as a modern professional.

On the dimension of self and power, I am impressed by the two extraordinary chapters by Anne Allison and Nancy Scheper-Hughes. Anne Allison deals with her son "playing with power" as he engages himself with the new morph toys introduced into the world market by Japan and producing a new phallic type of cyborgian hero. As Allison recognizes, this example has its wonderful parallel in Freud's own observation of his grandson, the little genius who invents the famous "fort da" ritual whereby he expresses the idea of separation and loss and provides a creative means of coping with it. Allison argues plausibly that morphing toys also provide creative vehicles for dealing with issues that cannot be verbalized or even communicated with adults. More disturbingly, Allison points out that the merchandising of these toys creates another space, a not-so-creative one, for late capitalism. However, these arguments ought not to close off a larger debate as to whether or not a culture of violence is created, reinforced or legitimated by these toys and their merchandising. For it is certainly possible for these toys to heal one sore, only to suppurate the body social with another. And it is here that Nancy Scheper-Hughes' chapter is disturbingly instructive.

Scheper-Hughes, like Freud and Allison, is dealing with her own loved ones, her parents who in their frail condition are interned in a place surreally named "The Happy Valley Nursing Home." There is no "fort da" here; no creative morphing with power. Quite the contrary, these omnipresent institutions of modern American society represent a "genocidal continuum," and Scheper-Hughes examines with an unflinching eye the closed arenas where peacetime genocidal activities take place and where an "institutional destruction of personhood" is being constantly enacted.

I have simply sampled some of the riches that this collection provides; there is not a single chapter here that I think does not make a contribution to the ethnographic interconnection between self/identity constructions, undoings and reconstitutions in the larger contexts of power plays and ploys.

1   Introduction: theorizing power and the self

Jeannette Marie Mageo and Bruce M. Knauft

Relations of power and the experience of people as subjects were two horizons of cultural theory in the late-twentieth century; they remain so in the twenty-first. But precisely how do these two sides of our human reality touch, mark, even remake one another? Where is the common ground between them? Our intellectual heritage from critical theory, all too often, has led us to focus upon the political structures and the economic circumstances in which people abide while disregarding the motivations, emotions, and meanings that modulate or vitalize these structures and circumstances. Our heritage from psychology and psychological anthropology all too often has led us to mistake the cross-cultural vicissitudes of people's sentiments and behaviors for reflections of a Western form of self. Not only have these two rich traditions frequently ignored each other's province; each has tended to define itself in opposition to the other. Until recently, many critical theorists were apt to denounce the very attempt to craft psychological models as essentializing – especially models emphasizing psychic universals of deep motivation or affect.[1] Meanwhile, many psychological anthropologists were apt to dismiss the study of power as derivative of a moral rather than an intellectual agenda.[2]

It grows ever more obvious that unmasking contemporary power relations and generating truly useful psychological models must lie at the confluence of these two heritages. As Fanon argued long ago (1967), one of the most crushing abilities of political oppression is to effect psychological forms of alienation in which people lose loyalty to themselves – to their profoundest feelings and to their love of self. Political perspectives that do not bring psychological theorizing into their purview must then be incomplete. Conversely, psychological theorizing that ignores power relations is liable to take human oppression for human nature. This liability has been evident since the dawn of modern Western psychological theory in ideas like Freud's "penis envy." It remains equally evident in evolutionary psychologists' recent insistence that natural selection favors females who are "slow to arouse sexually" and who are light-skinned (Ellis and Symons 1997:197–198; van den Berghe and Frost 1986).[3]

Earlier in this century there were noteworthy attempts to mediate this intellectual divide. Herbert Marcuse, a member of the post-Marxist Frankfurt

School, undertook a critical reading of Freud (1955).[4] For Marcuse, external power relations were internalized as cultural "performance principles," socially prescribed activities that channel human energy, demand renunciations, and universally disguise themselves as necessitated by the specter of scarcity (Marcuse 1955:35–40).[5] The result was "surplus repression" – gratuitous inhibitions that barred the unfolding of truly human capacities for love and for enjoyment.[6]

In anthropology, the culture and personality school took up the issue of power in studies of the psychologically coercive/permissive sides of culture. Their intent was to use ethnography to reformulate theories of the self – thereby broadening psychology's and anthropology's foundations as sciences. Margaret Mead, for example, offered a cultural relativist critique of Freud. Freud leaned towards the idea that conflict between the human body and the body politic was fundamental to the nature of society (1961:141–143). In *Coming of Age in Samoa*, Mead vindicated the utopian potentialities of human society that Freud disparaged. In Freud's vision, much human unhappiness derived from civilization's unrelenting demands upon the energies of the person, demands imprinted in the form of a punitive conscience, internalized through the agency of parental figures, and evident in sexual repression (1961). Mead countered that a culture could be created – in Samoa indeed had been created – which did not exploit but accommodated human needs.[7]

On the one rim of this power/self divide, then, we find continental philosophy on being and action oriented toward uncovering existential verities of the human condition. On the other rim we find American anthropology in the wake of Boas, seeking to use ethnography to gain purchase on Western personality theory. From these extraordinarily different vantage points began to emerge what is at least retrospectively a common ground. Alas, for decades to follow, mainstream psychological anthropologists obdurately insisted on conceptualizing emotional or cognitive schemata in synchronic/static terms – betraying lingering desires to unearth an ostensibly de-historicized and de-politicized human "nature" that was immune to the influences of power. Other anthropologists – in the tradition of Mead, Benedict, and Malinowski – continued to use ethnography to critique Western theory, but frequently abandoned the aims of these (often unacknowledged) predecessors. While earlier anthropologists had used ethnographic critique in the service of developing more comprehensive psychological models, these ethnographic deconstructionists were apt to insist that anthropology could at best aspire to a particularistic cultural relativism (cf. Strauss 2000). In the same spirit, many scholars who authored fashionable and intriguing studies of personhood or subjectivity in various cultures and historical periods seemed unwilling to acknowledge that their work had implications for psychological and anthropological theory.

Running in tandem with these divisive intellectual postures were efforts to develop the fertile space between the intellectual horizons of power and the self.

In this first chapter we begin by mapping this space. We then retrace fruitful twentieth-century efforts to cultivate it, which came from many disciplinary directions and out of which twenty-first century culture theory must grow. We also review the recent groundswell of interest in psychological anthropology in reaping this harvest – those works that are kindred to our own. In short, we aim to give this book, figuratively speaking, its homeland, its ancestors, and its family.

Mapping power and the self

To begin we offer a few words of definition concerning selfhood and power. *Self* we take to be as an encompassing domain term that includes within it virtually all aspects of personhood and subjectivity. The self is constituted by acts of identification with internal elements of experience and with persons, groups, and representations in the cultural world (Mageo 1998:3–36). As such, it is irrevocably implicated in power relations. *Identity* we take to be the sense of self that derives from acts of identification (Mageo 1998:38–39). In other words, one may identify with one's emotions, as women in Western societies were once encouraged to do (Lutz 1990), or with one's problem-solving capacity, as men were encouraged to do (Tannen 1991:49–50, 51–53). Both of these kinds of identification are with facets of the subjective inner self. Alternatively, one can identity with one's family, clan, lineage, or village – as people do in many of those societies anthropologists have traditionally studied. This is to construct identity through the relations of one's social self (e.g. Strathern 1990). In some societies people are encouraged initially to form subjective identifications, in others social identifications, but in the end both are ingredients in identity everywhere (Mageo 1998). Furthermore, while in any given culture certain experiences are likely to be hallmarked as definitive of personhood, the individual's personal identifications tend to shift continually, as in Stuart Hall's notion of "contextual suturing."

Hall (1996:3–6) emphasizes that identities are points of temporary attachment that "suture" an actor to a variety of subject-positions in the divergent social locations of his or her life. These subject-positions and social locations exist only within a specific cultural and historical context, which provokes situational ego-investments and fosters situational strategies. Subject-positions, furthermore, are galvanized by fields of cultural value and power that are embraced or resisted through the work of subjectivity – that is, by bringing one's own feelings and experience to bear on preexistent values and powers. This view is consonant in various ways with those taken by this book's authors.

Power can be conceived as socioeconomic and as entailing physical coercion or, alternatively, as an epistemic constraint of cultural assumption. The idea of power as socioeconomic or physical coercion easily associates with Max Weber's definition of power as individuals' ability to carry out their own will despite resistance – to exert *agency* over and against the will of others who oppose it (1958). By contrast, Foucauldian perspectives emphasize power as an epistemic function – the constraints of supposition and category that underpin our very form of knowledge and that shape the experience of being a subject. Unlike Weber, Foucault is interested in tracing how knowledge and subjectivity operate as power in an a priori sense – the power of epistemic assumption *within* which action takes place.[8]

Folk conceptions have long blended power-as-episteme and power-as-agency into one another, for example: (1) in the idea of gods and spirits influenced by magic, ritual, prayer, or (2) in notions of charisma or mana. Gods and spirits can be seen as personified versions of epistemic power subjected to human agency by religious practice. Thus ethics are one manifestation of an episteme and may be personified in a god to whom people may pray for justice. Prayer, then, is a method of exerting agency through the evocation of an episteme. Mana and charisma can be seen as epistemic manifestations invested in an individual's personality and body, resulting in enhanced agency. Mana is typically translated as efficacy, although it especially denotes an efficacy manifest in fertility (Firth 1949; Shore 1989:142). Chiefs who have mana are usually taken to personify epistemic values (to be noble, virile, and so forth), but correspondingly their hands and other body parts are believed to have the power to inflict or cure sickness. Obviously our discourse in this volume is intended to be philosophical/scientific rather than religious but, as in these folk models of power, we reject any essentialized dichotomy between social power and agency on the one hand, and epistemic power and experience on the other. Together, these "powers" constitute a continuum in which the poles are always shading into one another. Together they chart the domain of power in relation to self, as well as situating these essays and the theoretical frameworks on which they draw in a common field of inquiry.

Both social and epistemic uses of the word "power" can be found in Marx's nineteenth-century writings, the first well developed and the second incipient. For Marx, social power in the form of capital is dictated by who owns the means of production. But power also takes the form of ideology, the classic example of which is religion – the opium of the people. Twentieth-century critical theory sought to articulate these infrastructural and superstructural forms of power. Fully tracing the development of this twentieth-century problematic is a work that would require volumes, but it will be useful to briefly situate the major critical theorists drawn upon by the authors herein within its scope.

Twentieth-century articulations between power and the self

For contemporary anthropologists, one of the most influential early ideas that articulated agentive and epistemic power was Gramsci's notion of hegemony

([1948–1951]1992). Hegemony is what one might call "a naturalized ideology": that is, an ideology that presents itself not as a philosophy with which one might or might not agree, nor as a moral system that describes how things should be, but rather as the way the world *is*. Gramsci's idea that domination is as much a matter of worldview as it is of capital opened new questions. How did these structures of domination get inside people's heads? How were they naturalized? Early answers can be found in Vygotsky's activity theory ([1931]1992): interior worlds replay the culturally scripted social relations in which the child develops. Outer speech is interiorized and becomes conversation within the person, which then mediates between desire and the world. We tend to take what originates within us just as we take our bodies – as givens of the natural world.

Over the last several decades Foucault's considerations of how structures of domination are naturalized have pervaded anthropological studies. For Foucault, hegemony is constituted through discourse. Though discourses in the Foucauldian model tend to reflect the episteme of a specific historical-cultural world, they are "within" as well as without – a language of the self as well as for it. What enters into this language and what remains unspoken shape human awareness. Three internal agencies that are separate in Freud's model of the self – superego (conscience), ego (conscious awareness), and id (impulse) – are all implicitly constructed through discourse for Foucault. (1) Discourse operates as a form of surveillance, resembling Freud's superego – the internal, repressive presence of "civilization" that spawns "discontents." (2) Foucault's discourse also produces knowledge, resembling Freud's ego. Unlike this Freudian ego, however, discourse generates the very categories of knowledge and forms of facticity. In Victorian discourse, for example, sex became a new subject of knowledge and kind of fact (1990). (3) Discourse itself re-encodes, even recreates the domain of impulse. Nineteenth-century Victorian discourse incited a recognition and realization of sexuality in more personalized forms.

If Foucault cast light on the nature of hegemony, agency was bracketed in his work: those with social position and those without it were likewise compelled by discourses and the epistemes that authorized them. The issue of resistance was nonetheless pivotal for Foucault. Resistance was putatively the omnipresent "compatriot of power" (1980:142), but epistemes and resistances alike were ghostly entities – seemingly self-propelled. Indeed, it was unclear who was resisting just as it was irrelevant who was speaking. Here we had power forming the subject, but the subject rarely appeared as an agent.

Raymond Williams's notion of "counterhegemonic" discourse began to fill out the conceptual space highlighted by Foucault's idea of resistance (1977). Following Williams, scholars in Cultural Studies investigated discourses that, while sharing the basic terminology and presuppositions of dominant discourses, defined themselves in reaction to hegemony. Cultural theorists also began drawing heavily on Bakhtin's idea of heteroglossia ([1975]1981) at least in part because it complicated the hegemonic domination depicted so compellingly in Foucault's model of discourse. From a Bakhtinian viewpoint, hegemonies were never in any sense complete: there was always a multitude of discordant, contradictory "voices" within society and within the self. Bakhtin's voices engaged in and enlisted discourses but they were personified and dialogic rather than ghostly. Feminist and postcolonial theorists gave substance to these voices – showing us that they were embodied in people who had a particular social place, who featured certain forms of selfhood, and who were framed by a politics of knowledge.

Bourdieu's praxis theory (1992) also promised to supplement the deficiencies in Foucault's models of power and the self. If one considers "symbolic capital" as a kind of individual or in-group prerogative, *à la* Bourdieu, then epistemic power can be seen as symbolic capital writ large – enlarged in breadth and depth to encompass the very conditions of shared social being. Epistemic power is like a panopticon that oversees the most basic preconditions of subjectivity itself. But symbolic capital can also be seen as Foucauldian epistemes-writ-small, in fields of interaction where people exert social force on one another. Then epistemes become the unconscious orienting practices that play out in daily cultural life. As habitus, epistemes also code strategies for cultural games that can be played to advantage by actual people, especially those who are in privileged positions to begin with, and to a lesser extent those who would resist them (Bourdieu 1992:16–22). Further, in the form of symbolic capital epistemic power reappears as points that can be amassed like money in a game or like money in a fluctuating stock market and that can be drawn upon in future moves. In praxis theory, epistemes, while still tacit, became potential modes of practical domination rather than merely the invisible givens of consciousness and social life.

As resistance was central to conceptualizing power for Foucault, so was embodiment for Bourdieu. Bourdieu explored embodiment through his idea of "hexis," which in some ways seemed the physical instantiation of habitus. Yet it was unclear in his notion of hexis how bodily experience was an agentive mode of personhood. Hexis bore down like an imprinting stamp upon the body – shaping the movement styles, tastes, and bodily mannerisms of cultural groups and of gendered groups within cultures (1992:82, 87, 93–94). While Bourdieu's hexis helped to bridge the conceptual distance between epistemes and embodiment, it left obscure our ability to resist power relations as bodies.

The body is never mere corporeality. Everywhere the body encodes those aspects of the experiencing subject that are hypocognized in cultural ideologies and overlaid by dogma (e.g., Kleinman 1980, 1985; Martin 1987, 1995; Haraway 1993). Aspects of self that are impersonated by the body, figuratively speaking, are also those most likely to be excluded/repressed in epistemes.

As such the body is a likely nexus of personal resistance and of agency. Just as with Foucault's model of resistance, the conceptual space highlighted by Bourdieu's bodily hexis was incompletely filled in. Bourdieu's concept of practice accounted well for the person as exercising self-interested agency but not for the person as experiencing or resistant subject.[9] In this lack of attention to subjectivity, to feeling, to personal meaning, Bourdieu left untheorized our most private struggles, personal conflicts, and the small triumphs that remain so emotionally and intellectually sustaining.

Can psychological anthropology help traverse the conceptual distance between habitus and active agency on the one side, and affect and embodiment on the other? Let us begin our crossing by asking: has there been a model of the body as invested with agency or of the body as resisting power relations? In Freud's work, the id was an unconscious and instinctual dimension of our humanity and was a radical Other within the self. The id was the not-me that resisted civilization and was discontent almost in principle even if it was also, paradoxically, the very root of human happiness. From a more current perspective, the id could be rewritten, not as an inevitably alienated-dissociated part of self, but as a potential mode of affective and embodied agency that can be brought within the compass of conscious identification and intentionality. For decades now, feminists have explored a similar view in their models of emotion (Lutz, chapter 9). The core reactions of the affective/embodied self can become as mad, as hysterical, as destructive as any other part of the us; this potentiality has been documented by Freud, the psychoanalysts who succeeded him, and many others. Nevertheless, these reactions, deep within the self, are a vital source of human resistance to power relations. For present purposes, this affective/embodied form of agency may be roughly termed "psychic power." Psychic power is crucial to what Scheper-Hughes has called a "critical psychological anthropology" (1992a:221).

The implicit tension between epistemic and psychic power, we suspect, is one reason that psychological anthropology has trouble finding a center today amid an emphasis on universal motivations or cognitive structures, on one hand, and critical analyses that consider affect and identity on the other. This academic power struggle, so to speak, is not new but it persists. Like the layer-cake model of action bequeathed to anthropology from Parsons and Kroeber, these disagreements inappropriately stratify social life into discrete realms of the cultural or symbolic, the social or politico-economic, and the psychological.[10] By making the self the focus of analysis, and by considering agency *and* experience as dynamic and relational, the essays in this volume engage rather than undercut our sensitivity to articulations between such levels and to the nuances of psychic motivation. As such they create new ways for theorizing power and the self. In the process this book sheds light on some of the cardinal issues and tensions in contemporary anthropology.

Critical psychological anthropology: twenty-first century directions

Drawing lucid theoretical insights from original empirical research, the authors in this volume offer fresh approaches to opening the territory between the horizons of power and the self. The chapters wed a sweeping knowledge of relevant cultural theory with voices that emerge from case studies – studies that evince deep knowledge of and sympathy with their subjects. Together, we mean to fashion critical perspectives that encompass subjectivity and psychological models that comprehend power relations as an ever-present dimension of human psychology. We build on the existential and critical insights that cultural realities are created and recreated by human choices at the same time that human beings are shaped by political ideologies incorporated as modes of thinking, feeling, relating, performing, and embodiment. In line with the best work of the culture and personality school, and along with others in critical psychological anthropology, we use ethnopsychological studies of folk models to critique Western theory (see particularly Lutz 1988; Lutz and Abu-Lughod 1990; Scheper-Hughes 1992b).

Power and the Self is part of a larger effort in contemporary psychological anthropology to craft new theories by coupling local cognitive structures with broader conceptualizations of motivation, affect, and identity via the operation of epistemic and symbolic power (see for example Lave and Wenger 1991, Quinn and Strauss 1997, Holland *et al.* 1998, Mageo 1998).[11] Conversely, we combine critical theory and an advocacy for our subjects' human interests with theory-making about the self. These chapters trace the experiential journeys through which people achieve embodied, emotive, and strategic forms of agency within fields of social and epistemic power. They illustrate that forms of agency are intimately bound-up with the human capacity to innovate upon if not to reimagine existing schemata; these innovations and reimaginings are integral to the activity of self-making.

Ethnographic revelations emerge from these juxtapositions of power and the self, both in individual cases and in their relationship to each other. Our point is to use ethnography to discover non-essentializing ways of mapping structures and practices of power as they interact with cognitive and emotional schemata and with human experience. Doing so presents inherent problems because power and the self can each produce distortive knowledge about the world. Recent critiques of scientific inquiry expand upon Gramsci's idea of hegemony by demonstrating *à la* Foucault that power relations influence the questions asked, the manner in which questions are posed, and what counts as evidence in answer.[12] Psychological anthropologists have long argued that our sense of self is indelibly colored by the psychological economies in which we develop.[13] Working at objectivity in cultural terrain is like assuming an ongoing counter-transference on the part of the investigator, who must forever deconstruct the phenomena she observes but also her position as observer, shaded as it inevitably is by power relations and culturally specific psychological orientations.

Part I – Power differentials in the US

Part I begins in the cultural territory from which its authors originate. Here we focus on institutionalized forms of social power in the US, the epistemes that sanction them, and the personal dramas through which people exert agency within the confines of institutions and epistemes. American studies of the self are apt to envision power as at odds with individuals. Indeed, from Emerson's "Self Reliance" to Lucas's "Star Wars," Americans have tended to valorize the individual. In contrast, listen to an early Chinese philosopher of the state, Mo Tzu (479–438 BC).

In the beginning . . . [p]eople existed as individuals. . . . [There were] a thousand concepts of right for a thousand men, and so on until there were a countless number of concepts of right for a countless number of men. All of them considered their own concepts . . . as correct and other people's concepts as wrong. And there was strife among the strong and quarrels among the weak. Thereupon Heaven wished to unify all concepts of right in the world. The worthy was therefore selected and made an emperor (quoted in Chan 1963:230).

Here individuality is a suspect renegade force at odds with heavenly order.[14] When people identify primarily with their groups, individualism is perceived as the source of social discord, as in Mo Tzu's origin story. Alternatively, inasmuch as people identify with individualism they dissociate group needs, which reappear in projected form as autonomous demonized powers: organized crime, communism, big government, and evil empires. This does not negate American studies' view that the state jeopardizes individuals' human needs and legitimate interests. Rather, it is a necessary realization that all vantagepoints, including those in this volume, are culturally positioned. In a Foucauldian sense, the American conceptualization of "the individual versus social power" is a site for the production of knowledge.

Chapter 2, Scheper-Hughes's "The Genocidal Continuum," argues war crimes like genocide dramatically illustrate a failure to regard others as human, but this failure also underlies many peace-time practices. Through their treatment in insane asylums or retirement homes, for example, inmates may be reduced to the status of objects out of place that need to be severed from society like the mad in Foucault's *Madness and Civilization* (1965). Hsu (1961) has argued that Americans take self-reliance as a basic marker of personhood; correspondingly, socially dependent categories of people are in jeopardy of being treated as non-persons. Scheper-Hughes concludes with her own radical version of participant-observation: a visit to her beloved aged parents who are institutionalized in a state-run "home." There she confronts the questions: what can affective/embodied resistance mean when one must rely on agents of the state to perform even one's most intimate bodily functions? How can we survive in any meaningful sense as human subjects within contracting structures of social and epistemic power?

In Lachicotte's chapter ("Intimate Powers, Public Selves") our focus shifts to the late modern relatives of the inmates of earlier insane asylums – psychiatric outpatients. Here the state-as-institution is a Kafkaesque field in which it is nonetheless possible to exercise a degree of agency. Exploring the case of Roger – who is variously pronounced "obsessive-compulsive," "bipolar," "schizoid," "borderline," and so forth – Lachicotte considers the incipient heteroglossic character of psychiatric discourse. Although constituted to control people like Roger, psychiatric discourse turns out to be a source of symbolic capital that he can appropriate for his own ends. Lachicotte uses Bakhtin's view of the heteroglossic nature of discourses like Roger's to develop the concept of a "space of authoring" within which agency and resistance are possible. Drawing on Vygotsky for perspective on Roger's discursive practice, Lachicotte emphasizes the recursive rather than oppositional relationship between the social as the outward repetition of psychic life, and subjectivity as the interiorization of the social. The kind of psychic distance that Obeyesekere (1981, 1990) previously dichotomized as the difference between private identity symbols and public ones is here made a continuum – or better, it turns dialogic. This dialog crisscrosses the boundary between the ostensible self and the omnipresent social other. As such, social and personal life do not disappear one into the other; rather, as Lachicotte puts it, they subsist as "two mediations of human existence."

To extend this idiom, there are ways that a dialogic notion of identity can be used to comprehend human existence in ever-widening circles that spiral out from what Gilles Deleuze would call "pleats" or "folds" – those changing relationships that constitute membranes between the self and a world of external powers (1993). Analysis can move in widening arcs that touch progressively on interiorized motivational structures as well as the wider social and epistemic forces that interact with them and form their context. Here identity is constituted at the boundary between internalized and externalized forces – operating in that zone of contact between social and epistemic power, and the motivational responses that engage these as either accommodation or resistance. The pleats or folds of the self shift accordingly, sometimes pushing the envelope of subjectivity as resistance against established dogma and sometimes retreating inward in defense.

Part II – Transnational psychologies

Transnationalism is an important late-modern venue for critical theorization of power, yet the psychologies that derive from transnational experience are little studied. There are two ways one might consider the flows that are constitutive of transnationalism: the flow of global capitalism lubricated by the media, and the flow of people, particularly immigrants, across state boundaries. Part II investigates these flows and their relevance to power and the self through multinational marketing by Japanese manufacturers of children's toys (Chapter 4, Allison's "Playing with Power") and the life-history of a Turkish immigrant making her way in Dutch bourgeois society (Chapter 5, Ewing's "Consciousness of the State and the Experience of Self").

Like fantasy figures of global evil in James Bond or Superman or Batman movies, globalized epistemes in multinational marketing reflect an ominous constellation of power. The culture mixing that is inevitable in transcultural contexts, however, also intensifies heteroglossia in social and personal life. The essays in Part II suggest that this heteroglossia intensifies conflict within the self, even while it expands opportunities to play epistemes against one another and multiplies possibilities for agency. At the same time, larger aspirations for heightened personal success in the spiral of late modernity almost serve as a kind of Bakhtinian "superaddressee," against which alternative values and audiences are ultimately subordinated. The self in transnational perspective, moreover, raises anew questions as to what we share cross-culturally. These commonalities are not imagined as residing in essentialized cultures. Rather in transnational perspective they are discovered in cultural interactions within historical time as shared dimensions of our humanity (and inhumanity) are inflected by power relations. Transnationalism meaningfully re-draws lines of human difference and connection.

Taking us into their subjects' bodies and emotions – Allison, those of her own son, Adam, and Ewing, those of her friend Nergis – these essays depict the relentless presence of epistemic and social power in globalized human life. Bombarded with commercial indoctrination from the beginning of life, it may seem to children, as the Borg declare in *Star Trek*, "Resistance is futile!" In transit from one culture to another, one might think that Nergis has no leverage, no stable cultural standpoint from which to resist. Yet both essays reveal possibilities for embodied, affective *and* strategic agency opened by the complexities of globalization.

Adam and Nergis live betwixt and between cultural worlds; in Adam's case between a local and a global world, in Nergis's case between a Turkish and a Dutch one. Children playing with power in a realm of globalized commercialism and members of migrant groups inhabiting what Anzaldua has eloquently called "borderlands" (1999) are pulled in two (or more) directions at once. They discover and develop themselves from this liminal position. Their condition is postmodern; they live with differences and with attendant ambivalences as cultural givens that cannot be resolved. Previous theorizations of this condition, for example Jameson's (1981), portray the associated psychology as one-dimensional – personal affect flattened and personal narrative broken into disjunctive fragments lacking a center.[15] Allison's and Ewing's subjects are nothing like this; their reactions are transparently, touchingly human and familiar. But they are also reacting in and to a power milieu that forecloses certain possibilities and opens others; these need to be understood to fathom their distinctive cultural psychologies. Their psychologies may not be those of a "traveling culture" (Clifford 1992), but they are the psychologies of cultures that travel.

Part III – Colonial encounters: power/history/self

In the second half of the twentieth century, colonial studies were central to Marxist and post-Marxist analyses of power relations. An initial tendency in these studies was to see the colonized as socially disempowered – victims of progress with the term progress placed in quotation marks (Bodley 1975). Later works (see for example Taussig 1980; Wolf 1982; Comaroff and Comaroff 1991, 1992; Obeyesekere 1992) emphasized epistemic aspects of colonialism and resistance to power relations. Part III investigates how indigenous cognitive, emotive, and bodily schemata have been compromised by colonial epistemes but also how people renew themselves in those cultural encounters that punctuate historical experience.

In Chapter 6 ("Spirit, Self, and Power"), Dalton examines the colonial undermining of precolonial discourses and ways of emoting among the Rawa speakers of Papua New Guinea. Dalton argues that this produced two divergent forms of "normative schizophrenia" that resemble two linguistic disorders outlined by Jakobson (1971). Each of these linguistic disorders corresponds to the dropping away of one element of logical thinking, which is then replaced by fantasy processes. Two intriguing case studies illustrate these linguistic disorders – the case of an aspiring but disequilibrated cargo cult leader, Meyango, and that of a raskol gang leader, Tapa.

In chapter 7, "Self Models and Sexual Agency," Mageo traces the colonial decay and postcolonial recreation of Samoan women's traditional modes of discourse and agency. She argues that in nineteenth-century England, moral agency was attributed to women while agency for achievement was attributed to men. Attributions of agency had sexual correlatives; moral sexual agency was exercised by what one did *not* do – for example by not having sex prior to marriage. These gendered attributions traveled to Samoa with the London Missionary Society and gradually compromised Samoan women's sex roles, which Samoan men then took up in parodic and ludic forms of transvestism. In face of a colonial shrinkage of their discourse, sexual agency, and modes of political achievement, some women retreated into a psychic realm of spirit possession. There, women continued to act out the old modes of embodiment and discourse. The case Mageo explores, that of her former Samoan sister-in-law

Easter, shows how one woman retrieves agency from the spirit realm, partially revising colonial epistemes.

Part IV – Reading power against the grain

Part IV is dedicated to the idea that theory-making must always go hand-in-hand with critical reflexivity. It is only by continual efforts to remain critical towards one's own premises that the activity of theory-making can remain an open process. The volume's last two essays return to the reflexive stance of Part I but in a new key. First we ask: to what extent are the questions we pose on power and the self an artifact of our own cultural positioning? After all, concerns with power and the self descend to us from a Western tradition that stretches back at least to Hobbes's *Leviathan* (1973) and Rousseau's *Social Contract* (1923). Second we ask: is our way of conceptualizing selves as exercising meaningful agency *vis-à-vis* social and epistemic power a cultural construction that descends from these same Western sources?

Chapter 8, Whitehead's "Eager Subjects, Reluctant Powers," questions whether power is universally desired or is merely a Western obsession, sister to our obsession with the self – a mania to which the Seltaman of Papua New Guinea have not succumbed. Whitehead argues that in worlds where social power is not consolidated and when people are allowed to cultivate satisfying dependency relations early in life, they may be happiest riding "under the wing of power." Reciprocally, those taking power must be persuaded and cajoled to do so. Acceding to ritual power can be onerous; it imposes difficult, sometimes impossible, responsibilities.

The concluding chapter, Lutz's "Feminist Emotions," considers how a depreciative psychological designation – "Women are emotional" – became an epistemic ground within late-twentieth-century Western society. The self and power problematic has been fundamental to the history of feminist discourse on emotion and its critical analysis has helped provide a notion of self from which women have begun to renegotiate power relations. In turn, this feminist tradition is singularly weighty for the present volume; it explores what we have called psychic power in its own right – albeit in different terms than have traditionally been considered in psychological anthropology. From the perspective of late-twentieth-century feminist thought on emotion, an understanding of psychic power can help us contend against the social power of others and against the epistemes that would determine our perceptions, cognitions, motivations, and goals. This critical grasp of emotion, furthermore, has been an important arena for reformulating power relations and the self not only in Western societies but more widely.

At the beginning of each chapter we will discuss at greater length how these contributions bear on areas of current anthropological investigation. For the remainder of chapter 1, we confine ourselves to previewing cross-cutting themes and to a synthetic analysis of problems that recur throughout these chapters – one might call them landmarks that identify that middle ground between power and the self.

Power in experience

The people of whom we write come from extraordinarily different cultures and political circumstances. Nevertheless they have existential problems in common and there are significant commonalities in their efforts to solve these problems. Our ethnographic protagonists push against if not split from the quotidian reality of their social worlds. Lachicotte's protagonist, Roger, slips into a fantasized world of psychiatric esoterica that protects him from the normal demands of social life. Whitehead's Seltaman move off into a world of ritual secrets, whose tortures and shared imaginings cordon cult members off from everyday life and from those (women and children) who inhabit it. Allison's son Adam along with all those children who follow the pied piper's call of commercialized toys-games-films escapes the limited autonomy of childhood and family in the late-modern capitalist world. Ewing's Nergis begins to revise the social power relations in which she lives by splitting with her family, her husband, her culture – reaching the point of transition in her trip to an amusement park, a toyland, which symbolizes fantasy life, just as toys do for Allison's son Adam. It is there that Nergis in her own mind, as well as socially, confronts her demons – in the form of stares by young Turkish men – with impunity. Samoan girls enter a world of spirits in which differences between Western and Samoan values are reconcilable counterpoints. Dalton's cargo cult and raskol gang-leaders likewise retreat from the contradictions that their colonially wracked social world visits upon them to a fantastic realm. There, cultural contradictions do not weigh people down in paralyzing depression so much as stimulate creative if not manic reimaginings of social schemata.

In these chapters one often finds not just individuals but whole groups that split with normal social life, retreating into the fantastic. There people reconnect with their own psychic power – with emotionally incandescent and embodied reactions to the forces that buffet them in daily life. This infusion of psychic power helps people revise epistemic and social relations, suggesting that fantasy can serve as a realm for "thinking through culture," in Shweder's terms, or for the "work of culture" in Obeyesekere's – a creative space in which personal culture can be transformed.[16] In other words psychological departures are a necessary preface to creating a "space of authoring" (Lachicotte, chapter 3).

Creating this "space" not only necessitates a break with the social world but also a breaking down of what Ewing calls the actors' own fragile "illusion of wholeness" (1990). Freud believed that the function of the ego is to mediate

between the libidinous dimension of the self and conscience, which is tantamount to the internalized laws of social worlds (1961). When the ego is inadequate to this task, as in mental illness, a symptom replaces the conscious self
in this medial position. Dreams, for Freud, also play this medial role and are in
this sense the universal "symptom" (1955). Rather than consciously integrating impulses and inhibitions, dreams and symptoms symbolically concatenate
otherwise disjointed territories of the self (Freud 1955; 1966:394, 358–360).
Delusional worlds, even flights of fantasy, serve the same purpose. Freud saw
symptoms, dreams, and delusions as regressive, but he also believed that in certain cases regression could serve the self. It offered a safe harbor where people
could discover mediations that they had previously failed to find, not just to
ride out the proverbial storm, but to productively change in the process. Indeed
this was the point of psychoanalysis.

   It is in the imaginal realm that people regain touch with psychic power and
discover avenues of agency within fields of social and epistemic power. Critical
psychoanalytic anthropology is helpful in analyzing the nature of this process.[17]
Obeyesekere argues that conflicted individuals sometimes orchestrate their most
private experiences in public symbolic idioms provided by culture (1981, 1990).
Doing so enables them to find a meaningful place for their painful, disorienting
personal histories within the social order. For Obeyesekere this orchestration
is the way back from personal alienation and disempowerment to social integration and empowerment. His Sinhalese female celibate ascetics, for example,
begin as social victims but through fantasy articulate crushing life experiences
with religious symbols. In the process, they exponentially increase their own
symbolic capital and mediate social power as it bears upon their lives. These
ascetics use their "calling" to exert freedoms that other women in their societies
do not share: they exercise a high degree of choice in sexual matters, they have
respected careers and independent incomes. This articulation of psychological
experience and shared idioms carries the weight of being non-normative and
to some extent stigmatized yet empowers its authors in significant respects;
it is also a fertile source of epistemic change (Obeyesekere 1981:169–183;
cf. Knauft 1996:225–230; Mageo 1994:417–427; 1998:164–190, 218–239).[18]

   For Obeyesekere, epistemic change originates in the individual and is born of
tragic personal histories. The studies in this volume suggest that the epistemic
revisioning that Obeyesekere calls the work of culture can also be born of shared
social histories, like those of Rawa-speakers, or of Samoan Girls, or of children
coping with global capitalism.[19] But epistemic revisioning is also the work of
subjectivity (to expand Hall's term) and can refract creatively and disruptively
against various dimensions of power. Through the temporal twists of these
two inextricably interwoven projects, the work of culture and of subjectivity,
individuals and their groups along with them can powerfully re-author their
identities in ways that bear upon epistemic and social power.[20]

The question is: how is this possibility for change realized, or how does it fail to be realized? How do groups overwhelmed by the conflict between social or epistemic power and by their own psychic processes, marooned in personal fantasies that break with cultural epistemes and social power relations, effectively re-engage both? How does a generation (Allison's son Adam's generation), or a gendered cultural subgroup (Rawa men or Samoan women) find meaning or, alternatively, how do they fail to do so? How do they reconstitute Ewing's fragile "illusion of wholeness," not only within the self but also social cohesiveness between self and world?

Scheper-Hughes poses this question in her moving personal cry of despair at the end of her essay, which seems to offer no way out of "Happy Valley." This is why Roger is both a heroic and a pathetic figure: like some Alice forever in Wonderland, he cannot find the way out. Lost in fantasy, Roger subverts his own relation to the real, which he nonetheless endlessly seeks through the labyrinthine passageways of psychiatric discourse. He caricatures the discovery of the key, a relation between private experience and shared epistemes, in his attempts at self-analysis. Roger applies terms that would ordinarily place the patient's "delusions" or "neurosis" in relation to socially shared schemata of responsible adulthood, but he uses them to avoid responsibility – avoiding direct confrontations with power in what seems a quasi-conscious form of discursive guerrilla warfare.

Like Roger, Whitehead's Seltaman seem unable to overcome a profound ambivalence about power and about their own (potential) power and so would rather play power games than take real world roles invested with responsibilities. On the one hand, ambivalence results in seeking: young men seek power in fantasies made real by painful initiatory ordeals. On the other hand, ambivalence results in avoiding: mature men prefer to play with power in the imaginal realm, eschewing power roles in social life.

Allison's morphing tales return their hero/ines to everyday life – the seemingly insurmountable daily problems of development with which their stories open magically resolved. But one must ask: to what extent do these stories actually map such returns or merely proffer an empty promise of re-engagement, a promise that is addictive by virtue of the fact that it is never realized. Is it this addictive quality that is exploited to the hilt by manufacturers in multinational corporations? Allison's fantasy-possessed children are undergoing a commercial form of colonization. Like Dalton's colonized Rawa, they seem to be members of a late-modern cargo cult, desiring the latest toy in an action-figure series with the intensity of devotees. Do they, too, like the Rawa, suffer from normative schizophrenia, attempting to appropriate fantasized but non-existent capacities represented by their techo-enhanced heroes? Allison's son's partial deafness is a wonderful metaphor for the poignant and real problems posed by children's sense of limitation in face of the overwhelming social worlds that humans have created and the alienation that these precipitate, throwing them back on fantasy. How many children who play with action-figures would rather confine themselves to playing power games, as do Roger and the Seltaman; how many children are driven to do so by the toys they buy?

In the West, questions about the relation between public and private symbols, or between social life and fantasy life, are also ones concerning the relation between rationalist discourses and personal-emotional ones. In the writings of Lutz's feminists, emotion appears as a dimension of self that is open to the imagination rather than, as Enlightenment forms of reason, turning upon a disarticulation of logic and fantasy. Emotion is a holistic form of mind, constituted of ideas, feelings, and sensations, and stimulated by external and internal images (see Hillman 1964). The feminists of whom Lutz writes argue that emotion also organizes data as wholes.[21] Does this functional isomorphism mean that emotion is a form of mind linked to the imagination through which new wholes can be created? If so, then emotion has a central place in charting the way back from those splits through which people enter into more agentive relations to power as it is embedded in internalized schemata and in social relations. The volume's chapters thus reveal a temporal dialectic between affective and embodied resistance to power *and* the re-absorption of subjectivity into power-inflected fields.

For Easter, whose spirit experiences are explored in Mageo's chapter, talk about spirits is reminiscent of psychoanalytic "talking cures" that involve emotive work. Easter's narrative is a process of thinking about and through emotions, a process that takes place in fantasy life. Yet her spirit talk articulates new modes of agency that are efficacious in the social world. The potent emotions that animate Easter's story seem to hold the key to culling symbolic capital as well as rewriting epistemes (while at the same time, her emotions towards her father complicate her passage). Perhaps Ewing's Nergis finds the way back most successfully. She temporarily relinquishes her emotional ties – to her unwanted husband certainly, but also to her son and parents – but not to the emotions that anchor these people within her. As in Easter's case, Nergis finds a relation between her dreams and her social realities that appears to turn on a talking cure. This involves reliving the emotional past in imagination with the friends who take her in during her "liminal" period – that period during which she has broken with her natal sociocultural world.

Nergis' ultimate reengagement, furthermore, is coincident with finding ways to exercise social power while sustaining relations with loved others. Nergis evinces a remarkable ability to recapture, in Ewing's terms, an illusion of wholeness, not only wholeness within the self, but a social wholeness in which the self is situated in a shared world. This is how we would define the work of subjectivity but it is also the work of culture. Nergis does not act only for herself; her efforts produce a new way of being-in-culture for younger relatives.

They are allowed, even supported, to continue their education because of Nergis. Identity mediations like that which Nergis achieves may be adopted by ever-widening circles of social others, forming new "membranes" between the self and external powers.

Genders–identities–contexts

Other themes that traverse this book call for at least momentary reflection. Among the most obvious is gender. Studying gender in the context of power and the self highlights its fluid and symbolic character, but also gender's sexual underpinnings that are fed by what we have termed psychic power. In turn, the issue of gender in these chapters makes obvious how social and epistemic power plays a role in self-construction (and its tribulations).

In Allison's chapter, phallized images of what was once male gender become the second skin of superhero/ines of both genders – in Sailor Moon's case, transmuting into a costume of a highly eroticized femininity. In Mageo's chapter, culture history turns upon male role-play with eroticized images of what was once female gender. Mageo considers colonial adulterations of traditional sex roles, which Samoans convert in entertainments into ironic reflections on gender difference. Ewing's Nergis shows how multiple gender models, juxtaposed in time and space by transnational experience, complicate gender as a facet of personal identity but also make it a source of strategic possibilities. Mageo's, Ewing's, and Dalton's chapters highlight the recursive role of gender in self-configuration. Gender is also part of the symbolic capital that Easter, Nergis, and Dalton's cargo cult and raskol gang leaders use to develop a personal sense of self, yet through this development each revises cultural gender models and the epistemes from which they derive. Mageo argues that gendered discourses tend to articulate with cultural domains – most saliently public/private in Anglo-American cultures or hierarchical/peer in Samoan culture – and that shared understandings of these domains shift in parallel with gender models through cultural history.

In Lutz's chapter, gendered models of self become a mode of transit from pejorative characterizations of female inferiority to novel constellations of self-hood, knowledge, and power. Peripheral peoples, especially women, have emotions and selfhoods nested in them that were marginalized by an Enlightenment privileging of reason. Lutz's history shows that latent in marginalized portions of self are critical perspectives on the center that can be enlisted by those who lack symbolic capital and are exiled from social power. In this sense Lutz's chapter raises another issue of supreme salience in the volume – the relation between identity and episteme.

Like Lachicotte, Lutz shows how epistemes provide languages and tropes that can be played back against themselves, constituting what we might call "counter-identities." Scheper-Hughes' chapter surveys processes of identity erosion within epistemic power, specifically the personal erosion of her father's and her own identity. In Dalton's chapter, colonial epistemes erode indigenous identities and even generate aberrant and culturally dysfunctional identities. Lachicotte's Roger illustrates how the episteme of the sovereign individual can be bent and even cartooned in the process of identity construction. In Whitehead's chapter the episteme-as-religious-ideology is itself colonized for purposes of identity construction and hence fails to serve the purposes of social power. For her Seltaman, social power becomes little more than an identity trapping and an ambiguous trapping at that: those who have social power are suspected of trafficking in sorcery and their reputations are besmirched.

Lastly, many of the volume's chapters reveal how relations between the self and power pivot on the issue of context. In Scheper-Hughes' chapter, epistemes are most constricting when, in institutionalized forms, they freeze the normal flux of contexts. Her parents' retirement home suffers from a uniformity of context that seems to paralyze possibilities for self-construction. One can only die at "Happy Valley"; one can change neither oneself nor social nor epistemic power relations. In Lachicotte's essay, multiple psychiatric discourses and multiple life contexts (with spouse, with doctors, etc.) open the possibility of subverting social and epistemic powers. In Ewing's chapter, cultural contexts juxtaposed by transnational experience open inventive possibilities for self-construction and transform fixed epistemic and social power relations into negotiable realities. In Allison's chapter, morphing is a trope for traveling between contexts, the fantasized and the real, macro and micro, personal and social, as well as the medium of self-construction. Traditional contexts corrupted by colonial experience in Dalton's chapter almost irreparably confuse the activity of self-construction. For Samoans in Mageo's chapter, a colonial corruption of traditional contexts generates a recreative play with identity through which Samoan women in spirit possession negotiate their relation to male social domination and Samoan men in popular entertainments negotiate their relation to Western epistemes.

Much more could be said about these chapters, their contribution to bridging the distance between power and the self in psychological anthropology, in cultural psychology, even more broadly in studies of history/power/culture, and in culture theory. But it is time to let these fine essays speak for themselves.

NOTES

1. Essentialist ideas presuppose that fundamental characteristics are possessed by human beings, that there is a reliably fixed "human nature" beneath cultural and historical variation (Bocock 1986:112–117).

2. See for example the debate on objectivity and militancy in *Current Anthropology* 1995, 36(3):399–440, particularly Crapanzano's commentary (1995:399–408).

3. On these tendencies in evolutionary social science see further Mageo and Stone n.d.

4. Habermas (a student of Gadamer, another member of the Frankfurt School) later investigated the sphere of communicative action, which gave him a deep interest in psychoanalytic concepts of illusion such as projection and rationalization (1972).

5. "Performance principles" are the guises the reality principle assumes in different societies. This is not Freud's reality principle, although Marcuse's concept builds on Freud's. For Freud, the reality principle demands adjustments to *the* real world, with its inevitable limitations and difficulties (1911). For Marcuse, performance principles demand adjustment to *a* historical, sociocultural reality, with its specific demands on human energy. These sociocultural realities often mistake themselves for intrinsic reality, but are in fact arrangements that serve the interests of a privileged class.

6. In Reich's more embodied concept of "character armor," the self is also freighted with gratuitous inhibitions that diminish physical and emotional life (1972).

7. On Mead's critical reading of Freud, see further Mageo 1988:28–37. Unlike Marcuse, Mead feared that when one subtracted discontent from civilization, one also undermined intensity and involvement with life; these were the qualities she found missing in her Samoan model of Pacific harmony (1973:x). In Foucault's terms, Mead realized that when relations of power are moderated, so are forms of resistance.

8. Wolf distinguishes four kinds of power: individual capacity, the ability of one individual to impose his/her will on another, individuals' or groups' ability to control contexts, and structural power (1999:5). The first two of these assimilate to what we call agency, the third is intermediate on our agency/episteme continuum, and the fourth articulates epistemic and politico-economic dimensions.

9. For related critiques see Certeau 1984; Ortner 1984:144–148; and Quinn and Strauss 1997:47.

10. See further the analysis in Knauft 1996:10–13. Which features of each level were considered primary or determinant of those at other levels quickly became a major fault line of theoretical contention. In the wake of these debates, social and cultural theory has found it generally difficult to address actors' psychological plumbing, as Sherry Ortner (1984), among others, has noted. As noted in the text, it was to remedy this difficulty that scholars turned to practice theories in the 1980s and to epistemic notions of power in the 1990s. In psychological anthropology, this move was signaled by Catherine Lutz and Lila Abu-Lughod in the introduction to their important 1990 collection *Language and the Politics of Emotion*. They argue that if emotion is to be considered as a discursive construction, it cannot be divorced from the epistemic field of power within which discourse is located.

11. Although less grounded in psychological anthropology Battaglia 1995; Strathern 1990; Wagner 1991 also deserve mention here.

12. For examples see Laqueur 1990; Martin 1987; Haraway 1993; Scheper-Hughes 1992a; Taussig 1980 and Lutz, Chapter 9.

13. For examples see Benedict 1934; Spiro 1982; Hallowell 1955.

14. D'Andrade raises the question of Good vs. Bad power (1995:407–408). Power tends to culturally perceived as bad when it is at odds with fundamental cultural orientations to personhood and to be perceived as good when it is concordant with these models (Mageo 1998:11–14, 52–68).

15. For a psychological critique of Jameson, see Strauss 1997.

16. On fantasy processes and the revision of cultural schemata see further Mageo n.d.
17. In critical psychoanalytic anthropology Obeyesekere (1990) and Crapanzano (1992) worked at integrating cultural relativity, Ricoeur's textuality (1981), and phenomenology into a basis for psychological theorizing. Allison's *Night Work* (1994) and McClintock's *Imperial Leather* (1995) combined a psychoanalytic framework with Marxist and Gramscian perspectives on social consciousness, linking cultural schemata with forms of feeling, interaction, and embodiment. In psychology, Chodorow (1978) and Benjamin (1988) also evolved critical psychoanalytic approaches, considered in depth in Lutz's chapter.
18. Vygotsky's (1978) work on symbol formation also contributes to understanding the relation between imagination, psychic power, self-construction, and social worlds. See in particular the final chapter in Holland *et al.* 1998.
19. See further Mageo 1994:421–427.
20. This argument is further developed in Mageo 1996.
21. Lacan argues that imagination also organizes data as wholes (1968).

REFERENCES

Allison, Anne. 1994. *Nightwork*. Chicago: Chicago University Press.
Anzaldua, Gloria. 1999. *Borderlands – La Frontera*. San Francisco. Aunt Lutz.
Bakhtin, Mikhail M. [1975]1981. *The Dialogic Imagination: Four Essays by M. M. Bakhtin* (M. E. Holmquist, ed.; Caryl Emerson and Michael Holquist, trans.). Austin: University of Texas Press.
Battaglia, Debbora (ed.). 1995. *Rhetorics of Self-Making*. Berkeley: University of California Press.
Benedict, Ruth. 1934. *Patterns of Culture*. Boston: Houghton Mifflin.
Benjamin, Jessica. 1988. *The Bonds of Love: Psychoanalysis, Feminism, and the Problem of Domination*. New York: Pantheon Books.
Bettelheim, Bruno. 1976. *The Uses of Enchantment: The Meaning and Importance of Fairy Tales*. New York: Knopf.
Bocook, Robert. 1986. *Hegemony*. London: Tanstock Publications.
Bodley, John. 1975. *Victims of Progress*. Menlo Park: Cummings.
Bourdieu, Pierre. 1992. *Outline of a Theory of Practice* (Richard Nice, trans.). Cambridge: Cambridge University Press.
Burridge, Kenelm. 1969. *Tangu Tradition: A Study of the Way of Life, Mythology, and Developing Experience of a New Guinea People*. Oxford: Clarendon.
Certeau, Michel de. 1984. *The Practice of Everyday Life* (Steven Rendall, trans.). Berkeley: University of California Press.
Chan, Wing-Tsit, trans. and ed. 1963. *A Source Book in Chinese Philosophy*. Princeton: Princeton University Press.
Chodorow, Nancy. 1978. *The Reproduction of Mothering: Psychoanalysis and the Sociology of Gender*. Berkeley: University of California Press.
Clifford, James. 1992. Traveling Cultures. In *Cultural Studies* (L. Grossberg, C. Nelson and P. A. Treichler eds.), pp. 96–111. New York: Routledge.
Comaroff, John and Jean Comaroff. 1991. *Of Revelation and Revolution: Christianity, Colonialism and Consciousness in South Africa*, Vol. 1. Chicago: Chicago University Press.
        1992. *Ethnography and the Historical Imagination*. Boulder: Westview Press.

Crapanzano, Vincent. 1992. *Hermes' Dilemma and Hamlet's Desire*. Cambridge, MA: Harvard University Press.

  1995. Comments on Objectivity and Militancy: A Debate. *Current Anthropology* 36(3):399–408.

D'Andrade, Roy. 1995. Moral Models in Anthropology. *Current Anthropology* 36(3):420–421.

Deleuze, Gilles. 1983. *Anti-Oedipus: Capitalism and Schizophrenia* (Robert Hurley, Mark Seem, and Helen R. Lane, trans.). Minneapolis: University of Minnesota Press.

  1993. *The Fold: Leibniz and the Baroque* (Tom Conley, trans). Minneapolis: University of Minnesota Press.

Ellis, Bruce J. and Donald Symons. 1997. Sex Differences in Sexual Fantasy: An Evolutionary Psychological Approach. In *Human Nature* (Laura Betzig, ed.), pp. 194–212. New York: Oxford University Press.

Ewing, Katherine P. 1990. The Illusion of Wholeness. *Ethos* 18(3):251–278.

Fanon, Frantz. 1967. *Black Skin, White Mask* (Charles L. Markmann, trans.). New York: Grove Press.

Firth, R. W. 1949. The Analysis of Mana. *Journal of the Polynesian Society* 49:483–510.

Foucault, Michel. 1965. *Madness and Civilization* (R. Howard trans.). New York: Pantheon.

  1980. *Power/Knowledge*. New York: Pantheon Books.

  1988. Technologies of the Self. In *Technologies of the Self* (Luther H. Martin, Huck Gutman, and Patrick H. Hutton, eds.), pp. 16–49. Amherst, MA: University of Massachusetts Press.

  1990. *The History of Sexuality, Vol. 1: An Introduction* (Robert Hurley, trans.). New York: Random House.

Freud, Sigmund. 1911. Formulations of the Two Principles of Mental Functioning. (James Strachey and Anna Freud, trans. assisted by Alix Strachey and Alan Tyson). In Vol. 12 of *The Standard Edition of the Collected Works*, pp. 213–26. London: Hogarth Press and the Institute of Psychoanalysis.

  1955. Interpretation of Dreams (James Strachey, trans.). In *The Standard Edition of the Complete Psychological Works of Sigmund Freud*, Vol. 10. London: Hogarth Press.

  1961. Civilization and Its Discontents (James Strachey, trans. assisted by Alix Strachey and Alan Tyson). In Vol. 21 of *The Standard Edition of the Collected Works*, pp. 59–145. London: Hogarth.

  1966. Introductory Lectures on Psychoanalysis. In *The Standard Edition of the Collected Works*, Vol. 15 (James Strachey, trans.). New York: Norton.

Goldman, Irving. 1970. *Ancient Polynesian Society*. Chicago: University of Chicago Press.

Gramsci, Antonio. [1948–1951]1992. *The Prison Notebooks* (Joseph A. Buttigieg and Antonio Callari, trans.). New York: Columbia University Press.

Habermas, Jürgen. 1972. *Knowledge and Human Interests* (Jeremy J. Sharpiro, trans.). London: Heinemann.

  1984–1987. *The Theory of Communicative Action*, 2 Vols. (Thomas McCarthy, trans.). Boston: Beacon.

Hall, Stuart. 1996. Introduction. In *Questions of Cultural Identity* (Stuart Hall, and Paul DuGuy, eds.), pp. 1–17. London: Sage.

Hallowell, Alfred. I. 1955. *Culture and Experience*. Philadelphia: University of Pennsylvania Press.

Haraway, Donna. 1991. *Simians, Cy-Borgs, and Women: The Reinvention of Nature*. New York: Routledge.

1993. The Biopolitics of Postmodern Bodies. In *Knowledge, Power, and Practice* (S. Lindenbaum and M. Lock, eds.), pp. 330–363. Berkeley: University of California Press.

Hillman, James. 1964. *Emotion*. Evanston, IL: Northwestern University Press.

Hobbes, Thomas. 1973. *The Leviathan*. New York: Dutton.

Holland, Dorothy, William Lachicotte Jr., Debra Skinner, Carole Cain. 1998. *Identity and Agency in Cultural Worlds*. Cambridge, MA: Harvard University Press.

Hsu, Francis L. K. 1961. American Core Value and National Character. In *Psychological Anthropology* (Francis L. K. Hsu ed.), pp. 209–230. Homewood, IL: Dorsey.

Jakobson, Roman. 1971. *Selected Writings II: Word and Language*. The Hague: Mouton.

Jameson, Fredric. 1981. *The Political Unconscious: Narrative as a Socially Symbolic Act*. Ithaca, NY: Cornell University Press.

Kleinman, Arthur. 1980. *Patients and Healers in the Context of Culture*. Berkeley: University of California Press.

1985. Somatization. In *Culture and Depression* (A. Kleinman and B. Good, eds.), pp. 428–490. Berkeley: University of California Press.

Knauft, Bruce M. 1996. *Genealogies for the Present in Cultural Anthropology*. New York: Routledge.

Lacan, Jacques. 1968. The Mirror Phase. *New Left Review* 51:70–79.

Lacquer, Thomas. 1990. *Making Sex*. Cambridge, MA: Harvard University Press.

Lave, Jean and Etienne Wenger. 1991. *Situated Learning*. Cambridge: Cambridge University Press.

Lutz, Catherine. 1988. *Unnatural Emotions: Everyday Sentiments on a Micronesian Atoll and Their Challenge to Western Theory*. Chicago: University of Chicago Press.

1990. Engendered Emotions. In *Language and the Politics of Emotion* (C. Lutz and L. Abu-Lughod eds.), pp. 69–91. Cambridge: Cambridge University Press.

Lutz, Catherine and Lila Abu-Lughod (eds.). 1990. *Language and the Politics of Emotion*. Cambridge: Cambridge University Press.

McClintock, Anne. 1995. *Imperial Leather*. New York: Routledge.

Mageo, Jeannette Marie. 1988. *Malosi*: A Psychological Exploration of Mead's and Freeman's Work and of Samoan Aggression. *Pacific Studies* 11(2):25–65.

1994. Hairdos and Don't: Hair Symbolism and Sexual History in Samoa. *Man*, 29:407–432.

1995. The Reconfiguring Self. *American Anthropologist*. 97(2):282–296.

1996. Spirit girls and Marines: Historicizing Possession and Historicized Ethnopsychiatry in Samoa. *American Ethnologist* 23:61–82.

1998. *Theorizing Self in Samoa*. Ann Arbor: Michigan University Press.

1999. Dreaming Cultural History: Feelings, Sex, and Gender in Samoan Dreams. Paper delivered at the at the 28th annual meetings of the Association for Social Anthropology in Oceania, Hilo, Hawai'i.

Mageo, Jeannette and Linda Stone. n.d. The Trope of Female Orgasm in Science and Social Science. Unpublished Paper.

Marcus, George E. and Michael M. J. Fischer. 1986. *Anthropology as Cultural Critique*. Chicago: University of Chicago Press.

Marcuse, Herbert. 1955. *Eros and Civilization*. Boston: Beacon.

Martin, Emily. 1987. *The Woman in the Body*. Boston: Beacon.

  1995. *Flexible Bodies*. Boston: Beacon.

Mead, Margaret. 1959. Cultural Contexts of Puberty and Adolescence. In *The Bulletin of the Philadelphia Association for Psychoanalysis*. Vol. 9., No. 3.

  1973. *Coming of Age in Samoa*. New York: William Morrow.

Obeyesekere, Gananath. 1981. *Medusa's Hair*. Chicago: Chicago University Press.

  1990. *The Work of Culture*. Chicago: Chicago University Press.

  1992. *The Apotheosis of Captain Cook*. Princeton: Princeton University Press.

Ortner, Sherry B. 1984. Theory in Anthropology since the Sixties. *Journal of Comparative Society and History*. 26(2):126–127.

Quinn, Naomi and Claudia Strauss. 1997. *A Cognitive Theory of Cultural Meanings*. Cambridge: Cambridge University Press.

Reich, Wilhelm. 1972. *Character Analysis* (Vincent R. Carfagno, trans.). New York: Farrar, Straus and Giroux.

Ricoeur, Paul. 1981 *Hermeneutics and the Human Sciences*. (J. B. Thompson, trans.) Cambridge: Cambridge University Press.

Rosaldo, Michelle Z. 1980. The Use and Abuse of Anthropology. *Signs* 5(3):389–417.

  1984. Towards an Anthropology of Self and Feeling. In *Culture Theory* (R.A. Shweder and R. S. Levine eds.), pp. 137–157. Cambridge: Cambridge University Press.

Rousseau, Jean-Jacques. 1923. *The Social Contract, & Discourses* (George D. Hoard trans.). London: J. M. Dent & Sons.

Scheper-Hughes, Nancy. 1992a. Hungry Bodies, Medicine, and the State. In *New Directions in Psychological Anthropology* (T. Schwartz, G. M. White and C. Lutz, eds.), pp. 221–247. Cambridge: Cambridge University Press.

  1992b. *Death without Weeping*. Berkeley: University of California Press.

Shore, Bradd. 1989. Mana and Tapu. In *Developments in Polynesian Ethnology* (A. Howard and R. Borofsky eds.), pp. 137–173. Honolulu: University Press of Hawai'i.

Spiro, Melford E. 1982. *Buddhism and Society*. Berkeley: University of California Press.

Strathern, Marilyn. 1990. *The Gender of the Gift*. Berkeley: University of California Press.

Strauss, Claudia. 1997. Partly Fragmented, Partly Integrated: An Anthropological Examination of "Postmodern Fragmented Subjects." *Cultural Anthropology* 12:362–404.

  In press. The Culture Concept and the Individualism/Collectivism Debate: Dominant and Alternative Attributions for Class in the United States. In *Culture, Thought, and Development* (L. Nucci, G. Saxe, and E. Turiel, eds.) Mahwah, NJ: Lawrence Erlbaum.

Tannen, Deborah. 1991. *You Just Don't Understand: Women and Men in Conversation*. New York: Ballantine.

Taussig, Michael. 1980. *The Devil and Commodity Fetishism in South America*. Chapel Hill: University of North Carolina Press.

  1980. Reification and the Consciousness of the Patient. *Social Science and Medicine* 14:3–13.

van den Berghe, Pierre L. and Peter Frost. 1986. Skin Color Preference, Sexual Dimorphism, Sexual Selection: a Case of Gene Culture Co-evolution? *Ethnic and Racial Studies* 9(1):87–113.

Vygotsky, L. S. 1978. Tool and Symbol in Child Development. In *Mind in Society* (Michael Cole, et.al., eds.), pp. 19–30. Cambridge, MA: Harvard University Press.

[1931]1992. The Problem of the Development of Higher Mental Functions. In *The History of the Development of Higher Mental Functions* (Vol. 4 of the *Collected Works of L. S. Vygotsky*, Marie J. Hall trans.), pp. 1–26. New York: Plenum.

Wagner, Roy. 1991. The Fractal Person. In *Big Men and Great Men* (M. Godelier and M. Strathern eds.), pp. 159–173. Cambridge: Cambridge University Press.

Weber, Max. 1958. Politics as a Vocation. In *From Max Weber: Essays in Sociology* (H. H. Gerth and C. W. Mills, eds.), pp. 77–128. New York: Oxford University Press.

Williams, Raymond. 1977. *Marxism and Literature*. Oxford: Oxford University Press.

Wolf, Eric R. 1982. *Europe and the People without History*. Berkeley: University of California Press.

1999. *Envisioning Power*. Berkeley: University of California Press.

Part I

Power differentials in the US

2   The genocidal continuum: peace-time crimes

Nancy Scheper-Hughes

In "The genocidal continuum," Nancy Scheper-Hughes argues that theorists from Freud to Foucault tend to psychologize violence and domination, which can distract us from confronting their experienced reality. In modern warfare and in the hyper-modern state, highly organized forms of violence (torture, death squads, etc.) may be used to obtain unconditional civil consent. In American society, civil consent is more subtly extracted and then used to warrant peace-time violence, including the symbolic violence that articulates deeply with epistemic power. The inmates of prisons or insane asylums may be treated as objects or as dirt – as are street urchins in Brazil – polluting elements that require removal to better constitute some minimal definition of being human (see further Douglas 1966; Hinton 1996). For Scheper-Hughes, these everyday violences are epistemic microcosms of genocidal crimes.

One is reminded here of anthropologist John Bowen's timely article, where he argues that genocide does not result as if automatically from ancient and unchanging ethnic identities (1996). Indeed, contemporary ethnicity, and particularly its genocidal inflection, is in significant part a modern creation – if not a creation of modernism itself. As Bowen further emphasizes, conditions are shaped by concrete political choices and decisions of rulers and power elites. Though these draw upon deep ethnic associations if not deeper structures of genocidal ideology, their power to be violent as opposed to merely vestigial results from the way that social powers become harnessed with epistemic ones. This keeps our analysis from being constrained by the conservative if not reactionary assumption that psychic processes or those of subjectivity are "small in scale" while processes of political economics and history are "large in scale," which increases the analytic divide between power and the self.

Perhaps what is most significant about Scheper-Hughes's essay is the presentation of her own experience, her own suffering of social and epistemic power and those of her loved ones. She writes her existential condition as data, thereby making palpable the connection between social, epistemic, and psychic power. Her critical analyses of power and the self meet in the bodies of her own parents in a manner that goes far beyond Bourdieu's concept of bodily hexis. Most visibly in her father's bodily habits and enactments, one finds a refusal to be subsumed in overbearing forms of social and epistemic power. But this resistance is by no means ghostly or anonymous. In this most personal portrayal of her treasured father, Scheper-Hughes shows body, feeling, and meaning to be active forms of our humanity, existentially transcendent even when we cannot escape the epistemic and physical terrorism of our cultural worlds.

Scheper-Hughes brings the self to theorizations of power by implicating herself in this analysis. Peace-time crimes are so deeply inscribed in lifeways and in people's internalizations of them that no one is exempt; no one is innocent – even she herself. Social critique must extend to self-critique, to viewing how our own ways of thinking and loving are implicated in analysis. True to form, she reminds us that the demons have not fled: there are dimensions of power that are sustained by everyone turning their eyes away, and this turn too needs theorization. In this manner, Scheper-Hughes shows us how to read across scales of violent power to realize their connection rather than their separation. Our critical lens must move in and out, sometimes intentionally juxtaposing the different scales of coercive power – macro and micro, epistemic and personal.

Jeannette Mageo and Bruce Knauft

This chapter revisits a key theme in my work, which is derived from a radical tradition of social science: a concern with popular consent to everyday violence. By everyday violence I mean the legitimate, organized, and (above all) routinized violence that is implicit in particular social and political-economic formations. The everyday violence to which I refer is related to but distinct from Pierre Bourdieu's (1977;1996) notion of "symbolic violence"; it is perhaps closest to what Taussig (1989), citing Benjamin, calls "terror as usual." I want to suggest here that everyday violence – "peace-time crimes" (Basaglia 1987) – makes structural violence and genocide possible. So perhaps an alternative sub-title to this chapter might be "toward a genealogy of genocide." Nothing that I say here has not already been said before and more eloquently by those more expert in the field of genocide. My sole contribution lies in weaving together disparate threads of everyday life and everyday practice that participate in sanctioning genocidal-like behaviors toward certain *gens* – classes of people who are seen as dispensable. The chapter ends with a personal vignette through which I hope to demonstrate the ways in which we are all bystanders of sorts and all privy to structural violence, even when it is directed, unintentionally and unconsciously, against those we most love.

Since his early work on the military destruction of Algerian villages Bourdieu became less interested in explaining how violence operates when it is expressed directly and crudely and more in the way that violence structures quite ordinary and "peaceful" social (and gender) relations. Bourdieu saw domination and violence in the least likely places – in the architecture of the home, in the exchange of gifts, in systems of classification, in village matrimonial rituals, in all the ambiguous uses of culture. Violence, he suggests, is everywhere in social practice. It is mis-recognized because its very familiarity renders it invisible. One could interpret Bourdieu's move toward a symbolic theory of violence as analogous to Freud's decisive turning away from the real and bloody facts of child sexual abuse, which he encountered during his studies in Paris and his familiarity with the published research of Ambrosie Tardieu, the leading French forensic pathologist, in order to consider the universal symbolic violence of unconsciously sexualized family relations (see Masson 1992, chapter 2).

Following Gramsci, Foucault, Sartre, Arendt, and other modern theorists of power and domination Bourdieu treats direct physical violence as a crude, uneconomical, and unnecessary mode of domination. It is less efficient and, following Arendt (1969), it is certainly less legitimate. The Foucauldian narrative (1979; 1980; 1982), for example, suggests that over the past two hundred years torture as a legitimate tool of the state officially disappeared in civilized countries. More refined methods for extracting consent were developed and implemented by modern "technicians of the social consensus," including labor and management specialists, urban planners, entertainment and media technicians, educators and, of course, doctors, counselors, psychiatrists, and social workers. One need only think of the mad bureaucrats of South African apartheid, for example.

But, contrary to the expectations of the "gloved hands of the state" theorists, at the close of the twentieth century we witnessed a repugnant resurgence of the political uses of direct, explicit, and graphic torture – the modernization of the forms, techniques, mechanics, and uses of torture by militarized police and security as well as by liberation and resistance movements. In South America, for example, during the 1970s and 1980s, state torture was used preventatively – as a political inoculation to nip in the bud contaminating ("communist") ideas, relationships, and practices. In Argentina, Chile, Uruguay, and Brazil those being detained, tortured, and killed usually had nothing to confess except their unwillingness and refusal to be killed (Weschler 1990). This kind of highly organized state violence was carried out to obtain total and unconditional consent. In the final years of the anti-apartheid struggle, police sweeps against township youth were common. Children were carried off, interrogated, and tortured simply because they were wearing "banned" ANC T-shirts. In the late-twentieth-century hyper-modern police state crude and violent forms of political domination were once again free to reveal themselves for what they were.

Meanwhile, anthropologists of violence[1] have begun to address the shocking rebirth of late modern forms of genocide in Central Africa, Central America, South Asia, and Eastern Europe – the resurgence of what we naively thought (after the Holocaust) simply could not happen again. And so I return here to a question that vexed a generation of post-Holocaust social theorists: what makes genocide possible? How do we explain the alarming complicity of otherwise ordinary "good people" to outbreaks of radical violence perpetrated by the state, police, military, and ethnic groups?

Adorno and his Frankfurt School colleagues (see Geuss 1981) suggested that the seemingly willing participation of ordinary people in genocidal acts requires strong childhood conditioning in mindless obedience to authority figures in addition to powerful ideologies, such as anti-Semitism. But Goldhagen (1996), relying on compelling testimony, argues that millions of ordinary Germans participated willingly, even eagerly, in the Holocaust not for fear of the authorities but because of race hatred. Alternatively, I have suggested a kind of genocidal continuum, made up of a multitude of "small wars and invisible genocides" (see Scheper-Hughes 1996a) conducted in the normative, ordinary social spaces of public schools, clinics, emergency rooms, hospital charity wards, nursing homes, city halls, jails, and public morgues.

The question – what makes genocide possible? – has guided a radical tradition of social science inquiry ever since the Holocaust made it impossible for students of human behavior to deny that a great many people, at different times and places, have been capable of perceiving (and disposing) of certain designated "others" as despicable and dirty things, as disposable rubbish, as worthy only (and ultimately) of extinction. Under radical political conditions, and often with broad social consent, policies of mass destruction under the guise of "social hygiene" and "ethnic cleansing" come into play.

The role of the popular media – radio in particular – in galvanizing genocidal acts was identified in Rwanda. But Philip Gourevitch (1998:33–34) added another disturbing key factor, the role of "communal obligation" – the almost automatic "call and response" passed along among the residents of dispersed but congested and tightly structured village hamlets. While "calls for help" and immediate response could be used positively – to interrupt an attempted rape, for example – Gourevitch wondered what might happen were this system of community obligation turned on its head, so that a call to murder and rape became the rule to which villagers had to respond, immediately and automatically.

Another element is necessary, however: the capacity to reduce other humans to non-persons, to things. An analysis of this terrifying radical estrangement between self and other that I have elsewhere called "basic strangeness" (1992:410–412) has motivated much of my anthropological work on the structures, meanings, and practices of "everyday violence." It seems essential that we recognize in our species and in ourselves a genocidal capacity and that we exercise a defensive hyper-vigilance and hyper-sensitivity to the less dramatic and far more mundane (and normative) acts of violence (sometimes masked as "sacrifice") directed against certain "classes" of humans – whether the farm-inheriting last-born sons in rural Irish farm families who are virtually forbidden to reproduce (see Scheper-Hughes 2000:45–46) or the angel-babies of Brazilian shantytowns whose premature deaths are naturalized and spiritualized at one and the same time, or the street children of Rio de Janeiro, Salvador, and Reife who are exterminated in the name of public hygiene, or the "oldest old" in America who are consigned to social death in nursing homes that bear some resemblance to concentration camps. Perhaps a self-mobilization for constant shock and hyperarousal remains the only ethical response to Benjamin's (1969:253) view of late modern history as a chronic "state of emergency." Here "continual traumatic stress" is less a psychiatric disorder than an ethical stance.

The genocidal *capacity* to which I refer has nothing to do with instinctual drives but refers to the "purely" social sentiments of exclusion, dehumanization, depersonalization, pseudo-speciation, and reification which normalize and routinize behavior toward another or a class of others that would otherwise be seen as atrocious and unthinkable. In referring to "invisible genocides" I realize that I am walking on thin ice, while my suggestion of a "genocidal continuum" flies in the face of a noble tradition within genocide studies that argues for a strict and legalistic definition of genocide (see Chorbajian and Shirinian 1999) so as to prevent the absurd dilution of the term in rhetorical arguments against abortion, drug addiction, and the spread of AIDS in the African-American community, to mention but a few common metaphorical extensions and misuses of the term. Within the context of world courts and genocide tribunals an extremely specific definition of genocide is called for. But I am raising a very different set of questions that have nothing to do with legalities or justice-seeking and more to do with normalities and soul-searching. What is lost, what is gained in noting certain troubling institutional analogies among families, hospitals, schools, and prisons, or between nursing homes and concentration camps?

What is lost, obviously, is an understanding of the absolute *uniqueness* of genocide and of the Holocaust as the prototype of all genocides. The philosopher Emil Fackenheim argues, for example, in *God's Presence in History* (1970), that the Nazi genocide of the Jews has no precedent, either inside or outside Jewish history. The Holocaust, Fackenheim insists, is *sui generis* – exceptional and utterly unique. The Holocaust "was annihilation for the sake of annihilation" (1970:70). Because the slaughter of the Jews was "for nothing," the Holocaust presents a paradigm of "pure" and gratuitous human suffering. Woe to those who would reduce or trivialize the horror and the exceptional nature of the Holocaust by comparing (and thereby equating) it with other lesser forms of social suffering.

And yet I do make such comparisons, though I proceed cautiously and join others who have called attention to forms and spaces of hitherto unrecognized, gratuitous, and useless social suffering (Levinas 1986; Das 1996; Kleinman and Kleinman 1996). If there is a moral and political risk – and there is – in extending as powerful a concept as "genocide" into other hitherto unrecognized public and private/domestic spaces, the benefit lies in the ability to draw connections, to make predictions, to sensitize people to *genocidal-like* practices and sentiments hidden within the perfectly acceptable and normative behavior of ordinary, good-enough citizens. Why are we surprised at how easy it seems to be for ordinary people to cooperate in mass killings and genocides once the foundation has been laid in the many ordinary betrayals, the small wars and invisible genocides, already perpetrated against certain classes of sub-citizens.

Hannah Arendt paved the way in recognizing the potential within otherwise decent people to become dedicated technicians of genocide under particular social and historical conditions. Denial is a prerequisite of genocide. (Adolf Eichmann pleaded "not guilty" to each of the fifteen counts of genocide and other war crimes on the grounds that under the existing Nazi legal system he had done nothing wrong. What he was accused of were not crimes at all, he argued, but merely "acts of the state" [Arendt 1963:21]). Here, Bourdieu's partial and unfinished theory of violence is useful. By including the softer, symbolic forms of violence hidden in the minutiae of "normal" social practices, Bourdieu forces us to reconsider the broader meanings and status of violence, especially the links between "everyday violence" (Scheper-Hughes 1992) and more explicit forms of political terror.

In the bucolic countryside and family farms of West Kerry, for example, I found evidence in the 1970s of structural and symbolic violence toward later-born sons. Their role as farm heirs excluded them from matrimony and child-bearing and consigned them to a monkish existence serving their "sainted" elderly parents. As a village demographer and "clerk of the records" I had gathered enough stories and been present at enough family and community crises to know what a great many ordinary villagers knew without ever going to the university – that something was gravely amiss. There were too many psychological tragedies to account for – some taking the form of madness ("schizophrenia"), a greater number expressed in deep clinical depressions and, in more recent years, a shocking number of young adult suicides (Scheper-Hughes 2000:47–51). There was trouble in the system, a very "nervous system" indeed (see Taussig 1992).

Beneath the quaint thatched roofs of the rural farm households an extraordinary drama of masked violence and ritual sacrifice was taking place. Up through the 1950s, when family farming was still a valued and productive way of life, the first-born son would have inherited the farm, but by the time I arrived in "Ballybran" (i.e. An Clochan, the real name of the community, which I have restored in my new, updated, and expanded edition of *Saints, Scholars and Schizophrenics*) the first-born were being reared for export. And rural parents were faced with a new problem – how to retain at least one son for the farm and for the care of themselves in their dotage. The new family "selections" paradoxically privileged the first-born children by "disinheriting" them, thereby allowing them to leave the village with honor, and victimized the designated heirs in relegating them to the status of pathetic "leftovers" and stay-at-homes "good enough" for the village, a place not then generally thought of as very good at all.

This family dynamic involved considerable symbolic violence – a cutting-down to size of designated farm heirs, a sacrifice of their manhood and repro-ductivity to permanent celibacy, and exploitation of their labor. All this was accomplished silently and through considerable shaming and ridicule toward these captive men. The moral economy of farm inheritance constituted what Bourdieu (1977) would have called a "bad faith economy," one based on lies and secrets, and concealing the true state of affairs. In fact, the situation I described here was very similar to one described by Bourdieu (1962, 1989) with respect to the bachelor peasants of Béarn, his own home region of France. Bourdieu recalled a "simple" village scene – a small dance on Christmas Eve in a rural tavern – that had haunted him for more than thirty years. Later, he reflected: "I witnessed a very stunning scene: young men and women from nearby towns were dancing in the middle of the ballroom while another group of older [local village] youths, about my age at the time, all still bachelors, were standing idly on the sidelines. Instead of dancing, they were intensely scrutinizing the hall and unconsciously moving forward so that they were progressively shrink-ing the space used by the dancers." The resentment of the village bachelors who had been sidelined at the dance (as in life) spilled over into their angry, non-verbal challenge to the "townie" dancers.

The spurned farm heirs of Béarn, like the bachelor farmers of An Clochan, were fated to permanent bachelorhood and virtually "forbidden" to reproduce. The aggressive behavior of the village bachelors at the tavern dance was, in effect, a symbolic protest against the new "matrimonial market" that had emerged among the "emancipated" factory workers from nearby towns. The older, rural system of match-making, controlled by the elders, had since given way to a "free market" in which young men were now expected to manage their own marital and reproductive affairs counting on their own personal assets including their "symbolic capital": the ability to dress, to dance, to present one-self, to talk to girls, and so on. This courtship transition had almost completely disenfranchised the rural class of shy bachelors who had always depended on intermediaries to arrange their personal and romantic affairs.

The transition from arranged marriages to "free exchange" signaled the demise of an entire class of small peasant farmers which the French state was trying to eliminate through various "modernization" projects beginning soon after World War II (Bourdieu and Wacquant 1992:165). Although this "war" on the class of peasant farmers was accomplished without overt violence and bloodshed, the brutality of the process was grasped intuitively by the young anthropologist who observed with mounting horror the shame and impotent rage of the bachelor wallflowers sidelined at that poignant Christmas Eve dance in Béarn so many years ago.

In a nutshell this was also the situation of the young, angry bachelors of An Clochan. While some bachelor farmers adjusted to the new system, making their daily little accommodations to it without complaint, others could not bring themselves to do so, and over time they grew into angry, isolated, hurt, and bitter individuals, cut off from the flow of human life. Some became the depressed and alcoholic bachelor farmers who populated the several village pubs that catered to the village. Others become the saintly hermits who retreated to their barns and sought companionship in their dogs and cows, and still others became the long-term mental patients at St. Finan's hospital in Killarney, men who were often obsessed with fears of bodily encroachment and possessed by unfulfilled and unruly sexual and generative needs and fantasies.

> He wept for all that would no longer happen.
> He wept for his mother making potato fritters.
> He wept for her pruning roses in the garden.
> He wept for his father shouting . . .
> He wept for never being able to leave the farm for a single day.
> He wept for the farm where there were no children . . .
> He wept for the hay, still to be brought in.
> He wept for the forty-two years that had gone by,
> and he wept for himself.
>
> John Berger, *Once in Europa* (1987:29)

Here the social tragedy was masked by a myth of mental illness and mental incapacity so that the family and the community was served at the expense of its solitary victims. This bears some resemblance to Henry's (1963) notion of "culture against man." I trust I do not dishonor the victims of other forms of collective suffering in suggesting a link between the sacrifice of the bachelors of West Kerry in relative peace-time and the sacrifice of other "dispensable" people during war-time. But curtailing the reproductive capacity of an entire class of men, strikes me as implicitly genocidal towards that group.

I take my lead from the late Italian Marxist psychiatrist Franco Basaglia's suggestive though under-theorized notion of "peace-time crimes" (*crimini di pace*) because it imagines a relationship between war-time and peace-time, and between the behavior of ordinary families and the state. In his essay "Peace-Time Crimes" (Scheper-Hughes and Lovell 1986), Basaglia posits a continuity between extraordinary and ordinary violence, between the everyday forms of violence that are normalized, naturalized, and unmarked, and the explicit, sensational, and remarkable crimes and violations of war-time. The idea of peace-time crimes suggests the possibility that war crimes are merely ordinary, everyday crimes of public consent applied systematically and dramatically in times of war. Consider the parallel uses of rape during peace-time and war-time; or, the family resemblances between public consent in the US today for legal border raids and physical assaults by INS agents on "illegal" aliens and the government sponsored genocide of the historical Cherokee "Trail of Tears."

Alternatively, the term "peace-time crimes" suggests that the everyday forms of state violence are what make a certain kind of domestic "peace" possible (Patridge 1997). Internal "stability" is purchased with the currency of peace-time crimes. For example, how many public executions of run of the mill ne'er-do-wells are needed in Texas, Louisiana, and California to make life feel more secure for the affluent? How many new and improved prisons do we need in the US to contain an ever-growing population of incarcerated young black men? Are we comfortable with a 10 percent confinement rate? A 20 percent confinement rate? More? What can it possibly mean when jails become the normative social-izing experience for a certain category of young people? Ordinary peace-time crimes – such as the steady evolution of US prisons into alternative black con-centration camps – are the "small wars and invisible genocides" to which I refer. They are invisible, not because they are secreted away or hidden from view, but quite the opposite. As Wittgenstein observed, the things that are hardest to per-ceive are those which are right before our eyes and therefore taken for granted.

Franco Basaglia's own awakening occurred when he first entered an Italian *manicomio* (a traditional state mental asylum) as a psychiatric intern after World War II. He was immediately struck by a frightening sense of *déja vu*: the odor of defecation, sweat, and death catapulted him back to the prison cell where he had been held as a member of the Italian Resistance during the German occupa-tion. That single terrifying moment became the basis for his powerful equation of mental hospitals with concentration camps, the insight that allowed him to perceive the links between war crimes and peace-time crimes. As director of the mental asylum at Gorizia, Basaglia tried to reverse the regime of violence and terror that masqueraded as therapy and which contributed to premature deaths among inmates. International war tribunals had just been established to try those guilty of war crimes treated for the first time as "crimes against humanity." Dr. Basaglia struggled to unmask the invisible (because normalized and routinized) crimes against humanity practiced in public mental asylums in Italy after the war. The irony was that some of the more disturbed inmates were already suffering from war-related post-traumatic stress disorders only to en-counter medically indicated versions of solitary confinement, physical restraint, and professionally applied "strangleholds." Here the "public enemies" were the mad, and the public executioners were ordinary civil servants, bureaucrats, and clinicians: doctors, nurses, and social workers.

Analogic thinking enabled Basaglia (like Erving Goffman, 1961, before him) to perceive the logical relations between concentration camps and men-tal hospitals, and between "war crimes" and "peace-time crimes," between reified, despised, and depersonalized ethnic prisoners and mental patients. It further allowed him to see the willingness of ordinary people – Basaglia's "practical technicians" – to enforce, sometimes with gusto, genocidal-like crimes against types of people thought of as mere waste, as rubbish people, as "deficient" in humanity, and as "better off dead." The profoundly mad and the mentally deficient have often fallen into this category, as have the very old and the pauperized, especially the sick-poor, women in witch-believing societies, and severely disabled or disfigured children. Erik Erikson (1950) referred to "pseudo-speciation," by which he meant the human tendency to classify some individuals or groups as less than fully human.

Meira Weiss (1994, 1998) has, for example, exposed regimes of terror, rejection, and territorial seclusion practiced by parents against their severely appearance-impaired (disfigured) children. The babies in her study were discharged from hospitals in and around Jerusalem to the middle-class and working-class homes of their parents, many of whom were unable to see their appearance-impaired children as human. They were called "monsters," "devils," "beasts," "dirty things," and they were often secreted away in hallways, closets, basements, and exposed on balconies. Weiss testified on behalf of the rights of these rejected and stigmatized children to the Helsinki Committee on human rights abuses. Reification and pseudo-speciation are a prerequisite of dehumanization and genocide. As is collective and personal denial.

In *Death without Weeping* (1992), I explored the normalization and social indifference to staggering infant and child mortality in shantytown favelas of Northeast Brazil. Local political leaders, Catholic priests and nuns, coffin-makers, and shantytown mothers themselves casually dispatched a multitude of hungry "angel-babies" to the afterlife each year saying: "Well, they themselves wanted to die." (The babies were described as having no "taste," no "knack" and no "talent" for life.) In the shantytowns of Brazil analogies between maternal thinking and military thinking, especially triage and displaced (perhaps disorderly) mourning rituals during wartime, suggest themselves. The ability of economically threatened women to help those infants who (they said) "needed to die" required an existential "letting go" (contrasted to the maternal work of "holding on," holding close, and holding dear). Letting go required a leap of faith that was not easy to achieve. "Holy indifference" in the face of adversity was a cherished but elusive value for these mostly Catholic women, who sometimes said that infants died (like Jesus) so that others – especially themselves – could live.

The question that lingered, unresolved, in my mind was whether this Kierkegaardian "leap of faith" entailed a certain Marxist "bad faith" as well. I never intended to blame shantytown mothers for putting their own survival before that of their pre-conscious, pre-personed, pre-selved infants. These were amoral choices that no person should be forced to make, and that were over-determined in most instances. But the "bad faith" to which I refer concerns the women's denial, their refusal to accept the authorship of their acts, and their willingness to project the deaths of their supernumerary angel-babies on to the will and desire of the doomed infants themselves. ("They died, Nanci, because they themselves wished to die.")

I gradually came to think of the shantytown angel-babies in terms of René Girard's (1987) idea of sacrificial violence and the ritual scapegoat. The given-up-on babies had been sacrificed in the face of terrible conflicts about scarcity and survival. And it was here that maternal thinking and military thinking converged. Whenever angels (or martyrs) are fashioned from the dead bodies of those who die young "maternal thinking" most resembles military, especially wartime, thinking. On the battlefield as in the shantytown, an ethic of triage predominates (saving those first who are most likely to survive and benefit from the intervention), an ethos of "letting go," a passive resignation to the effects of one's "indifference," and an accompanying belief in the "magical replaceability" of the dead (see Scheper-Hughes 1996b). Above all, ideas of "acceptable death" and of "meaningful" rather than useless suffering extinguish rage and grief for those whose lives are taken and allow for the recruitment of new lives and new (and better) bodies into the struggle.

Just as shantytown mothers in Brazil consoled each other that their hungry babies died because they were "meant" to die or because they "had" to die, IRA mothers in Northern Ireland and South African township mothers consoled each other at political wakes and funerals during war-time and in times of political struggle with the belief that their sacrificed and "martyred" children had died purposefully and died well. This kind of accommodationist "maternal think-ing" is not, however, exclusive to wartime or to poor and uneducated women. Whenever we allow ourselves to attribute some meaning – whether political or spiritual – to the "useless suffering" (see Levinas 1986) of others we behave a bit like public executioners. While this is an extreme statement, it is meant to rup-ture the "bystander effect" without which genocide *or* lesser forms of structural violence along the genocidal continuum would not be possible. While blamed on white Afrikaners, South African apartheid could not have existed for so many decades without the passive, "bystander" acceptance of English-speaking whites who accepted the benefits that the "genocidal" system provided for them.

Likewise, in Northeast Brazil such common medical practices as prescribing powerful tranquilizers to fretful and frightfully hungry babies, Catholic ritual celebrations of the death of "angel-babies," and the bureaucratic indifference in political leaders' dispensing free baby coffins but no food to hungry families and children, supported and amplified maternal practices of passive euthana-sia such as radically reducing food and liquids to severely malnourished and dehydrated babies so as to help them, their mothers said, to die quickly and well. Perceived as already "doomed," sickly infants were described as less than human creatures, as ghostly angel-babies, inhabiting a terrain midway between life and death. "Really and truly," shantytown mothers said, "it is better that these spirit-children return to where they came from."

And while Latin Americans – and Brazilians in particular – are known for their love of children, they do not love so-called "street children," who have multiplied in great numbers following the transitions to open market neo-liberal economies and to more democratic structures (see Dimenstein 1991). Suddenly – or so it has seemed to a great many people in post-IMF structural adjustment Brazil, Venezuela, and Guatemala – in the favelas, shantytowns, and poor barrios, ruptured and "homeless" and "dirty" street children seemed to be everywhere displaying their "criminal" needs. Older street children are described as "dirty vermin" so that metaphors of "street cleaning," "trash removal," "fly swatting," "pest removal," and "urban hygiene" can be invoked to garner public support for police and death squad activities against them. The most infamous case was the Candaleria massacre in Rio de Janeiro in 1993 when off-duty policemen fired into a huddle of two dozen sleeping street children, killing eight of them and seriously wounding several others.

The term "street child" reflects the preoccupations of one class and segment of Brazilian society with the proper place of another (see Scheper-Hughes and Hoffman 1998). The term represents a kind of symbolic apartheid as urban space has become increasingly "privatized" (see Calderia 2001). As long as poor, "dirty," street children are contained in the slum or the favela, "where they belong," they are not viewed as an urgent social problem about which something must be done. The real issue is the preoccupation of one social class with the "proper place" of another social class. Like dirt, which is "clean" when it is in the yard and "dirty" when it is found under the nails, "dirty" street children are simply children "out of place."

In Brazil "street" and "home" designate more than social space, they are moral entities, spheres of social action, and ethical provinces. Home is the realm of relational ties and privilege which confer social personhood, human rights, and full citizenship. Street is an unbounded and dangerous realm, the space of the "masses" (o povo), where one can be treated anonymously. Rights belong to the realm of the home. "Street children," typically barefoot, shirtless, and unattached to a home, represent the extremes of social marginality and anonymity. They occupy a particularly degraded social position within the Brazilian hierarchy of place and power. As denizens of the street these semi-autonomous kids are separated from all that can confer relationship and propriety, without which rights and citizenship are impossible.

Happy Valley

But we need go no further than our own medical clinics, emergency rooms, public hospitals, and old-age homes in the US to encounter other classes of "rubbish people" treated with as much indifference and malevolence as "street kids" or angel-babies in South America. The following (and painfully rendered vignette) should suffice. A few years ago (1997) I stepped outside "Happy Valley" Nursing Care Center near Baltimore, Maryland, to take several deep breaths before returning inside to face what was left of (and left to) my impossibly dear and now impossibly frail parents, both in their nineties. A "late in life" child, I can only remember my father with gray and then later with white hair. No other 5-year-old I knew cried themselves to sleep after reciting bedtime prayers, certain that their parents would surely die before they woke. But my parents fooled everyone and outlived their much younger siblings, joining that small cohort that sociologists refer to as the "oldest old." With me living 3,000 miles away from my parents in New York City and an older brother living in Baltimore who spent a good part of each year traveling, the once unthinkable idea of a nursing home crept up on us after all else failed. My parents refused to move when moving close to one of us was still an option. As my mother's strength and independent spirit was sapped by Alzheimer's, and as my father's mobility was hampered by a broken hip and by Parkinson's disease, we tried to hire home care workers. Eventually, my parents sold their house and moved up state New York to join my mother's older sister in a retirement community for elderly nuns and a few ancient couples who appreciated the beauty of the mountains and the Hudson River and found solace in the presence of a small contemplative-based chapel that was part of the grounds.

As my parents' condition deteriorated they were asked to leave St. Joseph's Villa, a rejection that my mother, in her frail mental state, took personally as a sign of her own failure. In the small, pleasant-looking nursing home in Baltimore to which they were "temporarily" transferred, both parents soon became almost completely physically dependent, immobile, and incontinent, but only Dad, at 95, was painfully conscious of his reduced condition and circumstances. Mom was maintained in the end (against her and my wishes) by a plastic sack of brown liquid, suspended from a movable pole, and dripped by tubing into her abdomen. By this time she had lost language and she communicated by gentle and lady-like howls. When not thrashing about she seemed resigned but with the hopeless, open-eyed, and desperate stare of a hooked rainbow trout. Whenever Mom saw me and when – ignoring the nurse's rules – I would release her from her final hook and line and wheel her into the sunny courtyard, she would smile and she was attentive to the birds overhead and to the bright pink azaleas that were always one of her favorite flowers. She would hold the blossoms in her hand and try to speak.

Around the corner, virtually trapped in his semi-private room, which he shared with a more robust but ill-mannered bully who would steal his socks and shirts, my Dad was maintained by three or four tins of milky liquid protein that was calorie-enriched. At every given opportunity, he would spill the sticky stuff into his wastepaper basket into which he also occasionally urinated because he could not, he complained, get to his bedside porter-potty on time. And so the wise man who taught me courage under fire (*nil desperandum* was his lifelong motto), the organic intellectual who introduced me to multiple ways of seeing and knowing the world now disparagingly called himself "Little Jack Horner" (that is, stuck in his corner at Happy Valley).

Just as I steeled myself to return inside the nursing home high-pitched sirens announced the arrival of emergency ambulance and fire engines. The engines were killed in front of the entrance and several young men, dressed in white and in blue, jumped from their trucks carrying a stretcher, oxygen tank, and other heavy-duty medical equipment. I was frozen with fear, but not so much of my dear parents' timely deaths. Rather, it was for fear of their untimely medical rescue. But it was another bird-like fragile creature who was carted away under an oxygen tent as she clawed at the plastic tent flaps like a startled tabby cat. Her body was handled efficiently, even gracefully, by the boys in white who, nonetheless, eased their work by making sport of the absurd drama of rescue into which a resistant Ms. Kelly had been recruited.

As ever-increasing numbers of the aged are both sick and poor due to the astronomical cost of late-life medical care they are at risk of spending their remaining years in public or less-expensive private institutions for the aged like "Happy Valley." In private, "for profit," nursing homes the care for residents is delegated to grossly under-paid and under-trained care-takers who understandably protect themselves by turning the persons and bodies under their protection into things, bulky objects that can – once a new staffer gets the hang of it – be dealt with in shorter and shorter intervals. Economic pressures bear down on the "staffers" by their supervisors to minimize the personal care and attention given to the residents, especially those like my parents, whose limited life savings had been quickly used up by the institution and who were now supported by the state on Medicare.

Today in the US nursing facilities care for nearly 2 million elderly and disabled residents. They are part of a lucrative private industry that produces some $87 billion of business each year, of which more than 75 cents of every dollar comes from public funds through Medicare and Medicaid. To insure profits, most nursing homes are grossly under-staffed and to compensate for that somewhat active or rebellious residents are over-sedated. A federal study in 1997 found that nearly one-third of all nursing homes in California had been cited for violations that caused death or grave harm to residents (Bates 1997:12). My Dad saw through the sham of benevolence that was announced by a nursing-home poster welcoming new residents to Happy Valley's "circle of care" and informing patients of their rights. He often made sport of the poster to show that he was still on top of things, but it was with a prisoner's double-edged humor.

The underpaid staff needed, no less than myself, to duck away out of sight as often as possible, for a smoke, a snack, or a breath of air. But other work-survival tactics at Happy Valley Nursing Home are less defensible. The personal names of residents are dropped and they are often addressed as "you" instead of as Mrs. or Mr. Scheper. Little or no account is taken of expressed wishes so that sooner or later any requests based on personal preferences – to turn up or down the heat, to open or close the window, to bring a cold drink, to lower the TV or to change a channel – are extinguished. Passivity sets in. When the body is rolled from one side or the other for cleaning or to clean the sheets (body and sheets are equated), or when the resident is wheeled conveniently into a corner facing the wall so that the floor can be more easily mopped, when cleaning staff do little to suppress expressions of disgust at urine, feces, or phlegm out of place – on clothing, under the nails, on wheelchairs, or in wastepaper baskets, the person trapped inside the failing body may also come to see themselves as "dirty," "vile," "disgusting" – as an object or non-person. An essay by Jules Henry (1966) on "Hospitals for the Aged Poor" documenting the attack on the elderly individual's dwindling stock of personal and psychological "capital" by nursing-home administrators and staff rings as true today as when it was first written.

The institutional destruction of personhood is aided by the material circumstances of the home. Although individualized laundry baskets are supplied for each resident, the nursing aids refuse responsibility for lost or mix-matched clothing, even when each piece is carefully labeled. Several times I arrived as late as 11:00 in the morning to find my father in bed and under his sheets and completely undressed because, he explained, he had "no clothing" to wear. Arguments with staff were counter-productive and if anything could increase their passive hostility toward the complainant. When all personal objects – toothbrush, comb, glasses, towels, pens and pencils – continue to disappear no matter how many times they have been replaced, the resident (if he or she knows what is good for him or her) finally accepts the situation and adapts in other ways.

Eventually, residents are compelled to use other objects, which are more available, for purposes for which they were never intended. The plastic wastepaper basket becomes the urinal, the urinal the wash basin, the water glass turns into a spittoon, the hated adult diaper is used defiantly for a table napkin, and so forth. Meanwhile, the institutional violence and indifference are masked as the resident's own state of mental confusion and incompetence. And everything in the nature of the institution invites the resident to further regression, to give up, to lose, to accept his or her inevitable and less than human, depersonalized, status.

How can I write this so personal reflection without screaming? I *am* screaming. But I found myself unable to do the only thing that could have reversed this mad system: to run down the halls of Happy Valley Nursing Home, pull out the tubes, detach the liquid bags, knock over the porter-potties, and pick up my ancient and still beloved old ones and take them home to live with me. But God help me, this I was unable to do.

My point in revisiting this painful experience is neither to indict a business which indicts itself by its own "for profit" motives ("caveat emptor!") nor less to blame the nursing-home aides who are paid less than fry chefs at the local McDonalds to care for our old ones. My point is to ask what kind of civilization and people we have become when we – social critics and "militant anthropologists" among us – can fall prey to a lethal passivity toward institutional practices which compromise and erode the humanity and personhood of our own parents.

Postscript

On September 17, 1997, my father passed away in a hospital, but without too much labor. His final moments were peaceful. And at least in death his bodily dignity was restored. The young funeral director, Vinnie, who attended to my father's remains and supervised their removal from Baltimore to "home" in Queens, New York, for a simple funeral executed his tasks with extraordinary care and concern for my late father's dignity. In his dark blue suit with jaunty rosebud in its lapel, his handsome white beard trimmed, my father's charisma and personhood were ultimately returned to him.[2] A simple gift. But it is a deadly commentary on postmodern life (and on all of us) when the body we love is given greater honor and value in death than in the very last years of a long, gentle, and beautifully ordinary life. Forgive me!

NOTES

Acknowledgments: Sections of this chapter appeared in "Specifics – Peace-Time Crimes," *Social Identities* 3 (3) 1997.

1. Here I am referring to the writings of Veena Das (1996), Linda Green (1999), Lisa Malkki (1995) and Val Daniel (1997), among many others.
2. Following my father's funeral my brother's son, an industrial artist in Baltimore, read a poem at Dad's graveside, written by a Baltimore street poet. Its studied irreverence would not bother Dad, who once played honky-tonk music in a speakeasy in New York City.

       Untitled

       Tonight I'm eatin stars
       and yer not gonna stop me
       Travelin through bars
       with glitter on my stockings

My body parts are shimmerin
as I move through my own galaxy
My high heels kick up moondust
I got Saturn's rings for jewelry
Yeh, I know that times are hard
and you got yer shovel waitin on me
But tonight I'm eating stars
so you can shove yer goddamn gravity
The Sun fell down my pants
and I'm gonna dance till Gabriel blows
Search all night long till I find myself
a couple of celestial bodies
Go on you can dig yer hole
cuz tomorrow you might catch me
But tonight I'm eatin stars
and mother-fucker you can't touch me.

REFERENCES

Arendt, Hannah. 1963. *Eichmann in Jerusalem: A Report on the Banality of Evil.* New York: Vintage.
1969. *On Violence.* New York: Hartcourt, Brace & World.
Basglia, Franco. 1987. "Peace-Time Crimes." In *Psychiatry Inside Out: Selected Writings of Franco Basaglia* (Nancy Scheper-Hughes and Anne M. Lovell, eds.). New York: Columbia University Press.
Bates, Tovah E. 1997. "The Political Economy of Nursing-Home Care." Unpublished Ph.D. Dissertation. University of California, San Francisco.
Benjamin, Walter. 1969. Theses on the Philosophy of History. In *Illuminations* (H. Arendt, ed.) pp. 83–109. New York: Schocken.
1987. *Once in Europe.* New York Pantheon.
Bourdieu, Pierre. 1977. *Outline of a Theory of Practice.* Cambridge University Press.
1996. *In Other Words.* Stanford: Stanford University Press.
Bourdieu, Pierre and Loïc J. D. Wacquant. 1992. *An Invitation of Reflexive Sociology.* Chicago: University of Chicago Press.
Bowen, John R. 1996. The Myth of Global Ethnic Conflict, *Journal of Democracy* 7(4):3–14.
Calderia, Thersa. 2000. City of Walls. Berkeley: University of California Press.
Chorbajian, Levon and George Shirinian, eds. 1999. *Studies in Comparative Genocide.* New York: St. Martin's Press.
Daniel, E. Valentine. 1997. Suffering Nation and Alienation. In *Social Suffering* (Arthur Kleinmen, Veena Das and Margaret Lock, eds.), pp. 309–358. Berkeley: University of California Press.
Das, Veena. 1996. Language and Body: Transactions in the Construction of Pain. *Daedalus* 125(1):67–92. Special Issue on Social Suffering.
Dimenstein, Gilberto. 1991. *Brazil: War on Children.* New York: Monthly Review Press.
Douglas, Mary. 1966. *Purity and Danger.* New York: Routledge.

Erikson, Erik. 1950. *Childhood and Society.* New York: Norton.

Fackenheim, Emil. 1970. *God's Presence in History: Jewish Affirmations and Philosophical Reflections after Auschwitz.* New York: New York University Press.

Foucault, Michel. 1979. *Discipline and Punish.* New York: Vintage.

    1980. *The History of Sexuality.* New York: Vintage.

    1982. *The Subject and Power.* (P. Rabinow and H. Dreyfus, eds.), pp. 208–226. Chicago: University of Chicago Press.

Geuss, Raymond. 1981. *The Idea of Critical Theory.* Cambridge: Cambridge University Press.

Gilbert, Leah. 1996. Urban Violence and Health – South Africa 1995. *Social Science & Medicine* 45(5):873–886.

Girard, Rene. 1987. Generative Scapegoating. In *Violent Origins: Ritual Killing and Cultural* Formation (R. Hamerton-Kelly, ed.), pp. 73–105. Stanford: Stanford University Press.

Goffman, Erving. 1961. *Asylums: Essays on the Social Situation of Mental Patients and Other Inmates.* Garden City, NY: Double day.

Goldhagen, Daniel Jonah. 1996. *Hitler's Willing Executioners.* New York: Alfred Knopf.

Goldstein, Donna M. 1998. Nothing Bad is Intended: Child Discipline, Punishment and Survival in a Shantytown in Rio de Janeiro, Brazil. In The Cultural Politics of Childhood (N. Scheper-Hughes and C. Sargent, eds.). Berkeley: University of California Press.

Gourevitch, Philip. 1998. *We Wish to Inform You that Tomorrow We Will be Killed with Our Families: Stories from Rwanda.* New York: Farrar, Straus, Giroux.

Green, Linda. 1999. *Fear as a Way of Life.* New York: Columbia University Press.

Gramsci, Antonio. 1957. The Formation of Intellectuals. In *The Modern Prince and Other Writings.* New York: International Publishers.

Henry, Jules. 1963. *Culture against Man.* New York: Vintage.

    1966. *Sham, Vulnerability and Other Forms of Self Destruction.* New York: Vintage.

Hinton, Alexander L. 1996. Agents of Death. *American Anthropologist* 98:818–831.

Klinenberg, Eric. 1997. The Violence of Domination in the Work of Pierre Bourdieu. Unpublished ms., Department of Sociology, UC Berkeley.

Kleinman, Arthur and Joan Kleinman. 1996. The Appeal of Experience; the Dismay of Images: Cultural Appropriations of Suffering in Our Times. *Daedalus* 125(1):1–24. Special Issue on Social Suffering.

Levinas, Emmanuel. 1986. Useless Suffering. In *Face to Face with Levinas* (Richard Cohn, ed.). Albany: State University of New York Press.

Malkki, Lisa. 1995. *Purity in Exile.* Chicago: University of Chicago Press.

Masson, Jeffrey Moussaieff. 1984. *The Assault on Truth.* New York: Harper.

    1992. *Assault on Truth: Freud and Child Sex Abuse.* London: Fontana.

Patridge, Damani. 1997. The Violence that makes Peace Possible in a Global Economy. Unpublished ms., Department of Anthropology, Berkeley, May 1997.

Scheper-Hughes, Nancy. 1992. *Death without Weeping: the Violence of Everyday Life in Brazil.* Berkeley: University of California Press.

    1996a. Small Wars and Invisible Genocides. *Social Science & Medicine* 43(5):88.

    1996b. Maternal Thinking and the Politics of War. *Peace Review* 8:3:353–358.

    1997. Demography without Numbers. In *Anthropological Demography* (David Kertzer and Tom Fricke, eds.). Chicago: University of Chicago Press.

    2000. *Saints, Scholars, and Schizophrenics.* Berkeley: University of California Press.

Scheper-Hughes, Nancy and Anne Lovell. 1987. *Psychiatry Inside Out: Selected Writings of Franco Basaglia.* New York: Columbia University Press.

Scheper-Hughes, Nancy and Daniel Hoffman. 1998. Brazilian Apartheid: Street Kids and the Struggle for Survival in Urban Brazil. In *Small Wars: The Cultural Politics of Childhood* (N. Scheper-Hughes and C. Sargent, eds.). Berkeley: University of California Press.

Taussig, Michael. 1989. Terror as Usual. *Social Text* (Fall–Winter):3–20.

1992. *The Nervous System.* New York: Routledge.

Weiss, Meira. 1994. *Conditional Love: Parents' Attitudes Towards Handicapped Children.* Westport, CT: Greenwood Publishing Group.

1998. "Ethical Reflections." In *Small Wars* (N. Scheper-Hughes and C. Sargent, eds.). Berkeley: University of California Press.

Weschler, Lawrence. 1990. *A Miracle, A Universe: Settling Accounts with Torturers.* New York: Viking.

3   Intimate powers, public selves: Bakhtin's space of authoring

William S. Lachicotte

William Lachicotte's "Intimate Powers, Public Selves" takes up questions of affective and embodied resistance to state-sanctioned institutions. In Lachicotte's fascinating case study, Roger reproduces a sense of personal power through his borderline personality. Here Lachicotte's use of Bakhtin shades into Bourdieu – indeed, improves upon Bourdieu by showing how stigmatized actors can nonetheless exert agency that cuts across the grain of established hegemonies.

Roger's "alien-voice" – his penchant for speaking forcefully, quickly and loudly, but with little inflection, and often at odds with his gestural or facial expressions – defeats others' attempts to attribute to him a normal adult identity. In American culture normal identity has entailments of individual responsibility for one's life, one's relationships, and one's failures. Roger makes what amounts to a mockery of psychiatric culture (which would restore him to normality) by appearing to enthusiastically accept responsibility for his condition: he applies every possible pathological label to his case. Yet at any given moment Roger enlists those labels that are useful to resist the responsibilities that others would impose upon him. His identity is what one might call a pure pragmatics, evincing no stable sense of self.

Member of an individualistic society though he is, Roger adopts a highly social form of personhood in which identity fluctuates relative to group milieu, rather than being inner and independent. This culturally contrary form of personhood is a "mad" identity. It is also a form of non-identity – a failure to be a person in his culture's terms; one might call it "counter-identity." Like Raymond Williams' counter-hegemonic discourse (1977), Roger's counter-identity partakes of the terms of the dominant discourse – psychiatric labels. However, like Foucault's "counter-memory" (1977), this form of identity draws upon experiences truly foreign to dominant discourses; this is perhaps what makes it genuinely "borderline" and is its most subversive aspect. Through this form of personhood, Roger defends himself against the peace-time violence of his own society and carves out a "space of authoring" (Holland, *et al.* 1998) where a considerable degree of agency is still possible. Lachicotte thereby raises for analytic consideration, and in a newly creative way, the relationship between inner-speaking and social performance, the "complications of self-fashioning."

Jeannette Mageo and Bruce Knauft

The relationship between social and personal life is one of the most enduring topics of the human sciences. It has also proven to be one of the most obdurate and contentious, and a language or discursive practice that allows scholars to construe the interrelations of society and self, sociality and intimacy, is still in the making. In past work one or the other of these partners has too often become a kind of shadow or mirror of the other. So, for instance, social action becomes in some versions substantially a re-enactment or outward repetition of psychic life, habits, conflicts, and disorders. Or, in versions that have more currency today, subjectivity becomes a field of subjection to the interplay of social powers in the form of discourses and instrumentalities. I will use the works of M. M. Bakhtin and L. S. Vygotsky to suggest another figuration of this central human relationship.[1] Bakhtin and Vygotsky articulate a self that is everywhere a form of sociality and whose life (thinking, feeling, and willing) is necessarily a political practice, a play of mundane power. At the same time they understand society as concrete interchange and interaction that is carried through personal activity – inner-speaking and the imagination – transfigured into common means of association. Selves are powers in return, agencies of social and cultural production. Social and personal life do not disappear one into another. They subsist as moments, two mediations of human existence.

Roger and me

Let me try to concretize the complications of self-fashioning (as social practice) by a brief case history.[2] My account is located near a classic, Foucauldian venue, the institutions of psychiatric practice. Its interest resides precisely in the ways its protagonist subverts the relations of subject and object constitutive to biomedicine's hegemony and turns the objects of psychiatry – disorders or disease entities – to other uses. My commentary begins with precepts drawn from Vygotsky and Bakhtin and extends them to the practical fields in which Bourdieu has housed social life. It shows how self-fashioning takes the form not of an integral agent, but of strategies in Bourdieu's sense: registers of social actions tuned, through imagination and rehearsal, in consciousness and habit, to the variable play of our activities. And turnabout is fair play. In these registers, as Bakhtin insisted, personal life is made the vehicle of society only so far as society finds itself impersonated.

I first met Roger[3] at the time of his fourth hospitalization. He was a rather short and rotund man of 33, and looked the part of a prosperous, if not wealthy, middle-class salaried worker. He was well groomed and well dressed and showed few of the "irregularities" of self-care that were apparent among other patients. Roger had no obvious signs of thought disorders, behavioral abnormalities or disturbances of mood. It was hard to see why Roger was on the ward at all – until you spoke to him. Roger had a bad case of alien voice. He spoke loudly, with little inflection, yet with a force and speed that suggested agitation or excitement. His tone of voice (not the content of his speech) failed to match his other means of expression, either gestural or facial. There was something at odds about Roger. Although a college graduate, he had by his own assessment been consistently underemployed during the ten years he had worked. He was married at the time, and throughout the time I met with him, to a psychiatric nurse.

Roger gave the impression of someone who had come upon an explanation of his problems. "It's a major psychiatric illness . . . A sort of thinking and feeling disorder. I can't always trust what I'm thinking and feeling." He remembered, in a garbled way, the names the doctor had told him: "Obsessive-compulsive disorder. Bipolar. Schizoid-affective personality disorder." He preferred to call his illness "neurotic depression," however.

After discharge Roger bought into the therapeutic "system" in a big way. Each time I would ask, Roger would say that his "meds" (medications) were the best he had ever had. He took an active interest in "psychosocial" therapies as well, attending weekly sessions with his therapist, with his support group, and, from time to time, with his wife in couples therapy. As he told me one year after we first met, "I have a 200 page notebook upstairs that has notes on sessions with every doctor, social worker I've ever seen. It helps."

It was as if Roger had taken on his recovery as a job, and he worked quite hard at it. However, each of his attempts to complete the task – to return to "real" employment – ended quickly. Roger eventually settled into a routine of television, volunteer work, and the rounds of therapy. He applied for federal disability income (Social Security Disability Insurance [SSDI]) which he was granted after a year's wait.[4]

Though Roger professed a mental illness throughout our acquaintance, without hesitation, his ideas about this illness changed. Not only did he grow more knowledgeable about psychiatric disorders, his conceptions of the particular nature of his own illness changed in kind. By the second interview, the vague notions of six months prior had given way to an adoption of "manic-depression," a combination of "racing thoughts," and enduring depression – "how about just a guy feels lousy and there's no known reason?" The lack of apparent reason for both his cognitive and affective states clinched the argument for Roger. It had to be something within him, not outside and visible, and yet something medical, a somatic condition, and not, as his parents seemed to suggest, a problem of character or will.

By the third interview, one year after the first, Roger had again modified his ideas about his psychological problems:

I've always thought they were mainly chemically related and I still think they are. But there is some personality. When you're growing up, I believe – that affected the way I . . . my behavior, my thinking patterns. That has not changed. It's a combination of personality and chemical, that's what I feel . . .

Roger had begun working with a new psychiatrist who had changed Roger's diagnosis and the emphasis of his therapy. Previously Roger had "carried" a primary diagnosis of either Bipolar Disorder or a type of schizophrenia.[5] His new psychiatrist decided, putatively on the basis of psychological testing, that Roger was basically "borderline," that is, personality-disordered. He told Roger his conclusion and Roger had begun to take it to heart.

The next interview found Roger still learning his roles. In fact, during this interview, he reverted solely to speaking about his "racing thoughts" and "twisted, negative thoughts," symptoms he referred to his mania and depression and not to any character disorder. He was pleased about both a new cognitive therapy he had begun to learn and a new support group for manic-depressives which he attended. His medication was effective, especially the new drug (the now famous Prozac) recently prescribed for him. Roger was, in fact, quite upbeat and full of plans to return to normal life – though he did not expect, nor had he for a long time expected, a cure. He told me, with a sophistication that showed his continual reading: "No, you're always a manic-depressive. You never recover. You have a chemical imbalance that's always there in your synapses and all that, your serotonin uptake. It's always got to be regulated." At this time Roger was optimistic of his ability to manage the illness.

I encountered a chastened Roger six months later at our fifth interview. He had just returned from a three-day hospitalization, that was instigated by a severe bout of "suicidal thoughts." When I asked what had happened, Roger began to report problems of character. "I would say . . . borderline personality disorder. That means a manipulator, a liar, social behavior is sometimes you get abnormal – things like that. . . ." Alongside the straightforwardly biochemical factors of the prior interview he recounted different causes: "[M]y parents were highly critical of me growing up. I had to be perfect, get straight A's, so I was very hard on myself, so some aspects of my personality probably never developed as much as they should have. I – stunted growth, that's what happened." He sometimes mixed both sorts of understanding: "My mother's some traits of it. I think it's genetic, a lot of that stuff. It's how you're raised, according to that book, by your parents. Whether they uh, reward you or punish you, they're critical or loving. Or they're there when you need them. I mean there's a lot of factors involved in that, sort of like chemistry. There's a lot of factors." Roger had been reading again and was attempting to piece his ideas together.

In the two-year period from our first interview to our fifth, Roger consistently identified himself as a mentally-ill participant in the world of mental health care. His ideas of that illness had deepened and broadened in ways one might expect from a fuller involvement in that world. But these ideas never settled into one consistent way of interpreting his difficulties.

The virtual world

Before returning to Roger, I want to locate my analysis in the tradition of Vygotsky and Bakhtin without entering into an elaborate theoretical excursion. Let me send you a postcard instead: elements that help to establish the place of self in fields of power. These six pieces compose a landscape in which selves are worked and reworked in what might be called spaces of authoring (Holland *et al.* 1998): intimate and public fields of activity, established by both social and personal histories, and hedged by practical and discursive relations of power.

First, a key principle of Vygotsky's work, a person's higher "mental functions" derive from a career of social interaction, from dealings with other people. The intrapsychic is the interpersonal:

Every function in the child's development appears twice: first, on the social level, and later, on the individual level; first, between people (interpsychological) and then inside the child (intrapsychological). This applies equally to voluntary attention, to logical memory, and to the formation of concepts. All the higher functions originate as actual relations between human individuals (Vygotsky [1930] 1978b: 57).

This maxim is the conclusion of an argument, whose steps I will have to skip, that begins with the understanding of human activity as mediated, as labor which depends upon "tools." Vygotsky drew upon Engels' discussion of the role of tool use in human evolution (Engels, 1940, 1968). Engels held that not only human practice but also the human organism itself must be seen as the product as well as the producer of tools. If the form of the hand allowed the use of tools, the use of tools in turn shaped the hand, the musculature, the architecture of jointure and the cerebral and nervous elaboration of control. Vygotsky took this notion of the tool and extended it to the notion of the sign, of word and gesture, the tools of human communication (Vygotsky, 1978a [1934], 1987a). Just as tool use mediates people's interchanges with the environment and thereby changes them as well, so sign use mediates people's interchanges with each other and changes the interior person as well as the intersubject. The life of the sign, though intersubjective both pragmatically and referentially, goes into the "individual" in ways usually unnoticed.

Vygotsky uses the simple example of "pointing." At first, in the infant, the motion which will become pointing is only movement toward a desideratum. The associates of the infant respond to the movement, completing the action and fulfilling the desire. By repetition of the act-in-society, the child comes to conceive pointing as an instrument by which he or she can move others. It becomes dissociated from its original desire in play and, in the web of verbal commentary through which adults describe behavior, becomes associated with semantic and grammatical forms. Pointing becomes a symbol and acquires a meaning – which for Vygotsky is formally linguistic. At the same time the act of pointing becomes something more. Of its distantiation and formalization, the sign permits the "person" a means of intimate control, an instrumentality for the organization of behavior divorced from immediate organicity. It becomes a mediating device for desire internally as well as externally. Although the notion of internalization remains somewhat indistinct in Vygotsky's work (see Wertsch 1985), its importance is clear. It is the very process by which persons as self-aware beings – as socialized beings – are created.

Roger's "tools" – the behavioral profiles figured in diagnoses; the behavioral routines signaled in therapeutic exercises – are altogether more complex than pointing, but their lesson is much the same. It is hardly a new lesson; it is, in fact, the very point of psychotherapies. What one learns in interaction with the therapist, and with all one's colleagues in the realm of therapeutic practice, is meant to become the means of self-understanding and self-control. It is his insistence upon the durably social nature of psychic processes that sets Vygotsky apart from Freud and other theorists of psychotherapy.

To see this point, add to this foundation a *second* piece that is equally important and not obviously derivative. The transactions among people that are the wellspring of signification and self-construction come to be represented within the person by inner speech. Consciousness is literally hearing thought spoken, with the proviso that what is spoken in consciousness derives from others' speech. We are all familiar with this inner voice, the voice sounding in one's head. It provides direction and commentary – proaction and reflection – for actions: it is the "voiceover" that lets us know the consequences of activity. Since Plato, and perhaps earlier, this inner voice has been identified with thinking.

It is important to recognize that "the" sign in this mediation is not incorporated unitarily; rather its whole origination is internalized, as is the materiality, the medium, of its presentation. Roger does not grasp diagnostic categories as elements, or even as complexes of sign-elements, within an abstract or formal set of relations we call language. Instead, these "notions" are weighted with the speakers, activities, and locales in and by which signs are articulated. Inner speaking is thus somewhat of a misnomer or, rather, an ellipsis for inner activity, or sensuous human experience (Marx, 1975): the interior trace of the very webs of interaction and commentary in which each person subsists developmentally. Yet, as Vygotsky was able to show, inner speech (inner activity), once organized in the child, takes on a dynamic separate from the ongoing social life of the person (see Vygotsky, 1962, 1987a for the dynamic features of inner speech). The virtual reality of consciousness becomes truly mediate between the somatism of desire and the sociality of the person.

In this context, we can elaborate the two fundamental theses in several ways outlined by Bakhtin. A *third* step: the content of inner speech does not invoke a monotonous, single speaker. Rather, when we think, says Bakhtin, we hear the "voices" (it would be more accurate to say the vocal images) of those social persons with whom we associate. So Roger may engage with the voice of his psychiatrist, or with the more generic interlocutor (in Mead's sense) set by the diction of self-help books, as he thinks of borderline personality. One must recognize, with Vygotsky, the features proper to inner speech that make it less a simple transcription of dialogue and more a reconstruction of it within an economy already established. Still, Bakhtin reminds us that inner speaking preserves the social identifications that mark its origins in common activity. Discourses are not neutral media, but are infused and differentiated by social values, rank, prestige, and position. They are (in a very strong sense) other peoples' words. Bakhtin (1981, 1984a) made this point in his notions of heteroglossia and dialogism, definitive of modern self-fashioning.

The space of authoring

The *fourth* element then: self-consciousness and its identities, the voices of inner speech which seem to be mine, are created from an "orchestration," that is, the balance struck among the socially identified voices that comprise inner speech. A person of Bakhtin's world is always addressed and addressing, located socially not only by what is said and done "towards" her, but by what she says and does "towards" others. Roger is "pinned down" by the voices of his parents, siblings, wife, psychiatrist, nurses, therapists, and fellow patients that speak through his thoughts, and called to answer not simply what they say but the roles allotted him by their partnering his dialogue. Yet addressivity – as Voloshinov called this key principle – is never simple. We are for the most part multiply addressed and we, in turn, direct response to several audiences at once.

So, if it is true that we always speak and think through the words of others, still in the deployment of these voices, in their combination, sequence and disposition, in the time and space which are necessarily taken up, lies the actuality of authorship. Bakhtin tempered this conclusion, or, rather, extended it, by asserting that practical genres must exist which set out the means of orchestration. In Foucault's terms there must be available technologies of the self – whether specialized genres such as autobiography, or common ones like the life story – that provide the schemata, the cognitive and affective means, for self-formation (Lachicotte, 1986). The social world of therapy that Roger inhabits is of course replete with these devices and with the practices that give them flesh.

There is no one place, no transcendent or absolute ego, in which to locate such a self-process. Its home is rather the mediate world of human activity, which is both actual and virtual, creative and mimetic, a world that lives historically. One must begin with practices in a community of speakers and actors. A *fifth* constituent: the possible states of coordination for these identities, this self, are a question of authority, the relative strengths of the voices in the "self" configuration. We do not address, nor are we addressed by, equal partners. Their words carry different weight and we orchestrate unequal forces, even in thought.

Power – the capacity to instigate and organize activity – derives from institutional and interpersonal life. We are moved by the social bonds, the interdependencies and coercions that realize human sociality according to generic forms of association, institutions, expressed through cultural media. Neither Vygotsky nor Bakhtin deny, as I have intimated earlier, the somatic, nearly natural, impetus of desires and instincts. But species powers are organized, gain direction, and achieve productivity in social development, just as new desires are worked into us as dispositions toward social engagements. The social organization of activity reaches into us and becomes that intimate governor Foucault imagined. But, in Vygotsky's and Bakhtin's social world, these intimate powers, unlike those of Foucault's imaginary, never lose their distinctions and their identifications. People do not answer to Discourse, which is no conversation at all. Instead they answer to a variegate world of consociates, located at different removes, drawn in different perspectives, and indexed by different registers. The voices of inner speech, the landscapes of inner activity, retain specific forms and interrelations – both of concord and discord. They partake of "figured worlds" (Holland, *et al.* 1998).

The powers of such figured worlds are, like Foucault's power, generative. Through them, people author as they authorize their actions. The diagnostic figures of psychiatric practice, for instance, give shape to Roger's self-understanding of his behavior. In Vygotsky's view they also provide a means of intervention and control, a conduit that brings activity to an identifiable future. Incorporating the figure turns behavior from happenstance to production. To say "I have manic-depression" is tantamount to setting out, delimiting, a career. The identification locates Roger's behavior in the chronotope, as Bakhtin called it, the "spacetime" of psychiatry. It organizes a plot for his life that he and his associates play out. And it enforces that possibility by the power of institutional psychiatric practice. Authority invokes all these things.

For any subject, and indeed any intersubject, this question of authority is a matter of institutional, habitual (in Weber's or Bourdieu's sense), interpersonal, and psychological arrangements. So a *sixth* step, following upon the fifth: one's identities remain open to, and dependent upon, the field of continuing social discourse and everyday interaction. The person inside is always political. The suasion of a voice alters as the social position of its speaker changes relative to the other member voices in the ensemble and relative to the social field of activity. Psychiatric discourse has a generic authority for Roger and most of us, but its practical authority is diffracted by the persons who invoke it and by the contexts which frame it.

Hence the rhetoric of social life and self-fashioning may be remarkably complex, as the realities of "countercultures" and of movements of resistance remind us. Not only do instituted standards fail to reach universality in ordinary practice, but other sources of social valuation also abide where realms of interaction – games, arts, rituals – are established in the partial suspension of the "ordinary course of events." These arenas of "play," the powers of carnival, have much to do with social experimentation as well as social reproduction.[6] I would pair them with Foucault's notion of the disciplines, to which play is almost the negative, the dishabiting that sets the stage for the reinhabiting of new disciplines (Holland, *et al.* 1998).

As Freud would have it, the question of authority depends to some degree upon the psyche's own dynamic. With such a contention Bakhtin can agree. Any new "orchestration" of the self is shaped by extant as well as precedent arrangements. However, Bakhtin did not agree with Freud's reduction of what I will call the social scene of consciousness to a few "primal" scenes, particularly the Oedipal complex (Voloshinov, 1973).[7] Bakhtin rejected the unconscious and the means of reduction, repression, altogether, because he could not accept what he saw as its impoverishment of the social interplay of cognition and conation. Analysis of the psyche, in Bakhtin's and Voloshinov's (1986) sense, would still involve the reconstruction of the social scene of inner speech, the interpersonal foundation of the intrapsychic. But it would describe a larger historical notion of the social beyond the familial and early childhood forms that dominate Freudian and neo-Freudian analysis. My analysis tries to place Roger into such a present "psychosocial" world – a space of authoring – in order to make *his* case.

Identity/Politics

What is the social scene of Roger's "inner" life? As Roger left the public world centered upon work and the day-to-day accounting of common interaction, he entered into different means for the making and interpretation of behavior.

These psychiatric means are not, of course, completely alien to the everyday, but, the more removed one becomes from the ordinary arenas of interaction (which is itself an oddity) then the more important these special "technologies of the self" grow. Not all people who find themselves so secluded agree with, or even attend to, the psychiatric "line." Nonetheless, their opposition or indifference leaves them still in the same situation as those, like Roger, who fall in with it wholeheartedly. The power of social circumscription sets persons with psychiatric disorders apart, despite their wishes and sometimes despite considerable efforts to resist circumscription.

There were, however, other reasons for Roger's willingness to adopt psychiatric ideas, which I hope to clarify. His mental illness obviously entered into a longstanding dialogue among Roger, his wife, and his family. As his wife told me:

There's always been a big competition in the family. And he was the one that went to 4 years of college, and you know, everybody wanted him to be a lawyer, and here's his brother who didn't go to any college and took a few courses at IBM and has a very good position in IBM.

Or, as Roger himself admitted:

I'm very closely tied to my parents. I don't know why. They never – I'm probably trying to get what I never got from them. I don't know – love and understanding. All I got was criticism and "you can do better" . . . They wonder why I'm not at work now. They don't understand mental illness. They think, you know, if you get off the pills, get off this, everything'll be OK.

This sense of competitiveness in economic achievement, the emphasis on self-control, the giving and withholding of affection as motivation toward achievement, are stereotypical features of American "middle-class" family life. Roger's quite obvious failure to meet these standards, and the consequent disapproval he met from his family, was a lasting dilemma in his social life, and for his self-understanding.

If, on his family's part, Roger met expectations that he found hard to fulfill, he encountered an opposing pressure from his wife (and his psychiatrist). She told me:

when he sees a job in the paper that he really would want, I have to think in my mind, is he really going to be able to perform that type of work, and yet I don't want to be the one to be the bad guy and say "Roger, I don't think you can really do that." You know, I think he ought to look into job opportunities as he's been doing, but I think there's some things that he's just never going to be able to do.

She saw her task as helping Roger to lower his expectations about employment, in line with her notions of the functional impairment which mental disorders cause. From her stance as a professional, a psychiatric nurse, she had adopted in her domestic relations both the separation between Roger and his illness and the kind of unintended power of illness over person, a kind of possession, that is the popular way of figuring this separation. But this toleration too was a problem for Roger. With his family, the distress which mental disorder caused Roger disappeared in the disguise, the mask, of his defective will. With his wife Roger's own thoughts, feelings, and interests disappeared within the manifestations, the symptoms, of illness.

It is easy to guess what brought about Roger's conflation of "identity work" and work in its usual sense. What interests me is how Roger used psychiatric notions strategically in order to answer the dilemmas of his everyday life.[8] When speaking of his relationships with his parents and brother, and his relations with co-workers, Roger usually emphasized a manic-depressive persona. Here he talked of his family (second interview):

No, they don't understand really. They think I'm just a little depressed or a little blue or something. They really don't know much about mental illness . . . It's ten times stronger than that. At least . . . At first when I was four months at [the hospital] six years ago, I wanted to die day and night; I was that bad. I couldn't even think straight. Everything was fuzzy, I mean, it was just so depressed. And my parents didn't understand, "What are you? Down a little? Can't you – ?", you know, "Girl friend problems or something?" I was just trying to focus on my name and stuff, it was that intense for four months . . . Yeah, that disrupting. They tried different medicines and they finally found one that helped me pretty good so they let me go, but I was there four months. Day and night I just wanted to kill myself.

Both medical psychiatry and much of the popular psychological discourse conceive this illness, bipolar affective disorder, to be primarily a somatic one, caused by a dysfunction of neurotransmission.[9] Susceptibility to the illness is also thought to be genetically based. It is thus beyond one's control and remedy by willful action alone; having manic-depression is not one's own fault. Roger thus opposed its unwilled disruption of his own capacities to his parents' and co-workers' interpretation: Roger lacked the will-power, or the energy, to change his misbehavior.

No, I didn't come with some idea to do this, no. I tried to be there [at work] everyday I was capable of being there. [Interviewer: Did things just get to be too much or what?] Yeah, I just – racing thoughts and fearful thoughts and you feel closed in and "I can't do this job another minute," and . . . Yeah, they had me in something called the mini-stacker. And these big boxes would come down with hundreds of parts in them. I had to count all the parts; they're in bags; some of them weren't in bags. Then I had to put them on another conveyer belt, punch in a few things and it would take them to the racks and stick them up there in stock. But some days you'd stand around an hour. Your technician is looking at you the whole time. And I don't know what to do. And he'll give me some racks to fill and I've never done them before. And it just created a lot of tension, him looking at me all the time. You know, and other days you've got so much – on that conveyer belt, it's backed up around the corner someplace.

Roger borrowed the authority of medicine to answer other people's claims against him, against his failure at work. At the same time, the persuasiveness of this psychiatric identity, *vis-à-vis* Roger's other self-conceptions, increased to the extent that it provided Roger with a way both to legitimate his past activity and to maintain the relationships he valued. It is entirely appropriate when one is afflicted by a disease which incapacitates for one's therapy to become one's entire work. So Roger justified his withdrawal from the work-world through his identity as manic-depressive. As he ruminated: "Who am I proving it to: me, my parents, my doctor, my wife, myself, who? That's the question I've got to answer. Most 35's aren't home watching TV half the day or sleeping half the day, [but most 35 year olds don't have] what I have, yeah."

Yet, when speaking of his wife and his psychiatrist, Roger took a different line and emphasized a "borderline" persona. He spoke during the fifth interview about a spate of impulsive sexual behavior that led to his subsequent hospitalization:

[It's] Embarrassing, really. Cause you wish you could control yourself better. I shouldn't be going to a massage parlor or nothing like that. I have a loving wife who should meet my needs, and she does. I mean I feel guilty, and I feel embarrassed. I just feel bad about myself. Those are normal reactions. But I don't know why I keep repeating this behavior [indecipherable] . . . It's compulsive, yeah. I get the thought in my head, and I can't stop until I satisfy that need. Whether it's a cigarette, or going to a massage parlor, or calling somebody 1–900, or . . . asking a girl to dance at the Long Branch even though I'm married, or whatever it is, you know, I just get that thought, and it's impulsive-compulsive, really. Prozac's supposed to be working on that. It's helped some, but . . .

Roger's wife did not doubt his incapacity, nor the necessity of his treatment. Indeed, her fatalism and her obsession were even greater than his own. His life apart from illness – what he wants to do and what he can do, not what he is made to do by disease – was nearly lost in their dealings. Hence Roger sought to change the terms of interpretation. The personality disorders, to the extent that they are learned, remain within the scope of will, of one's self-control. One can unlearn what one has learned, if one wants to.

[interrupting] I don't know. Like I, I went to Dr. G's yesterday, and he says that you lie a lot. I told him certain things, I lied a lot, and I have compulsive behavior, and I said, "I thought I was a good Christian guy. I didn't know I had this evil side to me. I always thought I was almost perfect, like my parents wanted me to be." So that really struck me as a major breakthrough we had yesterday. There is a good and bad me, you know, and it's OK to have both. You know, you can't hate one and love the other. You got to accept both.

Yet, even in the midst of a "breakthrough," there is a reminder that the misbehavior itself, "the bad me," persists at its author's whim. Roger's belief that
"You have to accept both" keeps him in (ambiguous) charge – who or what else
ordains the necessary acceptance?

Roger drew upon the sense of willfulness that still adheres to the personality
disorders in order to oppose his wife's (or his psychiatrist's) reduction of him
to his disease. By becoming "borderline" at the proper times and places, Roger
enhanced his own sense of his agency, his active self-expression, without letting
go of the legitimate disabilities of illness. Borderline Personality Disorder is pe-
culiarly adapted to this kind of double posture because of its very "undecided"
position in psychiatric knowledge. It carries still the signs of schizophrenia, of
affective disorder, and of character disorder, in a kind of continually rebalanced
mix.[10] And the powerfulness attributed to its volatility, the fact that its balance
may come apart at any moment, served Roger well. It went far to insure that
he, the actor "Roger," would not be dismissed or overlooked. So Roger reproduced a sense of personal power through his borderline identity.[11] I should also
note that becoming borderline also moved the blame, the responsibility for the
illness, from a kind of neutral, bodily "dysfunction" to a decidedly partisan
"abnormality" of childhood development. It made Roger's parents historically
accountable for his current misdeeds, as one brief quote given above articulates. Roger never elaborated this charge against his parents, at least in the talks
I had with him. It remained more an abstract possibility, rather than an integral
element, of his expressed relations.

Impression and expression

Roger used various tools to revise and establish his new identifications and
understandings of himself. These mediating devices included the various behavioral schemata provided by accounts of diagnostic categories (borderline,
manic-depressive, obsessive-compulsive, etc.), by therapeutic techniques (cognitive "chaining" and replacement, deescalation, etc.) and by Roger's own
rehearsals (the therapy book) and others' advice (self-help and support groups).
Apart from these specifics, however, there was the structure, the means of
organization provided by the token of the activity itself. Performing therapy,
attending self-help groups, reading both popular and professional writings
express a dispositional lesson. They signal to ourselves as well as others where
we are headed and with whom we travel. They are the means one uses to
reproduce the desire for particular identities. But there is a price.

Access to these activities and to the specific identities they produce is a
matter of social position and negotiation: in a word, politics. By participation
one adopts specific affiliations, disaffiliations, and relations of self-production.
Roger's course was not smooth. He did not settle on one particular psychiatric

identity, maintaining instead several versions of himself as bipolar, as obsessive-compulsive, as borderline. These were tied to the activities and agents from which they were mastered. As either the situational or the institutional relations among these activities and agents changed, so did Roger's identifications (or, at least, so did the work needed to maintain them). The change of psychiatrists, of therapeutic groups, of the relations between wife and family, wife and psychiatrist, psychiatrist and group, even abstract changes in the authority of psychiatric diagnoses, all had "direct" effects upon Roger's self-conceptions. Bakhtin would say that such semiotic devices, even as means of the imagination, remain others' words and acts, others' speaking, others' voices. By using them we gain materials toward identity, but these materials come socially identified. At the same time that you inform yourself, you open yourself (even in your own thoughts and feelings) to the social world.

It is neither representation nor public relations (as symbolic interactionism's strategies or games of self-expression so often seem to be) but public work that is happening here. The self is literally made in the deployment of performances, pulled into shape by the force of its constituent discourses, by what Bakhtin (1990) called the architectonics of expression. But one must also remember that some vocations in this force field are already personal, the recognized places of precedent organization: history-in-person.

Here I cannot do analytic justice to Roger's history of self, to the ways in which prior self-concepts and self-relations shaped the course of his self-reformation. What his case shows, however, is that one's personal agency is not the creation of a self that is always uniquely one's own. Rather, agency takes shape in a field of contest, the "space of authoring." This space is formed, both within us and outside us, by the very multiplicity of persons who are identifiable positions in networks of social production, and of worlds of activity that are also scenes of consciousness. When we act, whether that act is instrumental or imaginative, we "move" through this space figuratively. None of us is occupied singularly; we are not possessed by one identity, one discourse, one subject-position. Each act is simultaneously a social dynamic, social work, a set of identifications and negations, an orchestration or arrangement of voices. And our sense of self comes from the history of our arrangements, our "styles" of saying and doing through others. The freedom that Bakhtin calls authorship comes from the ways differing identifications can be juxtaposed, brought to work with and against one another, to create a position, our own voice, from which we respond to life's tasks.

Roger opposed several identities drawn from psychiatric discourse to those cast for him by his wife, family, co-workers, psychiatrists, even by himself.[12] I would argue that he did so neither to destroy or deny, nor to assert or take up, any one identity – to say that he was truly one person or another. Rather he orchestrated these differing identities, differing voices, to shape a place for his own activity. His agency was no one personage, but an ensemble of persons that lived around and within him. It is therefore entirely conceivable that Roger saw no conflict between identities founded upon the two types of disorder: they simply coexisted for him, manifest at different times in differing forms.

Roger's case teaches this final, potent lesson: there is *no* necessary integrity to self-understandings – even within a given field of activity.[13] Though hegemonic discourses work to authorize a normal version of "us," persons are not simply surfaces of inscription.[14] They are also social workshops that forge new forms of association, hybrids of relatedness among the partial selves that respond to sets of our associates, our multiple others. Each articulate notion of self – each orchestration of identity – is a public creation of social relations. We are, ourselves, renderings of possible social orders: imagined worlds-to-be. Roger's own improvisations in self-fashioning figure in a popular culture of "personology," whose relationships with psychiatric discourse cannot be relegated to simple subordination. The future of that rendering, the playing out of new "imaginaries," of new "figured worlds" instantiated by communities of social practice, is a complicated history that exceeds the task at hand. It is a tale wrought also in power, moved by the struggle for a public: the coalition of legitimate practitioners. Few of the myriad voices at play in Bakhtin's carnival are broadcast, and no vocation attains generic force necessarily. Yet, selves remain powers in return: as we answer to the world's manifold address, so it must answer to ours.

NOTES

Acknowledgments. Scholarship is always a Bakhtinian affair, an orchestration of the works and voices of others to make what is at best a novel chorus. The figures at play are too numerous to recall, much less to give due consideration. However, I would like to thank, first, Jeannette Mageo, who organized the session in which this chapter was originally delivered, and who has shepherded the papers to publication. Her comments and encouragement are much appreciated, as were those of Bruce Knauft and the two anonymous reviewers who read the entire collection. I would also like to thank my colleagues – Sue Estroff, Terry Evens, Judy Farquhar, Jim Peacock – and my former colleague, Jaan Valsiner, who helped shape my understanding of the material. My collaborators, Carole Cain and Debra Skinner, are still co-authors in spirit: the ID group lives! Finally, untold (and sometimes told) thanks go to Dorothy Holland, who introduced me to Vygotsky and Bakhtin more than fifteen years ago. We have been working out the implications ever since. The fact that Dottie will never quite see my vision, but, in Bakhtin's terms, always sees the surplus of vision, has paid dividends for all my work.

1. Mikhail M. Bakhtin (1895–1975) was a critical theorist, semiotician, and philosopher of language, as well as a workaday teacher of literature and literary critic. He worked for many years in the obscurity of a provincial Russian university – an obscurity necessitated by the official censure of his work that led to his exile

from St. Petersburg in 1929. His accounts of human sociality, subjectivity, and expressive activity are now well known and influential among Anglophone scholars in various disciplines. See e.g., Clark and Holquist (1984), Todorov (1984), Holquist (1990), Morson and Emerson (1990) for the critical reception of his works. Lev S. Vygotsky (1896–1930) was the preeminent social and developmental psychologist of early Soviet Russia and founder of a tradition – now called the "sociohistorical" or "cultural-historical" school (van der Veer and Valsiner, 1991) – that has influenced both cognitive and developmental psychology widely in Europe and increasingly in the United States. Vygotsky's conception of psychological life as inextricably rooted in the social world shares not only a problematic, but also a common discourse, with Bakhtin's writings. They were both shaped by the intellectual ferment of post-Revolutionary Russia, a ferment occasioned by the encounter of a newly regnant Marxian tradition with the spectrum of European human sciences. See Wertsch (1985) specifically for Vygotsky's work and Joravsky (1989) for a more general account of the intellectual context of the time.

2. See Holland, *et al.* 1998 for a more complete exposition of both this perspective on self and identity and the case study. Parts of this section appear are reprinted by permission of the publishers from *Identity and Agency in Cultural Worlds* by D. Holland, W. Lachicotte, D. Skinner and C. Caid, Cambridge, MA: Harvard University Press, Copyright 1998 by the President and Fellows of Harvard College. In this chapter I will not compare our position to other "theories" of self in social life. The reader should see *Identity and Agency* (especially chapters 1 and 2), and also consult Mageo's and Knauft's introduction (chapter 1) in order to place the argument in its larger context.

3. A pseudonym. Fieldwork for the case study described in this section took place from 1986 to 1991. It was conducted by a research team at the University of North Carolina School of Medicine headed by Sue E. Estroff and was supported by the National Institute of Mental Health (Grant MH 40314).

4. The whole apparatus of disability determination is an institutional voice of great power in the lives of many persons with severe and persistent mental disorder. It is a largely unspoken presence in this chapter. See Estroff (1981) and Estroff, *et al.* (1997a; 1997b) for detailed accounts of the roles it plays in not only the economic, but social and psychological worlds of psychiatric clients.

5. The verb "carry," frequently used in professional discourse to describe the relationship between diagnostic label and person, echoes all the ambivalence that marks psychiatric illness. It denotes the (positive) separation of person and disease (not I *am* a schizophrenic, rather I *have* schizophrenia) and yet (negatively) marks the token of disease as something I bear – a weight, burden, and finally a stigma.

6. See Bakhtin, 1984b of course, but also Vygotsky, 1978c, 1987b and two classic works by Johan Huizinga, 1955, 1956.

7. Note my representation of the works published under the name of Bakhtin's friend and collaborator V. N. Voloshinov as equivalents of Bakhtin's own. There is today an active debate over these works' authorship and the implications of that authorship for the reception of Bakhtin's ideas and the proper conception of his politics. See Morson and Emerson (1990) who contest Clark and Holquist's view (1984, see also Holquist, 1990), that the Voloshinov books are Bakhtin's. I have neither the expertise nor the need to engage in these debates. I will continue to follow Todorov's policy (1984) and refer to Bakhtin's circle, "Bakhtin plural," under the rubric of his

       name. It is not the ideological heritage of these concepts that interests me but their concordance and productivity.

8. Buried here is a matter of some importance. I was not privy to Roger's interactions with wife, family, and friends; I *interviewed* him *about* his activities. And interviews, especially since Crapanzano's classic (1980) exposition in *Tuhami*, are recognized as notorious co-productions of their own participants, times, and places. They are not transparent reports of life, but construals that refract and remake what is represented of people's lives. True enough, but there is mitigation that allows ethnographers to draw interview materials out of their immediate circumstances. The interview is an everyday genre that sets interviewers up as audience – as we always are, to a certain extent, in Bakhtin's world eavesdroppers on the conversations of our interviewees with their materially absent, but imaginatively quite present, correspondents. Ethnographic interviewing is not just one's own conversation; it is also and even more strongly like overhearing a conversation on the telephone. As in Bob Newhart's classic comedy routines, one hears only one person speaking, but the sense, even the disposition, of the (absent) respondent is virtually audible. In this way, interviews are representative of more than their situations – or, rather, we must understand the situation of interaction as translocal and multiply populated by agents bound within those present, the discourses spoken and the landscapes taken over. We cannot afford to ignore the people on the other ends of the many lines that run in and out of every human scene.

9. The biopsychiatric conception of this disorder is memorialized in the handbook of contemporary diagnosis, the *DSM-IV: Diagnostic and Statistical Manual of Mental Disorders*, fourth edition (APA 1994). For a more popular account, see Andreason, 1984.

10. These signs may be read, traced, in the eclectic list of symptoms whose conjunction defines the disorder in the DSM, as well as in the array of disorders against which it is differentially diagnosed. For a detailed discussion of the history of borderline disorders, and the implications that history has for diagnosis and treatment, see Stone (1986), a volume which also reprints the most important sources of this mutable history.

11. The fascination – perhaps dread is a better description – which therapists display in their incessant talk about "borderlines" is captured well by Schwartz-Salant (1987). I have treated this issue at greater length in the context of the histories and collaboration of those vocations which comprise contemporary mental health practice (Lachicotte 1992). Unlike depression, or even manic-depression, borderline personality disorder is a connoisseur's illness, a creature of therapeutic "culture." In this regard, too, Roger's wife and psychiatrist are the proper audience for its performance.

12. Let me make explicit one subtext of the argument. The mode of analysis adopted here reworks the popular notion of "defense mechanisms" – psychological defenses – that derives from psychoanalytic accounts. Speaking crudely (a subtle treatment would be a chapter in itself), Vygotskiian perspectives locate the origins of defenses in social "coping" strategies – with this proviso. Strategies here, and elsewhere in this paper, must be understood in Bourdieu's sense. They do not consist purely of conscious, or even semi-conscious, counteractions on the part of an actor. Instead, strategies are "outlines of practice" drawn up within what Jean Lave and Etienne Wenger (1991) call "communities of practice." They are the embodied bases on which players improvise sets of moves contingent upon a

predicated (imagined) course of events realized under highly mutable contexts. In G.H. Mead's terms, they are "forms of social coordination." Neither the action nor the actor is singly identified: individual. Roger is not, despite my focus upon him, the producer and product of "his" activity. The person "Roger" and any person are social forms; authorship is always joint.

When a practical strategy is internalized – when it becomes something we might call a psychological defense – it becomes, in Vygotsky's term, "fossilized." The social lines of its production are erased in a process of abbreviation that leaves only the bodily and imaginal gesture: the metonym or trace of activity Bourdieu calls "disposition." ("Fossil" because only the "cast" of the living activity remains.) Though I doubt this process is the only mechanism of habituation, the only means by which habitus is cultivated, it is one source that Bourdieu does not elaborate. Habitus takes on, in this reading, the partial character of a "cultural defense system" – which may be related to the conservative tenor most commentators have remarked in the concept. Once again, the reader should see Holland *et al.* (1998) for an exposition that draws Vygotsky, Bakhtin, and Bourdieu together into an account of human identity and agency.

13. Which is not to deny that there exist "consistent" aspects of self. In analogy to Bakhtin's discussion of language's dynamics (1981), one may say that social self-processes are both "centrifugal" and "centripetal." Specific fields of activity differentiate identities so that "we" *shift* from one to another as we move from one field to another. Yet there also exist specialized and everyday discursive genres that link these shifting self-understandings into coherent genealogies and histories: (ethno)psychologies and sociologies; tales of lives and careers. One need not follow Bakhtin's next step – positing that centrifugal forces are actual or historically real, and centripetal forces are virtual or *simultaneous* (cf. Lévi-Strauss on the "reality" of structures) – to accept this complex topology of the self. See Allison's "morph-ology" of fantasy figures (chapter 4 this volume), Ewing's discussion of shifting identity and self-experience (chapter 5 this volume) and Ewing (1990).

14. Bakhtin spoke of the process by which persons are freed from authority as a struggle with two forms of alien discourse. The first, authoritative, discourse is distant from us, inert in interaction and fused with the social position of its issuance ("religion," "science," or other official lines). Authoritative discourse inhabits and speaks through us; it is "unrepresented," discourse that we repeat and do not refract. It is, in this sense, anonymous, but this anonymity does not mean that authoritative discourse is "voiceless." Rather, it is "de-identified": becoming the standard, the "unmarked" case against which other actions are judged, as its particular, historical origins (and the interests that impel its formulation) are "erased" (masked). In analogy to Gramsci's notion of hegemony, authoritative discourse is *made* anonymous by the cultural politics of silencing and normalizing that accomplish its colonizing of everyday life. It has a basis in the symbolic violence that realizes institutional practices of domination (Bourdieu, 1977). Cf. Scheper-Hughes (chapter 2): violence that is symbolic is not only symbolic. The second type of alien discourse, "internally persuasive discourse," is masked by its fusion with what seems "our" voice or word. It has a kind of "psychological" authority – persuasiveness – based less upon official powers than upon personal history. In either case, for Bakhtin, the first step toward freedom is imaginative. One historicizes and localizes, putting a contemporary voice and face to authority; one personalizes (as one objectifies)

internally persuasive discourses with the figures that mouth them in order to (dis)engage their social force. But these imaginative acts are also social practice (parody), a counteraction of hegemony that locates its media in a contestable, moral universe of actors. See Bakhtin (1981: 342–349) for his account of the genesis of "ideological consciousness."

REFERENCES

American Psychiatric Association. 1994. *Diagnostic and Statistical Manual of Mental Disorders*. Fourth Edition [DSM-IV]. Washington, DC: American Psychiatric Association.

Andreasen, Nancy C. 1984. *The Broken Brain: The Biological Revolution in Psychiatry*. New York: Harper & Row.

Bakhtin, Mikhail M. 1981. *The Dialogic Imagination* (M.E. Holmquist, ed.; Caryl Emerson and Michael Holquist, trans.). Austin: University of Texas Press.

    1984a. *Problems of Dostoevsky's Poetics* (Caryl Emerson, ed. and trans.). Minneapolis: University of Minnesota Press.

    1984b. *Rabelais and His World* (Helene Iswolsky, trans.). Bloomingdale: University of Indiana Press.

    1990. *Art and Answerability* (Michael Holquist and Vadim Liapunov, eds.; Vadim Liapunov, trans.). Austin: University of Texas Press.

Bourdieu, Pierre. 1977. *Outline of a Theory of Practice*. Richard Nice, trans. Cambridge: Cambridge University Press.

Clark, Katerina and Michael Holquist. 1984. *Mikhail Bakhtin*. Cambridge, MA: Harvard University Press.

Crapanzano, Vincent. 1980. *Tuhami*. Chicago: University of Chicago Press.

Engels, Frederick. 1940. *Dialectics of Nature*. New York: International Publishers.

    1968. The Part Played by Labor in the Transition From Ape to Man. In *The Origins of the Family, Private Property and the State* (Eleanor Leacock, ed.). New York: New World Books.

Estroff, Sue E. 1981. *Making it Crazy: An Ethnography of Psychiatric Clients in an American Community*. Berkeley: University of California Press.

Estroff, Sue E., Patrick, Donald, Zimmer, Catherine, and William Lachicotte. 1997a. Pathways to Disability Income Among Persons With Severe, Persistent Psychiatric Disorders. *Milbank Quarterly* 75(4):1–38.

Estroff, Sue E., Zimmer, Catherine and William Lachicotte, Julia Benoit and Donald Patrick. 1997b. No Other Way To Go: Pathways to Disability Income Application Among Persons With Severe, Persistent Mental Illness. In *Mental Disorder, Work Disability and the Law* (Richard Bonnie and John Monahan, eds.), pp. 55–104. Chicago: University of Chicago Press.

Ewing, Katherine P. 1990. The Illusion of Wholeness: Culture, Self, and the Experience of Inconsistency. *Ethos* 18(3): 251–278.

Foucault, Michel. 1977. *Language, Counter-Memory, Practice* (Donald F. Bouchard and Sherry Simon, trans.). Ithaca, NY: Cornell University Press.

Holland, Dorothy C., Lachicotte, William S., Skinner, Debra and W. Carole Cain. 1998. *Identity and Agency in Cultural Worlds*. Cambridge: Harvard University Press.

Holquist, Michael. 1990. *Dialogism: Bakhtin and His World*. London: Routledge.

Huizinga, Johan. 1955. *Homo Ludens: A Study of the Play Element in Culture.* Boston: Beacon Press.

1956. *The Waning of the Middle Ages.* Garden City, N.J.: Doubleday.

Joravsky, David. 1989. *Russian Psychology: A Critical History.* Oxford: Basil Blackwell.

Lachicotte, William S. 1986. Bakhtin and the Society of the Self. Paper presented at the Annual Meeting of the Southern Anthropological Society. Wrightsville Beach, NC, April, 1986.

1992. On the Borderline: Profession, Imagination and Authority in the Practice of Mental Health Care. Unpublished Ph.D. Dissertation. Dept. of Anthropology, University of North Carolina at Chapel Hill. Ann Arbor: University Microfilms.

Lave, Jean and Etienne Wenger. 1991. *Situated Learning: Legitimate Peripheral Participation.* Cambridge: Cambridge University Press.

Marx, Karl. 1975. Theses on Feuerbach. In *Early Writings* (Rodney Livingstone & Gregor Benton, eds.), pp. 421–423. New York: Vintage Books.

Morson, Gary Saul and Caryl Emerson. 1990. *Mikhail Bakhtin: Creation of a Prosaics.* Stanford: Stanford University Press.

Schwartz-Salant, Nathan. 1987. The Dead Self in Borderline Personality Disorders. In *Pathologies of the Modern Self: Postmodern Studies on Narcissism, Schizophrenia and Depression* (David M. Levin, ed.), pp. 114–162. New York: New York University Press.

Stone, Michael H. (ed.) 1986. *Essential Papers on Borderline Disorders: One Hundred Years at the Border.* New York: New York University Press.

Todorov, Tzvetan. 1984. *Mikhail Bakhtin: The Dialogical Principle* (Wlad Godzich, trans.). Minneapolis: University of Minnesota Press.

van der Veer, René and Jaan Valsiner. 1991. *Understanding Vygotsky.* Oxford: Blackwell.

Voloshinov, V. N. 1973. *Freudianism: A Marxist Critique* (I.R. Titinuk, trans.). New York: Academic Press.

1986. *Marxism and the Philosophy of Language.* Cambridge, MA: Harvard University Press.

Vygotsky, L. S. 1962. *Thought and Language.* Cambridge, MA: MIT Press.

1978a. Tool and Symbol in Child Development. In *Mind in Society* (Michael Cole, *et al.*, eds.), pp. 19–30. Cambridge, MA: Harvard University Press.

1978b. Internalization of Higher Psychological Functions. In *Mind in Society* (Michael Cole, *et al.*, eds), pp. 52–57. Cambridge, MA: Harvard University Press.

1978c. The Role of Play in Development. In *Mind in Society* (Michael Cole, *et al.*, eds.), pp. 92–104. Cambridge, MA: Harvard University Press.

1987a. Thinking and Speech. In *The Collected Works of L.S. Vygotsky, Vol. I: Problems of General Psychology* (Robert W. Rieber and Aaron Carton, eds.; Norris Minick, trans.), pp. 39–285. New York: Plenum Press.

1987b. Imagination and Its Development in Childhood. Lectures on Psychology, 5. In *The Collected Works of L. S. Vygotsky, Vol.I: Problems of General Psychology* (Robert W. Rieber and Aaron Carton, eds.; Norris Minick, trans.), pp. 339–349. New York: Plenum Press.

Wertsch, James V. 1985. *Vygotsky and the Social Formation of Mind.* Cambridge, MA: Harvard University Press.

Williams, Raymond. 1977. *Marxism and Literature.* Oxford: Oxford University Press.

Part II

Transnational psychologies

4   Playing with power: morphing toys and transforming heroes in kids' mass culture

Anne Allison

In Anne Allison's "Playing with Power," child's play discloses the interaction between psychic power and internalized epistemic power. The reduction of superhero play-toy characters to good versus evil within the not-really-human category suggests to Allison that in action-figure fantasy play power is being grappled with in a manner similar to fairy tales. Allison resituates Bettelheim's psychoanalytic insights on fairy tales in a transnational world, suggesting that multinational marketing is effective because this play engages the cross-cultural vicissitudes of psychosexual life and their attendant ambivalences.

Bettelheim views fairy tales as developing the self. "Playing with power in the realm of superheroes" likewise represents a moral process/progress. Typically the protagonist starts out in what one might call a state of "moral liminality." S/he is likable but impulse-indulgent, comically so, as is the teenage girl Sailor Moon in her Japanese TV show, who is whiny, boy-crazy, and over-sleeps. Magical transformation into a superheroine, "morphing," symbolically separates the protagonist's morally-positive and morally-negative aspects. Postmorphing, the protagonist appears as superhero/ine, personifying positive morality in counterdistinction to villains who personify the premorphed protagonist's moral negativity. These villains are not just impulse-indulgent; they violently pursue illicit satisfactions that represent technologically enhanced forms of power allied with bleakly materialistic impulses. Allison identifies this moral negativity with the capitalistic/commercialistic underside of action-figure play that transforms so many children into born-to-be consumers.[1] This underside is Baudrillard's (1988) virtual world, where copies of copies in high-gloss advertisements divert desire into a "system of objects." Its "ethics," Baudrillard tells us, are hedonistic; its mantra "Fulfill oneself" by buying the latest product. Freedom is reduced to the freedom to choose among objects that give off the impression of limitlessness but represent a range strictly delimited by profit margins.

This hyper-modern world stimulates new freedoms-powers all the while that it evolves ever-more advanced technologies of control. In this regard it is interesting that an explicit, consciously recognized notion of "power" is associated with superheroes and supervillains by children themselves ("This guy has POWER!" "He's POWERFUL!"). These socialized understandings of power simultaneously naturalize power while belying and effacing its psychic and cultural structure of indoctrination. It is by this very means that power is dehumanized and humans are reciprocally disempowered. That the explicitly human self (as in Clark Kent) is so disempowered (emasculated?) underscores this and links fantasies of power with gender, as Henrietta Moore argues in her important study on gendered fantasies of power, *A Passion for Difference* (1994).[2]

Play that emphasizes action-figure fantasies of control is in structural respects also disempowering to non-fantastic, everyday self. Again, it is crucial to link psychic and in this case fantasized dimensions of power back to lived social action. A critical analysis of how children themselves frame "power" creates a wider frame and theoretical context for looking at self and power. If the battle of the self is won in the realm of the child's fantastic, the child's life is often one in which parents or teachers (or other yet more external persons and forces) control what the child can or cannot do. This is particularly the case, with very distinctive inflections, in Japan. Perhaps a contrast between freedom and limitation in Japanese childhood (such as that sketched by Benedict 1967) helps to explain why Japanese are so generative of transnational fantasy play for children in many cultures. Japanese childhood may in some sense be a metonym for the archetypally late-modern or even postmodern dilemma in which children's (and our own) visions of power as a technological possibility contrast wildly to our feelings of being in control.

Allison's identification of the fantastically powerful body with the phallus is a neat jujitsu of epistemic depth. The cyborg comes full circle to link with the libidinous. Correspondingly, the most disembodied is brought back together with the most deeply embodied, at least in masculinist terms. Or do these cyborgs present Lacan's detachable phallus – masquerading as the body, substituting simulacra for body, although as intensely cathected as the body? What is effaced in this psychic process is not just the development of sexuality as socially negotiated but the sense that we have no more control over sexual impulses than we do over the hypertechno-world that confronts us. Masculinist notions of right-to-sex as an aspect of phallic power are thus brought to new heights by being totally affectless in the process. They retain the self but only as a reduced cyborg or a Data-creature (to use Star Trek images). These are the POMO version of a Humphrey Bogart or John Wayne, ever consistent and silent to emotion on the daily surface. This regenders masculine eminence in the denial of personal vulnerability or quotidian social sensitivity, but in a yet more heightened cyber-tech key. Yet it is just at this extreme where gender differences seem to collapse into play – for females too assume cyborg shapes. Gender identity loses its moorings in sex and becomes a power costume anyone can assume (or shed?).

While action-figure villains are affectless cyborg monsters, the heroes–heroines are productively split into two selves. Sailor Moon and her compatriots are able to be cyborgs, representing the creative/destructive potentials of the late-modern and postmodern social worlds (as these potentials exist both politically and within the self). Yet they also wear the human face of humorously incompetent adolescents trying to overcome painful daily-life dilemmas, trying to convert their vulnerabilities into the capacities of contributing members of society. Via this split, action-figure fantasies might be said to slide up and down the scales of power – from personal experience, to social relations, to power in its most hegemonic forms, and back again; this makes them compelling for children. We cannot but wonder to what degree in real life (as opposed to in action-figure fantasies) is the mediation between these two selves – morphing – an empty metaphor?

Jeannette Mageo and Bruce Knauft

Since the time he was young my son has played with action figures. Some call these "boy toys": the equivalent of dolls for boys designed in the likeness of the action heroes popularized in comic books, Saturday morning television, and movies. For Adam, his favorites – such as Batman, Superman, X-Men, and Spawn – fall within the genre of superheroes marked by their ability to transform from ordinary to extraordinary beings, in which capacity they fight evil and save the world from destruction. Often it is the appearance of a new incarnation of the hero – a new Superman comic or the latest edition of *Batman*, the movie – that triggers interest in buying or playing with the accompanying action figure. As often, though, Adam will pick up a figure he has played with for years and engage it with the same degree of interest he would show a new toy.

Figure-play seems transformative for my son. It can absorb his full attention and seemingly transfix and transport him, almost literally, to somewhere else. When playing he visualizes scenes, he tells me: scenes which come from stories he has either seen or read elsewhere or created on his own. Sometimes he imagines himself inside these scenarios assuming a key role, but other times he positions himself outside and watches as if an observer. In either case, Adam plays by animating and activating his figures; he propels them through the air, engages two or more in battle, and positions them in whatever space is nearby – the kitchen table or dashboard of the car. At times, this play is augmented by sound – the whistles of battles, zooms of motorized vehicles, and snippets of speech. And, at times, Adam dispenses with figures altogether and, transforming the pencil or ruler he is using for homework into a weapon, he slashes the air as (would) the warrior in his head.

I have long wondered what type of play Adam is doing with his figures, why such a tranquil and peaceful child is drawn to the scenarios and recreations of deadly battles, and how the theme of power so central to superhero stories gets translated and transfigured into his sense of self. It is the transformative nature of this play, in other words, triggered as it is by the motif of transformation, so ritualized and fetishized in all superhero stories, that piques my interest. In the case of my son, whose preoccupation with figures disappeared recently (around age twelve), the fact that he is deaf in one ear strikes me as connected to the pleasures he has taken in playing alone, and slipping into the imaginary world of empowered heroes. This play of and with power warriors has been psychically reassuring, even critical, for Adam: a psychical work that has also been noted by others in observing how children use the motif of morphing from *The Mighty Morphin Power Rangers* to work through dilemmas, situations, and issues they are confronting in the process of growing up (Seiter 1999). A child psychologist told me that children who visit her often use the vehicle of the Power Rangers (through playing with action figures, donning morphing paraphernalia, or acting out battle scenes) to act out particular problems they seem otherwise unable or unwilling to communicate.

Bruno Bettelheim (1976), of course, made a similar argument about the "enchantment" of fairytales for children, pointing out how psychically productive are stories that present the world as inhabited by evil and nastiness as well as good, and by personal motives that are mean and base and not just noble and pure. The brutality so commonplace in *The Grimm Fairytales* – such as stepmothers plotting to kill their stepchildren who are killed in turn by the more clever kids – provides a constructive vehicle for children to express and experience feelings prohibited or denied in real life – anger and aggression at parents, the belief that parents are self-serving, evil, and gross.

To present a world too candy-coated (as Disney's is, according to Bettelheim) stifles children at the level not only of imagination but also of psychic development. But children lead lives that are often laced with violence of multiple kinds, from facing conditions that are literally or emotionally painful to experiencing emotions of rage, hatred, and resentment towards even "good" parents. Working much like a dream, stories like *The Grimm Fairytales* yield a psychological, if not literal, truth; mothers, for example, are split between good and bad incarnations (resonating with the ambivalence children themselves feel toward parents), and heroes tend to be both victims (an experience known and feared by any child) and victors (a wish-fulfillment if there ever was one).

In this chapter I take advantage of the overall theme of this volume, self and power, to hone in on one element – the structure of superheroic transformation – of a much broader phenomenon which I am currently researching. Referred to as "character merchandising" by those within the business, this entails the marketing of tie-in merchandise that feeds off and into popular characters whose stories are produced and circulated in the multi-media of mass culture (movies, television, video games, internet). My interest lies specifically in both the commodification and transnationalization of children's entertainment: how fantasies for kids get enmeshed in the business of commodity goods, and what happens when this mix, produced for children in one environment (bred by certain socioeconomic conditions and histories of stories, events, ideologies, and values), is marketed elsewhere and/or globally. My project involves Japanese character merchandising and its marketing both domestically and abroad (in particular, in the US) for which I have studied three sets of Japanese superheroes: the *renja* (ranger) series, which has been successfully broadcast in the US under the name *The Mighty Morphin Power Rangers; Bishōjosenshi Se-ra Mun,* which, under the title of *Pretty Soldier, Sailor Moon,* ran in the US (1995–1996) on network broadcast for only nine months but has wide cult appeal and male as well as female following for its cable re-broadcasts, and *Kamen Raida,* which was broadcast for a nine-month run in the US (1995–1996) under the title of *Masked Rider.*

History and superheroes

Here I concentrate on the question: What precisely is entailed in the structural transformation superheroes undergo between ordinary human to superhuman warrior, and what effect does this trope have on children who view and reenact these power transformations themselves? Of course, there are multiple ways and levels at which to address this question. One is that of historicity,[1] though at some level the superhero myth is a timeless universal. Present in cultures around the world and from the beginning of (human) time, it encodes thematics basic to the human condition – the instability of the world, human frailty, good versus evil, and the fantasy of superhuman powers and heroism. As Joseph Campbell (1968) recognized in his seminal work on mythology and, as picked up by such luminaries as George Lucas in the business of children's entertainment, mythic themes such as the superhero speak powerfully to people of all ages and across borders – cultural, national, historical – of multiple kinds. Yet if the superhero is mythically universal, s/he is also constructed according to the mappings of particular worlds.

Using the lens of history and developments in technology (of, in Benjamin's terms, mechanical reproduction), Richard Reynolds has analyzed the modern or modernist mode in which superheroes first appeared as a part of US mass culture. Reproduced through the technology of comic books, newspaper cartoons, and radio shows (and, later, film and television), superheroes were part of modernity's social imaginary organizing subjectivity along the lines of Fordist rationality, efficiency, and individualism. *Superman* (written by Jerry Siegler and Joe Shuster and picked up by D.C. Comics in 1938) was certainly a hero in the worker mode: one whose transformation signaled a quantum leap both in job and proficiency – from bumbling and lowly newspaper reporter to skilled and lofty world-savior. As importantly, Superman's powers were tied to a particular worldview – filial piety, patriotic duty, and masculine bravery – which was served and re-enforced by Superman's ceaseless heroism and moral goodness (waged against enemies portrayed as unequivocally bad). Superman's identity comes from being as much an American as a modern hero; and it was as an icon of and for national identity (and symbol for American superiority) that Superman was popularized in the years preceding World War II when he accompanied American soldiers (as comic books and radio broadcasts) into war-time battlefields (Daniels 1995).

The historical moment I write about is different: the 1990s, characterized as postmodern rather than modern because of the socioeconomic terrain of fluctuating jobs, families, nations, economies, and identities which are described (Harvey 1989, Jameson 1984) more in terms of fluidity than stability. Marked by the flows of global capitalism, lubricated as they have been by the end of the Cold War, the framing given superheroes these days is less overtly national (the *James Bond* series, for example, has become increasingly transnational)[2] and, accompanying this, focused less on the battles and battlelines dividing foes and more on the constellation of (albeit different) powers assumed by enemy and hero alike. Packaged in this form where their powers are not explicitly marked by national identity, superheroes are better "suited," it would seem, to operate transnationally as global playtoys. Indeed, this is exactly the view expressed to me by a vice-president of Bandai when discussing the marketing of Power Ranger merchandise in the US. As an anthropologist still interested in questions of culture, I asked him if the story of the "Power Rangers," originating in Japan, had anything about it that would not register with children living here. Answering "no" and that "a good toy is a good toy anywhere," he elaborated that it was the concept of morphing (= transformation) so highlighted and stylized in *The Mighty Morphin Power Rangers* that has captured kid audiences the world over.

The fantasy of power is a universal, he added. It is also one his company capitalizes on and feeds by trying to suture this (universal) desire to that of (global) consumerism. If, as he put it, "The T.V. show is the promise and the toy is the fulfillment," then companies like Bandai stay in business by getting children to associate the realization of their power fantasies with the purchase of power toys. Bandai has certainly succeeded on this score: Power Ranger merchandise has landed them unprecedented profits (largely on the basis of their export market which they have greatly increased with Power Ranger toys) and remained their biggest selling line for years (Friedland 1997). But, from the perspective of the child, what meaning does playing with power assume within the geometry of capitalist consumption? Do kids learn to evaluate themselves and each other on the basis of the material possession of power toys: toys that stand for, and in for, "real" power? And what about the structure of transformation so ritualistically rehearsed in the superhero play world; is not power as much an absence as presence in these games, and if its acquisition is equated with the adornment of material things (a Bandai power belt, for example), won't the unadorned, pre-morphed state come to be associated with the anxiety (and unease) of disempowerment?

The morphing pose: the case of *Kamen Raida*

It is in the context of the present historical moment with the spread of advanced capitalism and its emphasis on consumerism around the world that I ask my questions here about the mythic fantasy of superheroic transformation. To limit my scope, I will use the remainder of the chapter to accomplish only one task: to pull apart the specific elements at work in the transformation sequences of superhero stories, and from this more structural or formal level (versus ethnographic-learning about play practices from children players and marketing strategies from those in the entertainment business – which I am currently writing on), contemplate the implications such play has on kids. At its most basic structure, the story of a superhero entails three main elements: the fight of good against evil, the difference between ordinary and extraordinary being, and the activation of power. These themes are articulated and developed in terms both of story and characters. The narrative typically begins and ends at the same place: a tranquil community of normal humans going about everyday routines. This scenario is muddied by the presence of two kinds of alien: the hero who is living amidst the humans in human-disguise, and the enemy (often there are multiple enemies and heroes these days, such as the team heroes in Japanese shows like *Power Rangers* and the trio of Batman, Batgirl, and Robin in the most recent *Batman* movie) who, arriving on the scene from outside, threatens to destroy, disrupt, or take over the human world. In order to save this world, the hero transforms into a super-being – signaled by a costume change and the acquisition of exceptional powers – and fights the enemy. As the enemy is also super-empowered, a fierce battle ensues. But the hero is eventually and inevitably victorious, thereby containing (or eliminating) the foe, gaining recognition (once again) as a hero, and returning the human community to order and the status quo.

The characters in superhero stories are identified according to different sets of principles. In terms of ideological or moral outlook – whether one wants to preserve or destroy the human world – characters are identified as good versus evil. The hero, of course, is good incarnate; the enemy is the symbol of/for bad. In terms of ontological status, however, there are two gross categories, human and other-than-human, and both hero and enemy share this latter designation (whether by being extra-terrestrial as Superman, bionic as Bionic Woman, genetically mutated as Spider Man, or a wizard at technological and bodily make-over as Batman), which differentiates them from all the humans. So, on this measure, enemy and hero are more alike than different and both deviate from a norm of normal humanness. Power is the third principle of identity and is a more fluid and critical determination in the following way. Both the hero and enemy are marked by exceptional powers and, in this sense, are similar as well as equal. But when the hero wins the final battle the power balance shifts, distinguishing the hero's powers as superior and unique. With this, any ambiguity in the relative places and merits of the two leading characters is resolved. What differentiates the two winds up being more meaningful and determinative than what unites them. With this "pinning down of meaning" (to use a Lacanian notion) comes a message too about morality, since being "good" (standing and fighting for the preservation of society) wins the day in the end. Right becomes might, and might becomes right – an arguably conservative worldview for children to weave into their play.

How does transformation get configured in this mythic structure? I take here the case of a particular Japanese hero, *Kamen Raida* (Masked Rider) who, debuting in 1962 on a live action television program in Japan (broadcast by Toei studios), ran for years (in a typical pattern in Japan where a show will do a nine-month run then reappear three months later in altered form such as *Kamen Raida Buraku* – Black Masked Rider – and *Kamen Raida RX*), and is still popular today. *Kamen Raida* is identified as a *kaizō senshi* – reconstructed warrior – who transforms from the boy, Minami Kotaro, into the suited, cybernetic warrior, *Kamen Raida*. His origins, as is typical for superheroes, are exceptional (and different in the Japanese and US-remade versions).[3] After a brutal motorcycle accident, the boy's body is cybernetically remade by evil scientists whose clutches *Kamen Raida* escapes with new powers intact (Ishinomori 1994).

In a book for young children on *Kamen Raida Buraku* (Hikarinokuni 1987), the hero's powers and transformation are mapped out in the following way. First, the hero is introduced in his boy-incarnation – the guise he adopts on earth with which he disguises his identity as super-alien (that is known only to inner circle). Presented next are the steps Minami Kotaro goes through to transform (*henshin*) into the reconstructed warrior, *Kamen Raida*. Called *henshin po-zu* (morphing poses), these are highly stylized stances that borrow on martial arts – a significant point given that most super-warriors in Japan (in the live action or animated genre of *sentai* produced across the multi-media of television, film, comic book, figures, and trading cards) are highly trained in martial arts. Martial arts, in fact, represent a continuity in the powers of the warrior between their pre-morphed and post-morphed states. It is as humans that warriors train and discipline their bodies in martial arts so their "superhero" powers, though coded as primarily the exceptional qualities (cybernetic, mechanical, extra-terrestrial) acquired at the time of transformation, are also powers honed through the very human labor of a traditional disciplinary art.

In the case of *Kamen Raida Buraku*, the *henshin po-zu* are treated as almost sacred and are always undergone in the same ritualized fashion. Constituting eight steps, the critical change occurs at step seven when the *henshin beruto* (morphing belt – sold, of course, by Bandai) emerges, seemingly and seamlessly, from inside the boy's body. Immediately the entire power suit appears, encasing Minami, now the warrior cyborg, *Kamen Raida*, in a *mecha* (mechanical) armature that fits his flesh as if it were a second skin. Indeed, fusion and transformation become the same thing here; by fusing with his power suit, the boy's essence has been transformed – a point symbolized, it seems, by the fact that his power equipment comes from inside rather than outside his human (-like) body. And, significantly, even as re-made, the hero's shape remains humanoid, despite the fact that, in this case, *Kamen Raida* has actually become a cybernetic grasshopper equipped with antenna, infrared eyes, and a greenish-black body.

In the rest of this and other children's books on popular heroes in Japan, readers are told mainly about the warrior's powers, foes, friends, and *mecha* (machines which include vehicles to ride, weapons, and often hybrids of the two usually in robotic form). These are the four most important components in the coding of transformation; friends and foes are what incite the change (to protect friends who are being threatened by foes), and powers and machinery are what constitute it (which appear as both the substance and the visual/visible signs of transformation). For many Japanese heroes, powers (*chikara*) are also called "secrets" (*himitsu*), which are endlessly mapped, diagrammed, explained, and discussed in the various hero materials sold on the market (comic books, children's books, children's magazines). In the case of *Kamen Raida Buraku*, his powers are interestingly referred to as "bodily secrets" (*karada no himitsu*) which include: arms said to be superbly powerful and used in the "*raida chyoppu*" (the rider chop – one of his brandname warrior stances), the "*henshin beruto*" (transformation belt) which releases his energy, legs which are so strong he can jump ten times his height (called the "*raida jyanpu*" – the rider jump, another signature stance), the squiggly mark on his chest which holds a "mysterious secret," and his infrared eyes which can see even in pitch dark.

Virtually all mass-mediated superheroes today have an arsenal of power machines which serve multiple functions; the two most important are weapons and vehicles. For *Kamen Raida Buraku*, the hero has two driving machines: one is a car with a feminine personality and voice, and the other, the more important of the two, is the masculinized motorcycle called *batoru ho-pa* (the battle hopper) referring to the grasshopper shape he shares with his master. Both these machines can operate as automatons,[4] but *batoru ho-pa*, in particular, also merges with the hero. *Kamen Raida* rides on him and the two serve to analogize one another – the motorcycle acts like a hero-boy and *Kamen Raida* is as efficient as a machine. These riding machines double as fighting machines, though there is also an important category of detachable weapons, called "*buki*," whose arsenal characterizes hero and enemy alike. Included here is a wide spectrum of devices and tools that launch an array of gases, sprays, bullets, blades, electric charges, vapors, and ices that variously maim, wound, incapacitate, disintegrate, transform (this is particularly true of the enemy's weaponry which may alter the victim's mind, instincts, or memory), kill, immobilize, or remove one's opponent. In his incarnation as *Kamen Raida* RX, such *buki* interestingly include not only the "*bi-mu gan*" (beam gun), a huge gun that shoots high intensity light, and the "*baio buredo*" (bio blade), marked by extraordinary sharpness and speed, but what is also called his "*sugoi himitsu*" (really big secret): the fact that he transforms into two other heroes, *Robo Raida* (Robot Rider) and *Bio Raida* (Bionic Rider), who are treated as a form of *buki* themselves.

Morphing/developing the self

What precisely is at work in the transformation Minami Kotaro undergoes to become *Kamen Raida*? As is a commonplace in the genre, the hero has two selves which he is constrained from embodying at the same time. One of these selves is or looks human, the other is and acts exceptional, so the movement between the two is an upgrade from lower to higher powers. For some of the heroes, the inadequacies of the prior self are played up, even exaggerated, in the story. This is true of Clark Kent who is a bumbling newspaper reporter and a fumbling man, the antithesis of the macho, super-efficient hero he crystallizes into as Superman. This is true too of Sailor Moon who, as 14-year-old Usagi (Serena in the English version), is an over-sleeping, boy-crazy, video-playing, lazy, whiny, distractible teenager who is notable (and much noted by her friends and talking cat within the context of the story) for her deficiencies. Once she triggers her moon-based powers to transform into Sailor Moon, however, she becomes all that she has not been before, namely brave, competent, focused, heroic, and even sexy and beautiful: a woman who is now desired as much as she is admired.

For children who watch and play superheroes, one of the appeals must be the opportunity to identify with a flawed (or just ordinary) person who metamorphoses into someone superior. But what message about identity is imparted with this? One is obvious; within every normal child lies a potential superhero. But another, and somewhat different, message is: superheroes, though admirable, are simply not real. The question in all this might be then: is the second self a transformed self or an other? Of course, the complexities of making this distinction are apparent to anyone conversant with any branch of psychoanalytic thought, whether Freud or Lacan or the object-relations theory of Winnicott, Benjamin, and Chodorow. But just to adopt Freud's theory of the fetish for a moment (1961), one might argue that superheroes wind up remaining forever pitched on a border – between self and other, real and not real, present and absent – and in this lies their attraction. They both are and are not human, and in our world but also other-worldly.

What propels this fascination in an ambiguous, border-crossing object is the child's own precarious balance between inner and outer worlds: between what is familiar and predictable (in surroundings, relationships, events) and what is alien and strange. As Freud noted, for the infant, the worlds outside and inside blur into one – an amalgamation ensured by the nursing mother, particularly the one so attentive she attends to the child at first cry. But, when the mother begins to pull back and leaves the child physically behind when she goes out (shopping, to work), the infant starts distinguishing self from (m)other – a lesson fraught with pain but also pleasure in the Freudian model. The child often starts sucking her thumb, for example: an act that not only comforts in the mother's absence but also stands in for the mother's act (of nursing) itself. As such, thumb-sucking signals both an absence – of a (m)other's constant care-giving – and a presence – of the child's ability to comfort herself (an activity over which she has far more control).

Freud is brilliant in recognizing the complexities involved in such bodily rituals; thumb-sucking cannot be reduced to either an act that merely compensates for the mother's (better) care or a gesture that is totally liberatory and satisfying. Rather, all the pleasure-seeking actions and interactions humans pursue following what Freud saw as the pinnacle of human bliss – the infant sucking at its mother's breast – try to recreate something unattainable: the Freudian principle of desire. But this does not mean that the medium we use to pursue desire (such as thumb-sucking) involves no pleasure. Rather, this pleasure is always complicated and mediated by frustration and loss. It is ambiguous, in other words, and generates feelings of ambivalence as important and central to the self as any fantasy of utter satisfaction, indulgence, or control.

Freud used two other concepts to contemplate the ambiguity at work when the developing child navigates the anxieties and thrills of finding her/himself in the outside world. The first is a game he observed with his grandson who, anxious when his mother left home to go shopping, would throw and retrieve an empty spool in her absence, repeating the words "fort/da" (roughly translated as "here"/"there"). Seeing the game as symbolic, Freud suggested that the child was re-enacting but also overcoming his loss, playing by means of a ritual that kept alternating between the anxiety, but also mastery, over mother's absence.[5] Fetish is a concept Freud used for slightly older children when first encountering the radical and horrifying (as he conceived it to be) evidence of someone's "difference." The Freudian example was the developing boy who, first coming to understand something about the importance of his own penis, is shocked to discover that his mother lacks the same organ. The fetishist is a boy who, incapable of accepting the reality of gender difference,[6] diverts his gaze onto a substitute object – the fetish – which, in being phallic (in shape or association), resembles his own anatomy more than his mother's. Significantly, however, the fetish is a representation, in Freud's mind, not of the boy's "real" penis but of the mother's imaginary one. That is, the fetish stands (in) for that which the boy once thought existed and whose absence the boy cannot psychologically face.

With all these examples – the fetish, the game of fort/da, and thumb-sucking – children are playing with power in the sense they are using things or acts that give them pleasure as a means to master an anxiety-provoking situation. The game though is always ambiguous in that it returns to, as much as transcends, the original loss so painful for the child. The importance of Freud's insight here, so commonly misunderstood, cannot be overstated; a child never totally "masters" his anxiety with a fetish or thumb. These never make up for what the child (any child, according to Freud) inherently wants: the undivided attention of (and mergence with) a loving care-giver. So, in its ritualistic repetition – the thumb is constantly sucked, the spool repeatedly thrown, the fetish continually brought out – emotions of anxiety as much as mastery are triggered by the play.

Superheroes are, by their very constitution, ambiguous entities. They, like the game of fort/da, are in constant oscillation, moving back and forth between different worlds, different identities, and different capacities. Significantly, I would argue, they rarely become definitively or permanently fixed to one spot and when they do (in the movie *Superman II*, for example, when Clark Kent has been "outed" by Lois Lane and decides to forsake his super-identity in order to stay and marry her), either some disaster happens (reversing the hero's decision to remain in one identity) or the appeal of the character/story quickly dies out. In superheroes then, it is the very movement between two states that is fetishized, giving children something both familiar and unfamiliar, mundane and fantastical, this-worldly and other-worldly to use in a play of constant oscillation/navigation between the other and the self (and the self as it incorporates the other). This leads to the emotion Freud (1927) associated with the fetish, ambivalence, and explains the excessiveness with which both parts of the superhero persona are played up – a humanness that exaggerates the prosaic, ordinary, and flawed, and an otherness that is decidedly over-the-top. The liminality[7] of the superhero and the identity/identities with which she is linked also explains, I suggest, the fetishized nature of the transformation ritual, which is carried out (as would be an initiation ceremony) precisely and spectacularly, always in the same way.

Playing with power in the realm of superheroes, then, becomes a way of playing with and developing the self. It also, of course, inflects this play with the fantasy of control. As empowered heroes, characters are in control of even impossible situations and come out literally on top. It is important to remember, however, that the vulnerability, weakness, and even incompetence of the pre-transformed heroes is constantly repeated as well: a state the hero overcomes only to return to by the beginning of the next show. The transhuman powers of the hero then are symbolic: symbolizing – as does the fetish, the sucked thumb, the spool in fort/da – not the mere fantasy of mastery or control as much as the relationship between the latter and a "reality" of lived anxiety, absence, or fear. As a Japanese psychologist (Fujimi 1998:20) has written about the cartoon character, Doraemon, a robotic cat that lives with the inept boy, Nobita-kun, whom he is constantly assisting with a plethora of futuristic machines,[8] Doraemon is what Winnicott called a "transitional object" – an object that mediates between the inner and outer worlds of a child. He is neither mere "fantasy" nor reality, but an intermediary figure which the writer, now an adult, regards as a much-treasured part of himself – a part that opens up another world as valuable as the phenomenal world in which he works. And, importantly, while Doraemon possesses exceptional powers, it is more his relationship with the klutzy boy who never really becomes empowered himself that makes Doraemon so endearing.

The symbolic nature of a superhero's powers, as I have argued above, is sometimes explicitly marked within the text of the story itself when the victory over the monster-alien is coupled with the resolution of some very human problem confronting one of the characters. This technique seems far more common, or at least overt, in Japanese superheroes such as The Mighty Morphin Power Rangers and Sailor Moon than it does with US-based heroes like Superman. Typically the story starts out with the hero (or a friend) in human incarnation struggling with some dilemma; one of the rangers is obsessively dieting, for example, because someone has told her that she is overweight. This scene jump-cuts to that of the "other world" where a monstrously mutated prehistoric-looking beast is attacking the planet and the rangers signal to one another to morph into battle mode. The heroes change costume, up-grade their powers, activate their weapons, and assemble their individual robots into the super-robot they collectively drive. Though the battle is fierce the rangers eventually win, disintegrating their enemy into thin air. The final scene returns us to the ranger who was struggling earlier with a personal problem. Now, however, the issue has been resolved with, in this case, the ranger accepting the fact that not everyone has the same body-type and figuring hers is just fine the way it is – a wisdom learned, it seems, in the heat of battle.

In the dynamics of power and identity played out in the above story, there are two important elements I see at work. First, transformation and battle are inter-linked; the two events always accompany and imply one another, and both signify the peak point in the plot-line of the story. Second, after the key battle/transformation, the hero returns to what is now a somewhat, somehow altered state. As in the Hegelian dialectic, the ranger starts out in one state, confronts her other/enemy, then emerges in a state that represents a synthesis of self and other.[9] So, collapsing these two elements, we could say that the hero in superhero mythology is both confronting an other (demon-enemy) and becoming an other (hero-ideal): two sets of othernesses that, in some sense, merge and stand for the same thing. In this reading, the resemblances between hero and enemy come to make sense. Both are powerful and somehow alien (other) to human. Both henceforth push the (pre-morphed) hero to face the limits of her being and put her into a position which, ultimately, she is willing and able to go beyond. The victory in the end then signifies defeat of not only an enemy outside but also limitations and resistances within the self. For those who find the show *Power Rangers* constructive, the reason most commonly given is this: that its battles are a metaphorical or symbolic device (rather than literally seen, by its critics in the US and elsewhere, to encourage children to mimic the fighting poses and incorporate more aggression in their own play) for confronting and working through one's own problems – a healthy model for children. Bettelheim's argument about fairy tales is quite similar.

Phallic powers: what shape is the phallus given in imaginary play?

This saga is repeated *ad nauseam*, of course, in the playworld of the superhero. The outcome is known from the beginning and what pleasures it produces are ones predicated on this guarantee. In this sense, there is something almost timeless about the formula of superhero mythology and something basic about its utopian ability to reassure and appeal. To return to my earlier comments about historicity, however, I close by contemplating how this more general, generic, structure of superheroism assumes a particular format in this era of the 2000s, questioning how its configuring of power reflects and affects behaviors that are specific to this age. To continue with Freudian terminology, I approach the transformation of identity and power here in terms of the phallus, particularly given the constancy with which superheroes come armed in mass culture today with machines and weapons, many phallic-shaped, such as the wand Sailor Moon waves when she invokes her "moon prism power."

As argued by Freud and reargued by psychoanalytic feminists (for example, Gallop 1982, 1985), the phallus is a representation of power that is modeled on the bodily lines of those subjects assigned power in society. In a masculinist society, this would be the male anatomy, namely the part treated as most distinctly "male" – the penis. This does not mean the phallus is the same thing as a penis, of course, nor even a realistic representation of it. Rather, it is something of a linguistic sign (of/for power), which means it is the semiotic language assigned the way power is sought, navigated, imagined, and secured by the members of a particular world at a particular time. So, the shape of the phallus comes from both the real world (of material relations) and beyond the real (into symbols and desires), and is an ideological construction as well as a fantasy.

When superheroes undergo transformation, both their bodies and powers are remade. The two changes occur together and the shift in appearance is a visible sign of the hero's reconstitution as a power machine. Thus, with *Kamen Raida*, his transformation from average human to superhero is signaled, first, by modifications to his body: his power belt, power suit, helmeted head, antennae, and infra-red eyes. Each of these body-shifts indicates a source of new power ("hidden," as the children's book states, "within the body"): powers that either enhance or totally exceed normal human abilities. Of the latter there are many, such as his ability to move through time, space, and objects; and his arsenals (launched sometimes out of his hands) of lethal rays, sprays, and fireballs. There are also many powers that are mere human extensions – higher performing eyes, ears (antennae in this case), legs, arms, and brain. This human(ized) power-source is significant for it works on something familiar and shared by the kid viewers, a human body that is reworked to become something uncommonly unique. Here too there is a symbolic message: the magic of transformation is simply a hyped-up version of what kids can and should do on their own – extend the borders of their bodies whether by study, sports, karate, or computer know-how. This mechanism, which is a form of anaclisis (inflecting that which is familiar) and involves the self such as breast-feeding with an outer or supplemental activity, meaning, or pleasure (Freud 1962), also serves to make the hero, as mentioned already, an amalgamation of self–other, familiar–unfamiliar, human–alien. Never totally alien, s/he is much more a cyborg in Donna Haraway's terminology (1991): a hybrid of being that melds the skin and flesh of a biological human with the technological engineering of (post)modern science.

Today's heroes are also empowered by acquiring new things, usually machines, that operate as extensions of their power-bodies. These are mainly riding vehicles and weapons, and hybrids of the two – vehicular fighting robots (which often not only accompany the transformation of the hero but also transform themselves, from vehicle to stand-up robot, for example). The heroes blend with their machines and machinery (*mecha*) constitutes the core of their bodily transformation. The degree to which morphing is constituted and signaled by the acquisition of mechanical powers in today's superheroes certainly represents a shift from the past. Superman in the 1930s gained X-Ray vision and the ability to fly, but lacked the technological arsenal accompanying, indeed characterizing, the superhero of today. Along with this, the site of transformation in the 1990s has been fragmented and separated into a host of parts in the following way. When Superman transformed, his change was signaled primarily by a costume change that covered his whole body: the red cape, blue suit, and yellow "S" insignia on his chest. He did not undergo further visible change or acquire additional powers or objects in the course of his heroic activities. Superman's phallicism came in and on his body, in other words, and it was consolidated on the site of the (human-looking) man.

In the case of the present breed of superheroes, the Power Rangers, for example, their powers are spread over a number of different domains: from animal or dinosaur spirits, training in martial arts, and link-up to the extra-terrestrial power-source of Zordon, to weapons, robots, and the coupling of these individual powers into collective super-machines. Power is much more diffuse and complex; its materialization also comes much more in the form of material things. The shape of the phallus here, I suggest, is significantly different than in previous eras of imaginary superheroes. First, phallicism has diffused, decentering it from the heroism and will of one individual. In some cases, power is literally or equally shared by a team of heroes such as X-men, Power Rangers, or Sailor Moon (where there are five girls who morph into sailor scouts). Here considerable weight is given to how these different heroes get along and how they must work together in cooperative units to achieve their goals – themes of inter-personal relations and communitarianism far less stressed in the more individualist-oriented stories like *Superman*. Though this trend in superhero models is still more prevalent in Japan and other Asian countries than it is in Euro-America, it coincides with other socioeconomic developments such as flexible accumulation and increasing transnational travel (of the multiple "flows" of not only people and goods but also money, ideas, and images (Appadurai 1991) that lead theorists to call the late capitalist world of today one that is characterized by the postmodernism of decentered and fragmented selves (Jameson 1984).

Second, the phallus is much more material and materialistic than ever before. Not only is power tied to and represented by things, these things are also sizable in number. The implications for tie-in merchandise are obvious; with the production and proliferation of characters with multiple parts, kid consumers are incited to buy ever more products. As a mother of such a child, I can testify to the desire kids demonstrate for the acquisition of not only one brand-name superhero but all that hero's many vehicles, weapons, teammates, and incarnations (all the different versions of Batman, for example, accompanying the stream of *Batman* movies). In the case of Adam, while he would play with an old figure, he still desired to have the newest and most accessorized model. And if a part was lost (a key weapon, for example), there would be a depreciation of the figure's value, at least for the moment. Commercialism is such an intrinsic part of the superhero playworld of today that entering into the stories (which are transmitted across an increasingly broad spectrum of media including television, film, video, video and computer game, trading cards, comic book, and magazine) comes sutured to the purchase of commodity toys. So, just as superheroes extend their human bodies by means of the power machinery they acquire through transformation, so too is the entertainment of superhero watching extended by means of the acquisition of material toys. Of course, the kids' market of superheroes is hardly the cause of consumerism at large. But it is part and parcel of a wider economy that is targeted to consumption more than ever before. And children are the targets of an increasingly aggressive campaign to (trans)form them into avid consumers who tie their identity, pleasures, and powers to the goods they buy at a mall.

The phallic shape given superheroic power is different in a third, more promising, way today. Its very diffusion into removable or detachable things – robots, belts, wands, guns – displaces its center from a naturalistic body. This differs from the age when virtually all heroes were male (apart from the occasional female bombshell, like Wonder Woman, made by her creator, Dr. William Marston, to appeal to the tastes of males) and power was phallically designed on and as a masculine body. In the 1930s and 1940s fashioning of Superman, for example, all his powers were housed within his body so it was his body itself that became phallicized through transformation. By contrast, today's heroes have powers that reach beyond the body and materialize into tools or machines that could and are operated by more than just men – women and bugs (popular in Japan with *Kamen Raida* and, more recently, *The Big Bad Beetleborgs*, a US-import), for instance. The prominence of machinery in today's breed of imaginary superheroes reflects the highly technologized world in which we now live and the place machines (computers, cars, nautilus, CD players) assume in our lives as well as our identities. As Donna Haraway (1991) has said about the progressive potential of new technology, it can open the way for undoing old lines of identity politics built on the naturalistic signs of the color or gender of one's body. If identity will increasingly be dependent on and (re)made through technology, then we can build cyborgs with a new sense of politics: a politics in which the assignation of power is not limited to only those with certain raced or gendered bodies.

Indeed, such a promise is implicit in the mapping of phallicism in today's superheroes. Powers have become less naturalized and gendered; and heroes have become differentiated in terms of types and shapes. Most notable perhaps is the increasing presence of female heroes: *Xena – the Warrior Princess* (popular with older kids in the US), *Sailor Moon* (who, as a cartoon and comic, is popular around the world), and *The Mighty Morphin Power Rangers* (where there are always one or two girls in the team of five or six heroes). This is to not to say that female heroes are just the same as their male counterparts (and whether this would be good or bad is another issue), but in *Mighty Morphin Power Rangers*, for example, gender is relatively unmarked in the postmorphing stage where all the rangers are similarly suited and empowered, although there are always more males and a male is always the *de facto* leader. By contrast, as is standard in the Japanese sub-genre of superheroes called "*bishōjo hi-ro*" (beautiful young girl heroes – a trend that has been popular and well-established for over ten years), Sailor Moon transforms by a ritual that emphasizes and exposes her female body. Twirling around in a sequence that shows her momentarily naked, Sailor Moon emerges with a sailor outfit (the school uniform of middle-school and upper-school girls in Japan) that has been mini-sized, showing off cleavage and thighs. She is now ornamented in jewelry and make-up, and is imbued with a definite air of sexiness. Importantly, however (and this is a point made by feminist scholars of the trend in Japan), Sailor Moon is also empowered and the powers she has – a moon prism wand, a tiara she throws – are as phallically charged as any man's (though, in the case of the tiara, with a set of associations far more female than male). Important as well, Sailor Moon relies on no man in fighting the enemies. In the dramas of power here, woman finally assumes a position other than victim needing to be saved by a (more powerful) man.

Conclusion

Play with superheroes, as I have tried to show here, borrows on a mythical structure which gets imploded with particular meanings and effects that accompany the world(s) in which it is set. At some level, all superheroes are stories about identity and power and the magical transformation of a normal human to a super-empowered hero. The imaginary play that kids do watching and recreating these stories is influenced by both the stage of development they are at and the kind of material world (where power and identity are formulated along specific lines) they inhabit.

As I reflect once more on the play of my son, I see a child whose love of superheroes has filled hundreds of hours of time he otherwise might have spent lonely and bored. This play has accompanied a maturation marked by increasing self-confidence. It has also accompanied (and perhaps encouraged) a love for consumption; Adam's room was once filled with action figures and he still jumps at the chance to visit the mall. This playworld based in mass culture is part and parcel of a world populated by material things. But it is also a site for play and imagination – an arena in which today's kids can play out and play with powers that both overwhelm them and represent ideals of themselves. It is important to stress, I believe, not only the pleasures of such play but also its psychic importance – the value of rehearsing scenarios of not only empowerment but also disempowerment from which the hero continues to survive. At the same time we cannot be blind to the real (in this case, material) effects such power play produces as well: the compulsion to graph out one's sense of security in/of the self not only in material things but with an increasing array of them.

What about the future of superheroes? If I were an activist in the playworld of characters and toys, I would advocate for two things. First, more development of superheroism away from any set shape, particularly bodies that are (only or primarily) male, white, American, and "perfectly" shaped. Second, I would like to see changes in the narratives away from the fetishization given to battle, aggression, and moral superiority and toward dramas in which heroes face and resolve their dilemmas in something other than battle mode. Both these moves would be aimed at encouraging Haraway's progressive agenda: to make cyborg creations that push rather than re-inscribe the parameters of our present world order, where power remains in the hands of a limited few, those whose origins are privileged and "special."

When Nicholas Cage was negotiating to play the role of Superman for the movie series, he stated that he too has the fantasy of remaking the superhero mold. For him this is to be playing the hero as a darker, quirkier, less clean-cut, and more ambiguous character: one with whom he hopes children who are themselves more marginal and less mainstream (in whatever sense) can better identify. His hero, in short, is to be a different kind of subject – one whose identity challenges, rather than mimics, the hegemonic ideal. This seems to be a step in the right direction. But we need and can go much further: heroes with identities that transcend (or offer multiple variations of) all power-linked borders of race, ethnicity, gender, and sexual preference. With such figures, "playing with power" implies a transformation of not only the self, but also the world.

NOTES

Notes to preface

1. On commercialism and late capitalism see also Baudrillard 1988 and McClintock 1995:207–231.
2. For a more detailed ethnographic comparison of gender identity and modernity across two world areas, see Knauft 1997.

1. Another, of course, is that of culture: Are there differences in how superheroes are constructed and received that differs (between Japan and the US) in ways that could be considered "cultural"? Though this question is central to my current research I refer to it only implicitly here in order to concentrate more fully on the issues of transformation and global capitalism.
2. The reasons for this are many. One is undoubtedly to sell *James Bond* to larger audiences. Thus, in an attempt to globalize the consumer audience, the product itself is constructed in more transnational than national terms. Other reasons for this switch in *James Bond* are more complicated and include the worldwide critique of Anglo and American nationalisms: an international atmosphere in which patriotism sells less well than it has in the past.
3. In the US version the boy was born on a distant planet where, as prince, he was given special powers by his grandfather, the King, who sends him to earth to save it from the devastation his evil cousin – and crew including an army of destructive insectivores – plans to wreak on it.
4. As described in the book: *Batoru Ho-pa* is *Kamen Raida's* riding supermachine. It is a *mecha* that thinks by itself and exists on its own" (Hikarinokumi 1987:8).
5. Jacques Lacan extended this further by arguing that the linguistic terminology used in the fort/da game (a ritual he suggested was universal, in some form, to all humans and the human condition itself) represents – in its here/there-ness – how inevitably "split" is the nature of the self. We alternate between being present and absent, and these existential states are only representable through linguistic terms – fort/da – which further demonstrates how the human self is grounded in not only a "split" but also a "lack" ("we" are only present through language which itself is ephemeral, constructed, and outside our control).
6. Healthy maturation depends, according to Freud, on being able to accept gender differences. The fetishist then is stuck at a pre-adolescent stage of development.
7. Victor Turner wrote about liminality as a stage of being "betwixt and between" by which he meant transitional points in the life of an individual or society that fall outside, or move between, fixed states. Analyzing initiation rites, he observed how commonplace is the structure of an "anti-structure" in which transition is marked by the transgression or inversion of normative rules: unkempt hair or promiscuous sex, for example, when the reverse is usually prescribed. Turner also noted how ritualistic initiation ceremonies always are.
8. *Doraemon* has been popular for years in Japan as a comic, cartoon, book, and character product. It remains one of the longest-lasting "contemporary fairytales" in Japan and Doraemon's figure is seen everywhere in the public sphere – on advertisements for national railways as well as Doraemon goods, as an event or presence in local festivals (*matsuri*), and stamped on top of the lunch-boxes children take to school, etc.

9. This process is particularly interesting in *Pokémon*, the Japanese kid hit that was a current rage in the US between 1998 and 2000. Here the aim of the player (in the Gameboy game which resembles that of the lead character, Satoshi, in the television cartoon) is to become the world's best pokémon trainer by capturing all 251 Pokémon (pocket monsters). To "capture" entails fighting and overcoming the monsters who thenceforth become one's own, lending their strengths and powers now to the human would-be master. Monster and human merge and in the battles, as is true of the genre of superheros (which *Pokémon* resembles if does not precisely fit), the hero is often vulnerable and, in this case, does not always win. Again the cycle of mastery–vulnerability repeats and playing here is with power, acquisition, and objects that blur the borders between "reality" and fantasy.

REFERENCES

Appadurai, Arjun. 1990. Disjuncture and Difference in the Global Cultural Economy. *Public Culture* 2(2):1–24.
Baudrillard, Jean. 1988. *Jean Baudrillard: Selected Writings* (Mark Poster, ed.). Stanford: Stanford University Press.
Benedict, Ruth. 1967. *Chrysanthemum and the Sword: Patterns of Japanese Culture.* Cleveland: Meridian Books.
Bettelheim, Bruno. 1976. *The Uses of Enchantment.* New York: Knopf.
Campbell, Joseph. 1968. *The Hero with a Thousand Faces.* Princeton: Princeton University Press.
Daniels, Les. 1995. *D. C. Comics: 60 Years of the World's Favorite Superheroes.* Boston: Bulfinch Press.
Freud, Sigmund. 1961 (1927). Fetishism (James Strachey, trans.). In *The Standard Edition of the Complete Psychological Works of Sigmund Freud.* Volume 19:147–157. London: Hogarth.
       1962 (1925). *Three Essays on a Theory of Sexuality* (James Strachey, trans.). New York: Avon Books.
Friedland, Jonathan. 1994. Kid Stuff: Bandai Stays on Top of Japan's Toy Market. *Far Eastern Economic Review*, June 9:61–62.
Fujimi, Yukio. 1998. "Doraemon towa Fujiko Fujio o Shōkai nishite de tekita Seirei aruiwa Tenshi no Yōnamono" (The Doraemon Introduced to Us By Fujiko Fujio is Something Like a Spirit or an Angel). *Hato* 8:20.
Gallop, Jane. 1982. *The Daughter's Seduction: Feminism and Psychoanalysis.* Ithaca: Cornell University Press.
       1985. *Reading Lacan.* Ithaca: Cornell University Press.
Haraway, Donna. 1991. A Cyborg Manifesto: Science, Technology, and Socialist-Feminism in the Late Twentieth Century. In *Simians, Cyborgs, and Women.* New York: Routledge.
Harvey, David. 1989. *The Condition of Postmodernity: An Enquiry into the Origins of Cultural Change.* Oxford: Basil Blackwell.
Hikarinokumi. 1987. *Kamen Raida Buraku.* Tokyo: Hikarinokuni.
Ishinormori, Shōtarō. 1994. *Kamen Raida-1.* Tokyo: Chūō Kōron-Sha.

Jameson, Frederic. 1984. Postmodernism or, the Cultural Logic of Late Capitalism. *New Left Review* 146:59–92.

Knauft, Bruce M. 1997. Gender Identity. Political Economy and Modernity in Melanesia and Amazonia. *Journal of the Royal Anthropological Institute* 3:233–260.

McClintock, Anne. 1995. *Imperial Leather*. New York: Routledge.

Moore, Henrietta. 1994. *A Passion for Difference*. Cambridge: Polity Press.

Reynolds, Richard. 1992. *Super Heroes: A Modern Mythology*. Jackson: University Press of Mississippi.

Seiter, Ellen. 1999. Power Rangers at Preschool: Negotiating Media in Child Care Settings. In *Kids' Media Culture* (Marsha Kinder, ed.). Durham, NC: Duke University Press.

5 Consciousness of the state and the experience of self: the runaway daughter of a Turkish guest worker

Katherine Pratt Ewing

Transiting and transformation are salient themes in Katherine Ewing's "Consciousness of the State and the Experience of Self." Ewing depicts a Turkish immigrant woman (Nergis) as she transits back and forth between her immigrant world and worldview and the world/worldview of Netherlands' bourgeois individualism. Nergis has mastered the epistemes of her two worlds: she is regarded as a "good girl" by her family and immigrant cohorts, while also acquiring a Western education and subsequent employment at a far higher level than that of her parents and most of her peers. Initially she plays by the differing life rules predicated by each of these contexts at disjunctive times and places. Eventually, she realizes that this compartmentalization will not get her what she wants and is inadequate for dealing with the complexities of her actual relations. Nergis evolves a strategic approach, adaptively combining discourses and practices from both Turkish and Dutch contexts. Acting as a strategist necessarily blurs the distinctions between these two cultural orientations, so that for a time they seem oddly interspersed – as when Nergis assumes the bodily habitus of a Turkish villager when speaking of her family problems in the apartment of her Netherlands business colleague. In time, however, Nergis evolves hybrid ways of talking and thinking that allow her to create a life that is personally fulfilling; she is once again positively evaluated by her Turkish community while garnering the advantages of a bourgeois Dutch world.

Resisting social power is the stuff of Western narratives are made of from history to television dramas. Theorists of power from Nietzsche to Deleuze think about how to resist epistemic power. In Nergis's case epistemic power is symbolized by her mother's attempt to sway her daughter with charms and secret inscriptions. Obeyesekere's concept "practical rationality" (1992:19–22) is useful for grasping the special nature of Nergis's resistance. Practical rationality is a reflective form of mind that appears in the face of a problematic situation. While practical rationality is not "culture free," neither is culture free from its scrutiny. Nergis clearly draws on a pragmatic-reflective rationality, testing the limits and power of the various cultural schemata in her bifurcated life. Moreover, this thinking seems augmented by her transnational context, which begs some scale of efficacy against which her competing cultural values can be assessed. Nergis's way of being in the world thus represents the possibility of psychic resistance even to deeply internalized schemata.

Studies of diasporas often focus on the hybridity of culture amid the victimization of immigrants. Ewing shows us how hybrid psychologies expand possibilities for agency and how transnationalism can be a rich medium through which to construct the self. Here the social negotiation of power and the construction of self are one and the same risk-taking enterprise. This is an instance when the pleats and folds of the self in subject-making are squarely locked in a *give* as well as "take" relation with the social and epistemic powers of alternatively impinging worldviews and life-styles, Turkish and Dutch. The larger subjective shift from subordinated Turkish woman encountering Dutch values at the beginning of the chapter, to the agentive Dutch woman engaging Turkish family relations on her own terms at the chapter's end, is a striking transformation. It suggests, as does Mageo's later chapter (although in very different terms), how power as renegotiated within the self has repercussions for power in the social world.

The power of agency – in the present case, to "risk all for recognition" – is a cogent reminder that resistant selves continually complicate structures of power, be they social, epistemic, symbolic, or psychically internalized at a deep level. They also complicate our analyses of power and selves, keeping us attentive and responsive to the individual and collective variations that make unexpected and sometimes unexpectedly progressive outcomes possible. There is room for ending on an optimistic note in which the crucible of social and epistemic powers melds with assertions of selfhood that are creatively informed by these but in no sense totally subordinated to them.

Jeannette Mageo and Bruce Knauft

Images of order and authority, based on both fantasy and practical experience, are an important aspect of self-experience and are profoundly shaped by one's social positioning and class. Such images create the "world" in which we live our daily lives and help to shape the identities in terms of which we negotiate this world. The individual's experience of self in relationship to the state occurs in multiple arenas, such as going to school, paying taxes, and getting a passport. Many of these arenas are a part of the taken-for-granted background of everyday life. Concrete experiences of the state such as going to school coexist with what for many in the middle class are more abstract and remote images of order and authority such as the police, the law, jails, and the courts. These apparatuses of order and authority are nevertheless enduring sources of fantasy[1] that contribute to self-constitution – as when one drives past an unmarked police car – even when they do not impinge directly on daily living.

State authorities have the power to bestow identity[2] – to "interpellate" the self.[3] Though a sharp distinction cannot be made between "identity" and "self experience," for the present purpose I use the term identity to refer to the assumption of categories that are articulable by the individual and others, in part because they are articulated in public discourse and ideologies, such as the law. Identities would, then, include such categories as "woman," "educated person," "Turk," "immigrant," etc. Self experience must, of course, include one's identities but also one's affective, historical, and bodily relationships to such identities. For example, "I'm smart," or "I don't feel authentically Dutch," "my parents embarrass me," "I'm in danger here," etc. The sense of being powerful would thus be a self experience.

Collier, Maurer, and Suarez-Navaz, building on Foucault's theory of the discursive power of disciplines such as medicine, penal practices, and the law to constitute the modern subject as an individual, have demonstrated how "bourgeois law" is a contradictory discourse that on the one hand declares everyone equal before the law yet on the other hand encourages people to imagine themselves as unique persons with natural differences, implicitly attributing to them inherent qualities that are beyond the purview of the law (Collier *et al.* 1995). The result in the twentieth century was the proliferation of legal categories of inherent differences – such as gender, race, ethnicity, nationality, and immigration status – that we now see. One source of the proliferation and naturalization of identities is modern immigration law, which "create[s] and police[s] categories such as citizens, legal immigrants, resident aliens, refugees, asylum seekers, guest workers, and illegal aliens" (Collier *et al.* 1995:18). These laws essentialize ethnicity as primordial or natural and maintain migrants as different from members of the dominant culture. The experience of multiplicity should be particularly salient for the children of immigrants, who have been raised and educated in their "host" country and who speak their "host" language as a "mother" tongue: the very terms in quotations embody the contradictions in self-positioning that such people experience just by speaking.[4] We may expect to see shifting identities and perhaps even shifting self experience as the individual moves from one arena to the next and from one set of discursive practices to another, particularly if that individual occupies a radically different structural position within each arena.

A key question is whether such divergent and shifting identities are accompanied by parallel shifts in self experience. My focus here is on demonstrating the process of negotiating multiple identities and considering whether such multiplicity entails corresponding shifts in self experience, particularly with respect to a sense of power. I argue that the experience of identities – the specific ways they are taken on as "self" – depends in part upon the significance to the individual of the authorities by whom they are bestowed. I also argue that the social contexts in which identity is bestowed – such as the "Turkish home" or the professional office where one is employed – do not always coincide with an individual's self experience and self-representations in a straightforward way.

I demonstrate how an individual negotiates shifting identities that have been produced by legal discourse[5] and the relationship between these shifts and self experience by describing a moment in the life of a woman temporarily suspended between apparently incommensurable worlds and identities. Her liminal situation exposes aspects of identity negotiation and self experience that are normally not articulated and hence are usually invisible to the casual observer.

I shall call this woman Nergis. In one world, she was a young professional in a well-paying job with a promising future. In another, she was structurally powerless – an ethnic Turk and new mother whose daily life was tightly constrained by her husband and family. She is the daughter of a Turkish guest worker in the Netherlands. I met and talked with her shortly after she had fled her husband and family and turned to Dutch and foreign colleagues at work for help. She had been thrown into a novel situation that suddenly altered her positioning both in her Turkish family and in the Dutch social and legal system. Contours of her self experience and identity negotiation *vis-à-vis* competing sources of authority that would normally be implicit were therefore visible. Particularly evident was her personal power to transform her position in her family and to use the legal system and her personal networks to accomplish her goals. Her ability to do this makes her story a good vehicle for distinguishing power associated with one's structural position and identity within a family or community and one's personal power to shape oneself and control one's environment. An individual may tightly compartmentalize incommensurable worlds and identities, as Nergis does, and these identities may be constituted by a hegemonic discourse such as that manifested in bourgeois law. Nonetheless, Nergis's actions demonstrate how an individual may negotiate shifting positions *vis-à-vis* the dominant discourse of bourgeois law and the spaces of naturalized difference it creates without simply reproducing the cleavages generated by competing discourses.[6] Nergis used strategies and maintained self-representations learned within an "ethnic" space to act effectively in a bourgeois space.

It is important not to assume that immigrants and their children simply shift between incommensurable worlds and identities, thereby accepting as an analytic starting-point the differences that law and public culture posit. Naturalized difference is to a great extent a product of a hegemonic discourse constituted by bourgeois law and the other disciplines examined by Foucault. From the perspective of this dominant discourse, any evidence of difference may be categorized, either explicitly or implicitly, as merely the relics of a frozen "traditional" discourse. But such labels render invisible the possibility that these spaces of "difference" are a locus for alternative discourses and strategies that are dynamic and emergent (see Certeau 1984).

Recent literature on "legal consciousness" (a term introduced by Merry 1990) has explored litigants' understandings and expectations of the legal process

(O'Barr 1988) and how the categories of law intersect with everyday life. While concerned with the phenomenon of legal consciousness, I choose to focus on images of order and authority because they are broader in scope than the terms "legal" and "consciousness." While most of the phenomena I focus on are manifestations of legal processes, other loci of authority such as politics, religion, and personal patronage relationships operate in similar ways as sources of images and fantasy that locate the self.[7] "Consciousness" carries echoes of Marxist usage and its association with class, which is only one of the dimensions that scholars using the concept of legal consciousness have explored. The term "consciousness" also recalls Freudian usage, where it stands in contrast to unconscious processes. The images and fantasies I point to are not all necessarily "conscious" in this Freudian sense, but may be implicit and unacknowledged.

In the US, several studies have focused on the legal consciousness of subordinate groups such as the welfare poor (Sarat 1990; White 1990), into whose lives the state intrudes more directly than for the typical middle-class subject. For individuals who belong to communities that have been labeled ethnic minorities by law, specific government policies for dealing with ethnic communities play an analogous role in constituting identities and shaping consciousness or experience of self *vis-à-vis* law and authority. These policies position members of the community in specific ways, framing for them the realm of the possible; they vary widely from one country to the next, constituting immigrant communities and individual experiences in specific ways.[8]

With the migration into Europe of large numbers of people from countries such as Turkey, Morocco, India, and Pakistan has come a growing salience of "ethnicity" and the issue of whether an ethnic identity competes with and functions as an alternative to national identity. Scholars are beginning to challenge oversimplified models that assume competition between these two sources of identity, as in the image of, for example, the "traditional" Turk who must "adapt" to a strange new society by giving up old ways and becoming modern (Cağlar 1990).[9] This model of the process of establishing oneself in a new society reflects the contours of the orientalist dichotomy between static tradition and progressive modernity. Focusing on legal and political consciousness and, more broadly, on images and fantasies of order and authority offers a source of more nuanced models for how immigrants negotiate identity. It also casts light on the extent to which identity is contextualized or compartmentalized and whether there are shifts in the experience of the self corresponding to the spaces of difference constituted by bourgeois law.

In Turkish guest-worker communities in northern Europe, young women often find themselves caught between worlds, negotiating identities that are radically disjunct. Such disjunctions are, of course, a common experience for immigrants globally. But for examining the process of identity negotiation itself, the situation of young Turkish women who are growing to adulthood in a country like the Netherlands is particularly instructive because, for some women at least, it involves apparently dramatic shifts of power and position from one social context to another.

Most Turkish guest workers came to the Netherlands, Germany, and other countries directly from small communities in rural Turkey in the 1970s. They eventually settled their families and established local institutions in self-contained communities such as the well-known Kreuzberg in Berlin (Mandel 1996). In the Netherlands the encapsulation of immigrant communities is suggested by patterns of school attendance. The state schools serving such areas are often called "black schools" because they serve exclusively immigrant populations and enroll few, if any, Dutch students. This pattern of encapsulation has in the past been reinforced by state policy. In the Netherlands, migrant populations are defined by their collective identities and are referred to overtly as "ethnic minorities." In the past, social, cultural, and political functions were organized along denominational lines, what were called "pillars" – Catholic, Protestant, and Secular – each with a separate system of schools, welfare and health organizations, and unions (Soysal 1994:49). Although the pillarization of Dutch society has gradually disintegrated in the postwar period and there has been less emphasis on promoting separate institutions for migrant groups, current policies toward migrants still reflect this legacy (Entzinger 1985). As Soysal has pointed out, "all of these measures are designed to provide a bridge between migrant groups and Dutch institutions, which are presumed to be in natural disparity" (Soysal 1994:50). This policy, in other words, creates and naturalizes difference, in the same movement by which it seeks to bridge it.

The policies specific to the Netherlands tend to place intermediaries between the individual and the state, a practice which has a direct impact on young Turkish women, making them more subject to community leaders and their families than they might otherwise be. In keeping with gender patterns in their home villages, where daughters were minimally educated and were given to a husband in an arranged marriage, many Turkish families maintain sharply differing expectations for sons and for daughters. Daughters in many families are closely watched, their movements in public space circumscribed and restricted, and they are given very little scope for making their own decisions about school and marriage. In the Netherlands the daughter of a guest worker is often discouraged from attending school past the state-mandated age and is commonly married off to a close relative who has been brought to the Netherlands, perhaps illegally, for the wedding.

Nevertheless, these young women do attend school and are influenced by Dutch and other European media, all of which expose them to a very different organization of gender relations and a different discourse concerning the nature of the individual and authority. The self as defined by its relationship to power is a central aspect of this difference. When such a woman moves between disjunct worlds and identities, does she also demonstrate shifts in her experience of self and in the forms of power associated with her experience of self?

Nergis' flight

Nergis was 23 years old, the daughter of a Turkish guest worker. I met Nergis in The Hague four days after she had run away from her husband.[10] She was temporarily staying – hiding out, really – with the family of an American woman she knew from work. She had already been there one night. Engaged to her cousin at age 11, Nergis had, by her own account, been forced into an arranged marriage at age 18. The fight that precipitated her departure from her husband was the final round in a long-term dispute over money. She and her husband had sent money that she had earned to her in-laws in Istanbul to buy an apartment for them. One of the conditions that Nergis had insisted upon was that the apartment be in her own name, since she had paid for it. They had originally agreed that it would at first be in Nergis's mother's name (her mother is the sister of her husband's mother, making Nergis and her husband first cousins) and then be transferred to her own name. The fight erupted when her husband informed her that they would not transfer the apartment into her name. When she protested, her husband said to her, "Who are you that you think they should put it in your name?" That was the last straw. She complained that they treated her like a money machine, and she decided at that moment that her in-laws would not suck away her money any longer.

In her story, Nergis articulated a frustration with a self-experience that she represented to me as being a "money machine." Where does this image of herself come from? In her description of the fight, the "money machine" stands in implicit contrast with her own desire to be recognized as someone who earns money in her own right and who owns property. This desire is one that is supposed to be "natural" to a self that is discursively constituted by "bourgeois law" (Collier *et al.* 1995). Her professional status and income give her an identity as an autonomous individual, a potential property-holder, in keeping with the model perpetuated by bourgeois law. Her husband, articulating the perspective of his own family, speaks from a different discourse – not that of Turkish law, which is also informed by a bourgeois discourse of the individual and bourgeois notions of private property – but from a discourse in which the family collectively controls resources, including those of adult sons, and the husband is officially the sole authority and decision-maker, the representative of the family to the outside world.[11] Nergis's claim disrupts that discourse. It is Nergis's situation as the primary wage-earner that puts her in the middle of this clash of discourses.

But it is important not to simply chalk up this clash to the immigrant experience by assuming that in Turkey the "traditional" Turkish wife would be fully embedded in a "traditional" discourse. On the contrary, the phenomenon of dual career marriages is widespread in Turkey today, and many of Nergis's relatives, especially those who have moved to the major cities (as have her in-laws), follow this pattern. Many dual career families in Turkey manage to work out reasonably stable decision-making arrangements.[12] What creates a glaring contradiction for Nergis is the fact that she is the *primary* wage-earner – a professional who was married off to an uneducated, unskilled worker (who now works on an assembly line in a pillow factory). Though in some Turkish families the wife may actually earn more than her husband, this difference in the status of their employment is more unusual. This discrepancy *is* a direct result of her immigrant status as a resident of the Netherlands. If she had lived in Turkey, her family would more likely have found her a spouse with a similar educational background. But in this case, she was used as the vehicle for bringing another relative into the Netherlands, a common fate for young "Turkish" women growing up there. Her situation was thus a direct product of Dutch immigration law, which forms a part of the background reality in which she lives.

Having been labeled a specific ethnic minority, members of her family and community are subject to constraints on their mobility that they respond to strategically. Marriage choices are a key strategizing response that partially derive from pre-existing cultural patterns but are not simply a reproduction of those patterns. They are a "tactic" (Certeau 1984) for maximizing economic opportunity. As several Turks in the Netherlands, some from the guest-worker class and others from more elite strata who came to the Netherlands under very different circumstances, such as diplomatic service, told me many times, "The Turks here are more backwards and traditional than Turkish villagers back in Turkey." But their encapsulation as an ethnic minority is reinforced by marriage patterns that are encouraged by Dutch immigration law, even as these marriage patterns are perceived by the Dutch as a difficult-to-shake-loose "natural" or "traditional" pattern.

But the young women are beginning to rebel. Nergis described the situation in these terms: "Within the past 3–4 years, lots of girls have begun to run away. This is the first generation that is growing up and knows Dutch society. They do not want to live in the closed Turkish community, which does not even know what it is like in Turkey today – they live the way Turkey was in the 1960s. They do not want education, especially for the girls."

To illustrate this community problem of rebellious girls, she described the situation of another young woman whom she knew well.

My friend was Alevi [a different Muslim sect from that of Nergis's family], and my parents would not even let me go to her house after school to study [emphasizing how restrictive these Turkish parents are]. Eventually my friend fell in love with a boy and married him, against her parents' wishes. When it did not work out because he gambled and beat her, they took her back. But she eventually went back to him. When she left him again, they would not take her back. Then I lost touch with her – I often wonder what happened to her.

Her musings indicated that this woman had crossed the social boundary surrounding the Turkish community – a boundary that is both restrictive and protective – and was now completely beyond the pale.

On the day she left her husband, Nergis had been sleeping in a room separate from her husband because of their fight the night before. When he left for work at 6:30 a.m., he said goodbye. She was still in bed and just waved him away. Then she got up, packed her things, put her suitcase in her car, and dropped her 18-month-old son off at her mother's, as she usually did when she went off to work. She told no one what she was doing and had no idea where she would go. When I asked her whether she had been concerned about leaving her son behind, she explained to me that she had left her son with her mother even though she was defying her mother's expectations by running away because she felt that it would be easier for her son to be in a place he was used to until things settled down and she could get him back.

As she spoke, she recalled when she had gone to Curaçao for a week for a work-related seminar (her work involved overseeing the provision of support services for conferences), leaving her son behind to be cared for by her mother. Given her tightly constrained and closely monitored life, I was surprised to hear that she had made such a trip. In my eyes, she suddenly seemed to take on a new identity that was incompatible with the image she had been projecting as someone who fully inhabited a "traditional" Turkish world, confined by the demands of her family and the needs of her child when she was not at work. She explained that she had bent the truth a bit and told her family that she would lose her job and income if she did not go to Curaçao with her colleagues. Given that experience of separation from her son, she figured that this current separation, so far no longer than the earlier one, was no more traumatic for him.

After she had dropped off her son, she drove to work and told her boss what she had done. In previous weeks she had already revealed to him some things about her situation, and when she told him that now she did not know where she would go next, he offered to take her to stay with him and his wife. So the first two nights after she left her husband, she stayed at her boss's home. When he drove her to work each morning (she had left her own car parked in the company's locked garage), she would ride lying flat on the floor between the seats, covered with bags so that her relatives could not catch a glimpse of her. But on the third day Nergis learned that her family had guessed where she was staying, and so she felt that she had to move again.

In the meantime, an American co-worker had had an encounter with Nergis's mother, who had been hanging around the secured parking lot at Nergis's office. The mother, a stranger to the American woman, had approached her and asked her to hold the garage door open so that she could go in, "Just to look to see if a car is there." The American woman (who was an acquaintance of mine) would not oblige her but brought her into the receptionist to help her to page Nergis on the intercom. It was at this point that the American woman learned that Nergis was hiding out from her family. So she offered to take Nergis in herself, figuring that Nergis's family would not be able to trace her there. Nergis took her up on the offer, and it was at that point that I met Nergis.

For several days they maintained a routine in which Nergis's boss continued to pick her up on his way into work, hiding her on the floor in the back of the car each time. Nergis's boss also arranged for her to meet with a lawyer, who could both act as a mediator with her family and initiate divorce proceedings. Her boss had, in effect, become her patron.[13] In the meantime, Nergis had also enlisted the aid of many of her co-workers and myself. All were sympathetic to her plight. Her stories of coercion were outrageous from the perspective of a discourse grounded in bourgeois law and the principles of human rights and freedom. "Emancipation" of minorities had long been an explicitly articulated official ideology of the Dutch government. To put all of our actions within the frame of this discourse: a Turkish woman had become sufficiently enlightened to desire emancipation but needed help to escape her natural, traditional community, which has not yet evolved to the point of recognizing basic modern values such as equality and freedom.

Nergis's concern with hiding from her family indicates that it took several days for her to realize that her family did not have the power to physically recapture her or to hurt her, except through sudden, unexpected violence, a kind of terrorism often associated in European and American public culture with Muslims. Even the Dutch and American colleagues helping her accepted this reality, taking great pains to seal out any of her family members from the office building and to hide her completely from view. Public space was not safe. It was being constituted in terms that also reproduced aspects of public space in rural Turkey: a woman has no right to be out on her own or to disobey her family and can get away only by relying on a network of friends to hide and protect her. Violence against a young woman is, in some circles at least, legitimate (even if illegal according to Turkish law). The streets and parks of The Hague, even those far beyond her neighborhood, had filled with the imagined eyes of her legitimately angry relatives.

On the sixth day, two days after I had met her, her sense of space began to shift. By this time, she knew that the next day (Monday) she was to meet with her mother and brother, two of the main people she was hiding from, in the presence of the Dutch lawyer. It was now Sunday, and she did not have to go into work. Wanting to get to know her better and give her something else to do, I asked her to join my family on a trip to Efteling, one of Holland's largest amusement parks, which was more than an hour's drive from The Hague. The invitation felt quite incongruous to me, and I would not have thought of it except that my family already had plans for the trip with some colleagues. Otherwise, I probably would have been affected by the hide-out mentality and joined her for an afternoon at the apartment in which she was staying. At first she was startled when I suggested the outing – it was beyond the realm of possibility – but as we talked it over, she realized with some surprise that there was nothing stopping her and no immediate obligation to keep her from going with us. And it was well beyond the sphere of her family's influence: they would never look for her there. So we went. Ironically, shortly after we arrived at Efteling, she spotted several young men from her neighborhood. At first she went to great lengths to avoid being seen but eventually said, "What does it matter? They don't know who I am with. They can't do anything to me. So let them see me. But I must prevent them from talking to me." It felt at that moment that she had adopted a new sense of herself in public space. She defied their gaze and their identification of her as a wayward woman. She had become something else – at one point she said, "I have a right to be here with friends" – and now felt safe in that space. At first she had seemingly moved beyond the gaze of the Turkish community. But when its gaze extended even there, she realized that she was beyond its reach in a more profound way.

I thought I was drawing her into a new experience. She had described to me a life in which during childhood and even her college days she had never been allowed to associate with friends after school, always returning straight home, where she and her family virtually never went out to socialize in public. And then she had been married off before she had finished school. Even as a working woman, she had always returned straight home after work. But when I asked her if it was her first time at Efteling, she admitted (and it sounded like an admission) that she had once come with some of her schoolmates without her family's knowledge. In a story similar to the one she told her family about the Curaçao trip, she had told them she had a project that would keep her after school, and then she and her friends had cut classes to spend a day at Efteling. So it was not the first time that she had evaded their expectations. Returning to Efteling, it seemed, was tantamount to returning to a forbidden space.

For years Nergis had lived a compartmentalized life, embedded in worlds with little commensurability. At work she dressed and moved like any professional woman. Even her English had become fluent on the job, and she operated within the cosmopolitan world of The Hague's high-level business and government travel. In this world, she was an autonomous, talented individual. This identity was one that had been shaped during her years of schooling, often in defiance of her parents' efforts to control her. She described how her parents had taken no active interest in her schooling. When she did not want to go to the "black" school near her house (which, according to her, was "100% foreigners," from Morocco, Surinam, and Turkey), she found a better school, which was quite far from her neighborhood but which had only three or four Turkish girls. Nergis had had choices when it came to schooling because she had always gotten good grades, and so was able to go to the top-level high school.

Though in these stories of her schooling she emphasized her own initiatives in getting out of a "black" school, it is likely that as a young girl she had been noticed by her Dutch teachers, who then took it upon themselves to guide her into a school with better opportunities. Shifting to another, distant school must have involved some adult initiative, and she was explicit that the initiative had not come from her parents. Her current situation – including her willingness to share her story with me and her comfort in relying on her boss and other colleagues – suggests an established pattern of negotiating her incommensurable worlds by enlisting the patronage of those with the power to open doors for her.

Being in a school with a majority of Dutch classmates exaggerated the incommensurability of Nergis's worlds and the barrier between them. Her school friends had been primarily Dutch. Nergis never visited their houses nor they hers. She had never told them about her engagement at age 11 or her marriage at age 18, and with me, she used this incident as an example of the depth of the differences in their experiences and concerns. But her contacts with school friends from this Dutch world gave her alternative sources of identity that carried over into her Turkish world. As a teenager, she resisted community and family images of her career trajectory, even in her first employment experiences, because she had these alternative images as guides. When she was younger, her parents one summer made her take a job cutting up herring at Scheveningen (a tourist beach resort on the edge of The Hague). "That's what a lot of these girls do. Really low-level work. I couldn't stand it. I wouldn't do it, and so I got a job in a laundry." Her image of her social status was not consistent with her family's or her Turkish friends' images. She could have gone on to university because of her success in school, but she knew her parents would never have let her finish, so she elected to go instead to a professional school, where she was able to get a degree after three years (at age 18 or 19). The degree was in business, with a specialization in tourism. She had always known that getting a good education and a good job was the only way out. But she said that most other girls just did not have the desire to do well.

The marriage

In contrast to her days in school with Dutch classmates, Nergis told stories of how her family had over the course of many years prepared her for marriage and how different her family life had made her from her Dutch classmates. One day when she was just 11 years old her grandmother (who lived with her family in The Hague) gave her a beautiful ring and instructed her to take care of it. Her grandmother explained that it was her engagement ring. Nergis said that she had not really understood at the time what that meant. Every year her family would travel to Turkey for a holiday and would visit her mother's relatives while there. As Nergis grew older, the stays with her relatives became gradually longer, and she finally realized that she was to marry her first cousin, that these visits were to her future in-laws. She never told her Dutch friends about this side of her life. Finally, when she was only 16, her mother informed her that she was to be married. She tried to resist, but her parents insisted. Her parents brought her fiancé into the country (on a tourist visa, I believe), and the Turkish Embassy approved the marriage.

But things did not go exactly as her parents had planned, thanks to the intervention of Dutch authorities. Before the wedding could be finalized, the Dutch authorities captured her fiancé as an illegal immigrant during a routine identity check at a Turkish grocery store in her neighborhood. They deported him to Turkey, even though he was engaged to a legal Dutch resident. According to Dutch immigration law, Nergis was too young to make a spouse legal. Once he got to Turkey, he was promptly drafted for his required military service and was thus forced to remain in Turkey for a year and a half. This had been for Nergis an extended reprieve.

Thus, during the present episode, Nergis had a memory of Dutch intervention on her behalf. This intervention was based on the legal age of marriage. Legal marriage age is in turn grounded in a theory in which marriage is understood to be a contract entered into by two consenting adults who have the freedom and maturity as autonomous individuals to make the decision for themselves, a capacity not presumed to reside in children. This model of marriage is in sharp contrast with her parents' and grandmother's insistence that they had the authority to arrange her marriage for her. Islamic law also requires the consent of the bride. But this "official" public consent can occur in conjunction with coercion at another level. In this case, the *imam* who served as the family's religious advisor had firmly sided with her relatives and lectured Nergis on her duty according to *Şeriat* (Islamic law) to accept this marriage.

Nergis presented the tale of her marriage and her resistance in terms of Dutch norms and law. But not all of her resistance to her mother's marriage plans was grounded in a bourgeois legal discourse. She was also embedded in a reality defined by her family and the Turkish community in ways that were visible even when talking with us Americans. In the liminal world of the American woman's apartment where we listened to her stories late into the night, these two worlds collided and began to blur. As she became engrossed in telling stories of her marriage and her childhood she frequently repeated a gesture that looked slightly bizarre in that setting, a habit perhaps carried from Turkish village life. She would pull out the neck of her sweater and pretend to spit into it as a kind of expletive of anger and disgust. Her stories transported her (and us) back into her family's kitchen and habits.

This alternative world is further suggested by a story in which she described her resistance to her mother's daily efforts to convince her to want this marriage – back when she was 18 and her fiancé was near completion of his military service.

My mother went to the *imam-hoca* to get some magic. It is something written on a piece of paper that you put into water and the writing dissolves. Then you put the water in food. I noticed one day that my mother was smiling when I came home from school. She really urged me to eat a snack, and I got suspicious. Later I looked in the cupboard and found a glass with paper in it. The next time she offered me food like that – all smiling and coaxing – I told her I would eat it upstairs in my room. I took it up and threw it out.

She told several similar stories of evading her mother's magic.

Another time, I noticed that there were two carpets on the floor. I picked one up and found another piece of paper with writing on it. It was there for me to step over. And there was one under the carpet in my room, too. My mother carries a little bag where she keeps money and valuables – she tucks it in her bra when she goes out. One day it was hanging in the bathroom. I looked into it to see what was there, and I saw a little case with a hair inside and my name. It was my hair. So I went to my brother and told him I wanted to pretend to cut his hair, like a hairdresser. I picked up his hair and really cut a small bit as if by accident. Then I took the hair and replaced my hair with his in my mother's case. She kept doing this to try to change my mind. She didn't know that I knew what she was doing.

She resisted her mother's wishes, but even in the telling, she nevertheless shared her mother's world: magic works but can be escaped through careful and clever maneuvering. While at home, she did not stand outside that world and say "there is no magic."

The kind of resistance to her mother's magic that Nergis displayed can and often does occur even in a young woman embedded within a consistent environment who does not move among radically different cultural worlds. In fact, it is a hallmark of relationships within the restrictive environments in which many young Muslim women grow up. Scholars assessing cultural norms of psychological development within such extended families have often confused the kind of interpersonally enmeshed situation that many young Muslim women find themselves in within the extended family with psychological dependency and lack of autonomy. I have argued elsewhere (1991) that, on the contrary, a woman socially embedded within the complex dynamics of a large extended family, as in rural Pakistan or Turkey, must be able to maintain self-evaluations and an awareness of her own desires that are distinct from the terms in which her immediate interlocutors see her if she is to function successfully within the family. Such women speak of the "politics" of everyday life and describe strategies for getting one's way by working around the wishes of those who occupy the overt positions of power. This form of resistance is grounded not in a discourse of the bourgeois individual but in a discourse of local politics and patronage within a social system organized in terms of structural inequalities.

From the perspective of this discourse, one way of characterizing Nergis's ability to maneuver successfully through the school system and even through the corporation where she works is that she is very skillful at negotiating patronage relationships in a style that is reminiscent of so-called "traditional" power dynamics within a Turkish extended family and village. Skill at this kind of local politics is a source of power.

Ultimately, however, her mother and grandmother won, and Nergis was married off to a man whom she vehemently did not want to marry. Why did she yield? As evidenced by her school career, Nergis had always been a powerful person within her family's world, though occupying a subject-position that was very subordinate. She had known how to operate within the limits of this position. As she described her strategy, the struggle with her parents seemed to be a periodic phenomenon. She would push her parents to accede to her wishes and pull back just before they retaliated by setting limits. Strategically, she had not pushed to get a full university education, because she had feared that they could prevent it, leaving her with nothing: "I let my mother know how much I did not want this marriage, but at a certain point, I hid my objections because I was afraid that if they thought I would not go through with it, they would prevent me from continuing in school." When things escalated too much and her resistance became more overt, her parents would threaten to take her out of school: "Then I would submit and be quiet about my feelings." The decision to accede to the marriage had thus been a product of strategic negotiations, in which her parents and her fiancé agreed to let her finish the training program that she had selected as a shorter alternative to the university, allowing her to continue to attend classes even after marriage.

Another powerful factor in her submission was her identity as a "good girl," which she had wished to preserve. When she was describing her late adolescence, she contrasted herself with her best friend and with other young women who had run away with men or who had gotten involved in activities defined as "corrupt" by the Turkish community. To maintain this identity as a good girl, she had let there be a discrepancy between her parents' view of her and her "feelings." Similarly, she mentioned several times how people in the community thought it was an ideal marriage, because she always went along with things in public. When she left her husband, she let go of this image of "good girl." And then she replayed the letting go at Efteling, at the moment when she stopped hiding from the young men who knew her and defiantly returned their gaze. But the only time that she was moved to cry during that first late night conversation was when she talked of what she had had to sacrifice to retain her identity as a good girl in her parents' eyes. She broke down just as she was explaining how her 18-year-old sister is now living without all the restrictions with which Nergis had lived. As she cried, she said, "I've lost my youth." Her parents have learned that they made a mistake with Nergis, and they are pushing education for her younger siblings much harder now. She was sure that her parents would let her sister choose her own husband and felt sadly jealous. Her sister was on her side in the current crisis and had spoken with her on the phone, filling her in on what had happened after she left, providing a link with her son and her family.

Identity and self

The example of Nergis's situation offers a balance to the notion that the self is constituted by the gaze/judgement/power of the other or by a discourse such as the law in any simple way. Nergis has not been fully constituted as an autonomous, individual self by a bourgeois legal discourse, nor has she been located as a Turk who is naturally different from the Dutch. Nor does she simply jump between incommensurable worlds. Her particular strength would seem to lie in her ability to hold onto more than one frame of reference (i.e., the perspectives of everyone involved in a situation) at a time without losing herself in the gaze of the other. *This* sense of her own desires is not the autonomy of the subject as constituted by Western Enlightenment discourse, but if it has an external (i.e., a discursive or cultural) source at all, it would seem to be an outcome of her experiences of coercion and hierarchy within her family, which created disjunctions between her self experience and others' perceptions of her. These disjunctions within the world of the Turkish community became even more salient once she was established as a "married woman."

Her statement that people cope with a bad situation by saying to themselves that it could always be worse demonstrated this persistent strategy of holding two frames of reference in mind at once. It is this ability that gave her the power to go with friends to Efteling without her parents' knowledge, or to avoid telling even her best friend that she was already engaged to be married. This strategy is a source of power, an intimation of an ability to shape worlds and others to one's own desires by retaining another frame of reference apart from the one that appears to be the immediately present, socially agreed-upon reality. Given her schooling and professional experiences, Nergis was well-practiced in the strategies needed to operate as a bourgeois individual with rights, autonomy, and a successful career in one context and as an obedient Turkish daughter in another. But her effectiveness did not rest solely on her position within that bourgeois world. On the contrary, many of her effective strategies were learned in her "Turkish" world of family, politics, and patronage. She had a rich store of self-representations as an effective strategizer, with skills that could readily cross the ethnic divide.

In earlier work (Ewing 1990), I argued that self-representations and self-experience are context-dependent and discontinuous in ways that the individual may be quite unaware of. One of the reasons for this is that self-representations are maintained in relationship to representations of others and are often unself-consciously consistent with the image(s) that the other holds of one. As I have demonstrated here, these self representations, such as effective strategizer or bad girl, may cross-cut legally or culturally articulated identities such as Turk or educated professional.

Both Shamim (the young Pakistani woman described in my earlier paper) and Nergis saw themselves as strategizers and both were negotiating a conflict of near-crisis proportions that forced the confrontation of formerly contextualized, or even deliberately compartmentalized, inconsistent self-representations and experiences. For the purposes of my present argument, the key difference between the two women is that, at the moment of the conversation analyzed in the earlier paper, Shamim had not yet resolved a conflict between her own desire to marry the man of her choice and her parents' opposition to the marriage. She therefore shifted between inconsistent self-representations and alternative scenarios for the future, fully living each within the moment. Nergis, in contrast, had already made a decision and had broken the compartmentalized social frame of her everyday life, leaving her in a liminal situation. Within this situation, she was in the process of reorganizing her relationship to her past, creating narratives that repositioned her *vis-à-vis* her husband, parents, and other authority figures such as the *imam-hoca*.

Visible in Nergis's narratives are transitional self-representations that had worked in the past. In the current situation she used them defensively to minimize the appearance of rupture and to avoid an experience of negative self-representation. For instance, when imagining herself in relationship to her infant son, she adopted the self-representation of professional "as if on a business trip" rather than taking on the self-representation of (bad) mother who has abandoned her son. Both representations, however, were present during the course of our conversation, if only because I created a discursive context for the bad mother image through my own questions about what she had done with her son when she left her husband. But her ability to refuse or set aside the latter self-representation as bad mother while experiencing and convincing others of the former is an aspect of her personal power and effectiveness. Yet it is important to remember that I saw her only in one social situation – one in which she had firmly made up her mind and had taken on a set of self-representations (e.g. "money machine") that enabled her to act decisively through strategies learned within her family and to risk taking up new identities in the legal and social worlds she inhabited. In another time and place – such as the weeks leading up to her separation – her self presentation and the self-representations that would have been salient to an observer would no doubt have looked quite different. And even after these repositionings, it is likely that she will retain other, inconsistent self-representations that are relevant only for interpersonal contexts that she has not had to renegotiate during this crisis.

Nergis had deliberately compartmentalized two legally distinct identities, dividing her time between these "Dutch" and "Turkish" worlds, but her marital situation and her income had created a contradiction, turning her self experience into a "money machine." It was ultimately this contradiction, at one level a result of Dutch immigration policies, that pushed her to disrupt the balance she had achieved: her husband and family wanted to exploit her earnings while denying her the power and respect that she felt should accompany her ability to earn. In a manner characterized by Hegel in his theoretical description of the struggle between the psychological positions of master and slave, she ultimately seized power by being willing to risk all (even her life, as her family threatened her with physical violence if she tried to divorce her husband) for a new kind of recognition by her family. She redefined her rights in Dutch terms, filed for a divorce, and ultimately regained custody of her son. But she did not move wholly into a Dutch world. Her parents were the ones who capitulated. They accepted the divorce, and she moved back in with them, now in control of her finances, her son, and her free time. She had reorganized the family, transforming the environment for her siblings as well.

A year after I last saw Nergis, the American woman who had first introduced me to her emailed me the following message:

She seems to be fine now – the last I heard, she had moved into her own apartment with her son, her mother takes care of her son during the day, the divorce was in process and her husband wasn't bothering her. She and her husband sold the apartment they owned jointly (which covered what they owed on it), she gave the house in Turkey to his parents, his papers were in order for Holland and that seems to be about all he was concerned about. It's amazing how it all wound up in such a civilized manner when it was such a drama just a little over one year ago. One important factor seemed to be the mullah who acted as arbitrator. Everyone seemed to accept his word and abide by it.

The "mullah" was the man whom Nergis had called the *imam-hoca*. His position had apparently shifted during the course of the dispute. When she had been resisting marriage, he had done everything in his power to urge her into it, giving her mother amulets and lecturing her on her duties according to *Şeriat* (Islamic law). But even he had capitulated, accepting a mediatory role parallel to that of the Dutch lawyer.

Nergis had removed the contradiction and even become a "good girl" again. This was possible in part because even her rebellion had been thoughtfully timed. In contrast to her Alevi friend who apparently had pushed the goodwill of her parents to the breaking point, Nergis patiently tolerated the marriage for five long years – enough time so that her husband's immigration status had changed. After five years on a residence permit, he obtained an establishment permit,[14] which meant that he was now safe from deportation following divorce. She had not acted vindictively, her husband had gotten what he wanted, and he no longer needed her. She was able once again to compartmentalize her worlds and her identities, allowing the fragmentary hegemonies of everyday habits to flow through her once again. But she was now savvy in how to mobilize tactics learned in the space of ethnic difference to further her career and her friendships in the "Dutch" world of the corporation and the law. Her self experience as effective strategizer had transcended the borders of her domestic "Turkish" identity and become a position from which she could act in this Dutch world. While images of authority profoundly shape us, through fantasy and practical experience we also shape them. Like Nergis, we re-create the "world" in which we live our daily lives in the cumulative acts of authoring our identities.

NOTES

1. By fantasy I mean in this context stories of the self in which relationships to power and authority are played out.
2. The state and the law of course are not the only sources of identity or even of authority.
3. This is a process encapsulated in Althusser's example of the police officer who shouts "Hey, you!" to someone on the street, thereby momentarily fixing the self in a state of guilt even before it is clear who the officer is addressing (Althusser 1971). Freudian-influenced models of the mind suggest that fantasies of order and authority are a key component in the organization of the self, articulated in concepts from Freud's "superego" to Lacan's "symbolic order." Althusser and more recently Žižek have sought to link up these intrapsychic images of authority, as well as the dynamics of desire, with political processes, creating models for the structure of political fantasy.
4. At several workshops and conferences I participated in while in the Netherlands during 1996–1997, this issue of multiple identities and shifting selves was fore-grounded. I met a number of students and scholars who are themselves positioned as ethnic minorities, and their reactions to one of my earlier papers (Ewing 1990) indicate that the experience of "shifting selves" as part of the process of negotiating multiple identities is a salient one for many.
5. In passing, Collier *et al.* allude to the possibility that people may actually experience themselves as having multiple identities as a result of the ways they are positioned before the discursive power of the law (Collier *et al.* 1995:20).
6. Foucault characterized power in terms of resistances to it – particularly when attention shifts from discursive formations and technologies to selves (as Foucault himself began to do at the end of his career). These points of resistance, according to

Foucault, are transitory and mobile, "producing cleavages in a society that shift about, furrowing across individuals themselves, cutting them up and remolding them, marking off irreducible regions in them, in their bodies and minds" (1990:98). Given the possibilities for disjunctions of experience within immigrant communities, such communities are a prime site for identifying such "irreducible regions" and fragmentary hegemonies that produce disjointed individuals. From this perspective, Nergis's actions are vehicles for examining how, precisely, this irreducibility is manifest in individuals, and how, precisely, an individual's experience may not be disjointed in ways that might be expected. In other words, the lines of cleavage, while they may exist (and, I argue elsewhere, do exist), do not correspond to and are not constituted by the cleavages between competing discourses and associated identities one inhabits.

7. The difficulty in focusing on the experience of law in a narrow sense is illustrated by the experience of Carol Greenhouse (1986) who set out to do "legal anthropology" in a Baptist community in the American South but ultimately wrote an ethnography focused on other strategies of conflict resolution.

8. Various European countries that have experienced large influxes of immigrants have developed very different policies and laws for managing, providing services to, and policing immigrants and immigrant communities. In response, individuals and communities adapt in different ways to these diverse policies. The question of how immigrant identity, both community and individual, is shaped by perceptions and experience of the state is thus a salient one for the various governments, who must assess the consequences of their specific policies.

9. Çağlar critiques the scholarly practice in guest work literature of giving images of the unadjusted or "lost" Turkish migrant, which justifies the tradition/modernity dichotomy and legitimizes state policies that appropriate the same language (1990).

10. Nergis's father had come to the Hague as an unskilled worker in 1971 and brought the rest of the family in 1977, when Nergis was 3 years old. This extended separation and ultimate reunification of the family was a consequence of specific constraints on immigration imposed by the Dutch government.

11. For an analysis of the power dynamics within Turkish village families, see (Sirman 1990; 1995).

12. For an analysis of marital power dynamics among working-class Turkish couples where the wife works, see (Bolak 1995).

13. A similar use of a kind of patronage relationship to help negotiate the legal system is illustrated by the case of an American housekeeper who called upon her employer to help her escape a guilty verdict in an auto accident (Ewick 1992:742).

14. According to the Aliens Circular, the alien authorities must inform the alien who has resided in the Netherlands for five years of the possibility of applying for an "establishment permit." It is estimated that more than 90 percent of such persons hold this permit (Stewart 1987:876).

REFERENCES

Althusser, Louis. 1971. Ideology and Ideological State Apparatuses (Notes Towards an Investigation). In *Lenin and Philosophy and Other Essays*, pp. 121–173. London: New Left Books.
Bolak, Hale Cihan. 1995. Towards a Conceptualization of Marital Power Dynamics: Women Breadwinners and Working-class Households in Turkey. In *Women in Modern Turkey: A Reader* (S. Tekeli, ed.), pp. 173–198. London: Zed Books Ltd.

Caglar, Ayse. 1990. The Prisonhouse of Culture in the Studies of Turks in Germany. Institut für Ethnologie, Freie Universitat, Berlin, Sozialanthropologische Arbeitspapiere 31.

Certeau, Michel de. 1984. *The Practice of Everyday Life*. Berkeley: University of California Press.

Collier, Jane F., Bill Maurer, and Liliana Suarez-Navaz. 1995. Sanctioned Identities: Legal Consciousness of Modern Personhood. *Identities* 2(1–2):1–27.

Comaroff, John L., and Simon Roberts. 1981. *Rules and Processes: The Cultural Logic of Dispute in an African Context*. Chicago: University of Chicago Press.

Entzinger, Hans B. 1985. The Netherlands. In *European Immigration Policy: A Comparative Study* (T. Hammar, ed.), pp. xi, 319. Cambridge: Cambridge University Press.

Ewick, Patricia and Susan S. Silbey. 1992. Conformity, Contestation, and Resistance: An Account of Legal Consciousness. *New England Law Review* 26:731–749.

Ewing, Katherine Pratt. 1990. The Illusion of Wholeness: "Culture," "Self," and the Experience of Inconsistency. *Ethos* 18(3):251–278.

——— 1991. Can Psychoanalytic Theories Explain the Pakistani Muslim Woman? Intrapsychic Autonomy and Interpersonal Engagement in the Extended Family. *Ethos* 19:131–160.

Foucault, Michel. 1990. *The History of Sexuality*, Vol. 1. New York: Vintage Books.

Greenhouse, Carol J. 1986. *Praying for Justice: Faith, Order, and Community in an American Town*. Ithaca, NY: Cornell University Press.

Mandel, Ruth. 1996. A Place of Their Own: Contesting Spaces and Defining Places in Berlin's Migrant Community. In *Making Muslim Space in North America and Europe* (B. Metcalf, ed.), pp. 147–166. Berkeley: University of California Press.

Merry, Sally. 1990. *Getting Justice and Getting Even: Legal Consciousness among Working-Class Americans*. Chicago: University of Chicago Press.

O'Barr, William M. and John M. Conley. 1988. Lay Expectations of the Civil Justice System. *Law and Society Review* 22(1):137–161.

Obeyesekere, Gananath. 1992. *The Apotheosis of Captain Cook*. Princeton: Princeton University Press.

Sarat, Austin. 1990. The Law is All Over: Power, Resistance, and the Legal Consciousness of the Welfare Poor. *Yale Journal of Law and the Humanities* 2:343–379.

Sirman, Nukhet. 1990. State, Village and Gender in Western Turkey. In *Turkish State, Turkish Society* (A.F.a.N. Sirman, ed.), pp. 21–51. London: Routledge.

——— 1995. Friend and Foe? Forging Alliances with Other Women in a Village of Western Turkey. In *Women in Modern Turkish Society: A Reader* (S. Tekeli, ed.), pp. 199–218. London: Zed Books.

Soysal, Yasemin Nuhoglu. 1994. *Limits of Citizenship: Migrants and Postnational Membership in Europe*. Chicago: University of Chicago Press.

Spinosa, C. and Hubert Dreyfus. 1996. Two Kinds of Antiessentialism and Their Consequences. *Critical Inquiry* 22(4):735–763.

Stewart, A. H. J. 1987. The Legal Position of Aliens in Dutch Law. In *Die Rechtsstellung von Auslandern nach staatlichem Recht und Völkerrecht* (The Legal Position of Aliens in National and International Law) (J.A.a.T.S. Frowein, ed.), pp. 869–918 Vol. 1. Berlin: Springer-Verlag.

White, Lucie E. 1990. Subordination, Rhetorical Survival Skills, and Sunday Shoes: Notes on the Hearing of Mrs. G. *Buffalo Law Review* 38(1):1–58.

Zizek, Slavoj. 1989. *The Sublime Object of Ideology*. London, New York: Verso.

Part III

Colonial encounters: power/history/self

6 Spirit, self, and power: the making of colonial experience in Papua New Guinea

Douglas Dalton

Apart from Frantz Fanon, early scholars of colonialism were often reluctant to theorize its psychological dimensions. Among other things, this stemmed from a fear of reenacting colonialism on a new level – of assimilating the colonized to Western psychological schemata in which their differences would be pejoratively interpreted or erased. Indeed, this assimilative project was evident in much early anthropological writing, which suggested that people's minds and emotions in non-Western places were like those of children and/or women in our own society. This understandable hesitation has left many gaps in our models of interconnections between power and the self.

Douglas Dalton's "Spirit, Self, and Power" complicates Fanon's (1967) perspective on the psychological consequences of colonialism. While Fanon sees colonialism as resulting in self-repudiations in relation to an idealized colonist other, Dalton portrays Rawa men in Papua New Guinea as caught in colonially generated contradictions that complicate their sense of self. These contradictions can lead to feelings of inadequacy that are then compensated for by fantasies of empowerment and of violence. In his analysis, Dalton pushes to new and more contemporary levels our comprehension of the transactionally collective Melanesian self – which has been anthropologically important at least from Mauss' *The Gift* in 1925 to M. Strathern's *The Gender of the Gift* in 1988, and since. Drawing in poststructuralist perspectives on self, Dalton articulates his analysis with a subtle critique of the continuing Western attempt to view selves as coherent – even if "dividual" rather than individual in social coherence. Hence Dalton's wonderful trope of "normative schizophrenia" and the Rawa male double bind of "having to be what they cannot be." In a sense, the deeper cosmological power of Rawa culture is its own best tool of de-familiarizing "self"-ish assumptions about power.

As in the chapters of Part II (this volume), in Dalton's analysis, selfhood emerges through interplays of transnational power rather than merely within a culture. He investigates two cases, that of Meyango, a would-be cargo cult leader, and that of Tapa, a raskol gang-leader. For both Meyango and Tapa features of colonial politico-economic power and social domination inform competing vantagepoints for viewing society and self. It makes sense that Tapa, having gotten the goods away from the raskol police, would not use these items in exactly the same self-less way as indigenous notions of Rawa selfhood would have suggested. Indeed, Karen Sykes (1999) has dramatically shown new forms of "self"-ish consumption by raskols in Papua New Guinea. There is a lurking notion of possessive selfhood, if not selfishness, that is all the more alluring because it is outside colonial or national political control and yet still in tension with more traditionalist possibilities. Kenelm Burridge (1969) effectively uncovered similar features in his analysis of "self-willed" components of Tangu indigenous identity and showed their colonial expansion, including in cargo cult orientations. For Burridge, the cult leader, Mambu, epitomized the "new man" who drew on and hybridized a range of selfhoods and powers. Whether one wants to view these via culture-as-constituted (as Dalton seems to) or as cultural transformation, they are both sides of a combined process.

Jeannette Mageo and Bruce Knauft

In their introduction to this volume, Mageo and Knauft describe the "self" as a site where social political hegemonies and their resistance take place. Thus the "self" is always involved with power. In this chapter, I elucidate a similarly contextually active and engaged "self" among Rawa-speakers of northeast Papua New Guinea using local notions of human spirits and associated fantasy imageries.[1]

My purpose is threefold. First, I reflect upon two complementary enigmatic interstitial discourses involved in modern colonial history. One is the discourse of the leader of a fledgling "cargo cult" movement – the remnant of an earlier widespread movement – whom I call Meyango, and the other of the leader of a "raskol" gang incident whom I call Tapa. With these two examples, I aim to show how this Rawa "self" is contextually historically conditioned. Stephen (1989:228) has pointed out that Melanesian concepts of self cannot be understood outside of a religious context and without reference to emic ideas of spirits (cf. Wagner 1981). Yet Papua New Guinea idioms both about "selves" and about "spirits" are characterized by "innumerable idiosyncrasies and permutations . . . [and] random and inexplicable diversity" (Lawrence and Meggitt 1965:25). This is because Melanesian selves are flexible and fluid as well as contextually and historically engaged.

Second, I sketch a Rawa model of the "self" based on ideas involving gendered emotions which have important everyday behavioral correlates but also cast light on these interstitial discourses. As Strathern (1988) has shown, in Melanesian cultures human agency is predicated upon gender difference, which is both elicited through cultural imagery and evocative of this difference. "Power" is an effect and condition of gender difference. I intend to show that among Rawa-speakers, the embodied gendered "self" is processual and exists in a permanent liminal state. This state is one of "giving" and is ontologically between birth and death, and between different modes of behaving in relation to this transitional becoming. I argue that this Rawa "self" involves a kind of "normative schizophrenia" entailing a double bind that comes about as a result of having to repay ontological debts. This "self" reflects Rawa cultural tensions among gendered emotions, pollution ideas, and types of power and I relate these aspects to what are conceived of as two inimical yet mutually necessary spheres of activity or exchange: those encompassed within acts of sharing and those without.[2]

Last, enriched by a deeper understanding of models of power as a condition of gender difference, the chapter returns to the leader of a fledgling "cargo cult" and the leader of a raskol gang incident with whom it began. I find that the engagement of the Rawa "self" with Western colonial culture needs to be understood in terms of the dimensions of classic Rawa indigenous ideas and Bateson's idea of double binds, and further that the colonial global economic situation has stretched and skewed the gendered emotions of the Rawa "self." Thus the liminal Rawa "self" is simultaneously indigenous and colonially influenced: as Rawa-speakers delimit their own contexts and spheres of activity, they also engage in the modernist world. I find that in so doing, Rawa-speakers define a relation between sociocentric and egocentric orientations, but in entirely local terms of giving and expenditure.

Cargo and gangster talk

The two discourses I consider here as "interstitial" in that they both fell through the cracks of my fieldwork notes. Both discourses were entirely unsolicited and mystifyingly abstruse, so I was neither able to obtain verbatim texts nor had any basis at the time on which to pursue detailed personal histories or in-depth interviews which would help to make sense of them. My fieldwork techniques did not entail tape-recording outside of relatively formal interview contexts. In the case of the "cargo cult" leader, he sought me out secretly to inquire about the source of whitemen's power and to disclose his thinking on the matter. Both discourses were outside the bounds of prevailing public social discourse I encountered among Rawa-speaking villagers, and of the logical grammatical structures that I needed to make sense of and even coherently recollect these discourses. I found much of what he said so incomprehensible that, not having recorded it, I was unable to recollect with any detail or much accuracy most of what he said. So odd and unusual were his musings that I could not even imagine how to structure a formal interview to elicit a linguistically coherent text. The "raskol" leader's discourse was similar. His story was offered in a highly informal context as a source of amusement among a very few intimates and the narrative text of his discourse was so fantastic and unbelievable that I did not consider it worthy of further investigation.

Were I able to obtain a text of their actual speech, I might be able to subject them to more rigorous linguistic analysis, but I also believe that would miss the point. What was most characteristic of both discourses was precisely their odd quality – the fact that the lexical substitutions or narrative sequences necessary for the construction of coherent metaphors, metalinguistic cues, or storylines were missing. Grammatical, lexical, and textural analysis of discourses can only get one so far in understanding them. Indeed, as Silverstein has shown, one can hardly construct a sentence without referring to the context in which it is spoken (1976). The analysis of grammatical structure betrays a Western cognitive bias where what is most urgently needed to understand linguistic meaning is the analysis of cultural and historical context (Hymes 1962). I shall suggest, however, that one way to try to make sense of these discourses is to suppose that they are particular instances of grammatical and cultural structures being distorted in particular ways according to the strategies they employ in their historical colonial context.

I do not know Meyango, the cargo cult leader, very well. He is from a village some distance from the one in which I resided and came to visit me several times in my house, alone and furtively. I also had a few short discussions with him and his cohorts while visiting another village where he also happened to be visiting. He is evidently a politically ambitious man. He has subsequently become a leader in the local level government of his village, although he has not given up his "cargo cult" thinking. In a recent visit, Meyango came to find me and asked to interview me – to find out if I could "help" him – but was unable to get me alone and so abandoned the effort. As with the Seltaman and other Melanesians (see Whitehead, chapter 8), for Rawa-speakers power is obviously manifest in the world but the source of power is also external to the "self." It is generally assumed that someone somewhere knows more about it and one therefore strives to establish an intimate connection with it.

Among the most coherent things Meyango ever said to me was that he would like to take me to his house and have me stay there while he and his wife indulged me with every sort of hospitality to get me to give him whitemen's secrets. I therefore take him to have been attempting to establish an intimate relation with power through his visits to me. Hospitality is an entirely usual behavior for Rawa-speakers. It is also efficacious in that it establishes relations of giving and mutual interdependence. Rawa hospitality for whitemen is espe-cially extravagant because whitemen are so wealthy and Rawa-speakers wish to entice them to give, much as they elicit giving behavior in their own families. However, Meyango was unique in supposing that what he would entice me to give him was the "secret" that allows white people to have so many material objects. The fledgling cargo movement in which the man who came to question me was involved can be seen as an elaborate form of mimesis in which, among other things, Rawa-speakers emulated the happy, unfettered, rich lives of the "whiteman."

This man's discourse consisted of a vague incoherent random series of allusions, which I take to be mimetic contiguous connections with something he-knew-not-what. I can give only an indication of what his discourse was like:

White men have lots of things, lots of knowledge ["thought" or "cognizance," in Neo-Melanesian *save*; Rawa *ingodundu*], know how to take care of things, Papua New Guineans don't have lots of things, certain knowledge, know how to look after things, Papua New Guineans are different than whitemen, the same as whitemen, weren't given something, something got lost, he felt very close to having something, he had tried all sorts of things and failed.

The two explanatory comments he supplied, and which stuck in my Western mind, were that he was sure that whitemen were given a certain sort of knowledge by their mothers which allowed them to have lots of stuff, and that he had had intercourse with his wife while she was menstruating and so was unable to obtain the power he sought. The former comment indicates that the power whitemen have is one of domestic sharing (which for Rawa is a feminine gender proclivity, as I shall explain below), while the latter indicates that it entails the power which Rawa magicians competitively seek by obviating sharing (a male gender proclivity). The conjunction of the two in this discourse is striking. It suggests that the power whitemen supposedly have transcends the opposition Rawa-speakers feel between domestic sharing and external competition, or between the embodied gendered states of women and men.

Meyango's "self" would seem to be comprised of a loose orchestration of constituent voices with no necessary integrity, as in Lachicotte's analysis of the case of Roger (see chapter 3). However, Roger was institutionalized for an apparent "psychiatric illness" whereas Meyango is a rural Melanesian villager with aspirations for power. "Cargo cults" were made illegal by the Australian colonial government, and, were Meyango to express his beliefs more widely and openly, it is not unlikely that, as many "cargo cult" leaders before him, he might find himself in jail. In addition, one can easily suppose that had the Australians thought to bring a tradition of psychiatry to Papua New Guinea, someone like Meyango could just as easily find himself in a mental ward instead of in jail, leaving him, like Roger, to coordinate some sort of "self" identity among various diagnoses. Instead, as many "cargo cultists" do, he was working with the discourses of missionaries and colonists according to which Melanesians are in some way or other inferior to whitemen, which supposedly accounts for why whitemen have so much and Melanesians so little.

This colonial discourse was mixed with his own understandings of power and gender. While Rawa believe the source of power to be remote, power is elicited and realized through gender difference. Power itself is secret and un-knowable. Wagner (1986) shows a general characteristic of Melanesian cultures among the New Ireland Usen Barok when he elucidates their notion that knowl-edge is obtained only through physical enactment rather than verbal instruction because it centrally concerns unglossable power. Power can only be known as it is manifest through physical experience and in the enactment and the embodiment of it. Cultural images both stimulate and work to elicit physical enactments and bodily performances through which power is achieved. Strath-ern (1988) shows that this agency is predicated on gender difference. Through his behavior and discourse, Meyango was trying to imagine and connect to a kind of power foreign to Melanesian understandings – not thought of as re-mote but as present, and not predicated upon difference but on transcendence. In this way his imagination was very different from that of the raskol leader Tapa.

Tapa was a resident for a time of the village in which I resided, and I knew him fairly well. He was orphaned when he was young and raised by a leader from another village, but had left his step-father to claim land from relatives in the village where I lived. He participated in village activities but eschewed church social regulations when he took a second wife and in other ways flaunted village authority. He used to enjoy defeating prominent village men in card games, for which he cultivated magical power, marking him as an outsider, although he was also clearly a village member. He acted as someone who had not gotten the extremely intense nurturing experiences of most Rawa children because he sought power in ways that could be socially destructive. I believe that other "raskols" may have similar personal histories. They are always an orphan type. One does not generally hear about their illegal activities until they are killed, so it is impossible to know who they are beforehand. All one knows about them is that they are young men living in some town or with relatives other than their natal families. The only other raskol from the area that I had ever heard about was the son of a man who was very active in the supra-local church organization. I therefore suspect that like Tapa he didn't get the nurturing he needed from his father. The fact that he was living away from his father with relatives in town is telling.

When I first moved into the village Tapa was more open and forward than most, coming to my house, telling stories about himself, and wanting to know about everything I had. He struck me then as somewhat frenzied – a live-wire – which made him both witty, interesting, and fun as well as intelligent. Yet Tapa was not very contemplative, as one might like an important informant to be. When he visited he often wanted to take my possessions and use them in his own home. Other villagers warned me that he was someone who would "foul" my things. But their reaction was not to exclude him as Westerners might someone they deemed a "bad" or "evil" criminal element, but instead to provide him with greater nurturing, giving him even more food and things than they generally did others.

Tapa once told me a tale of breaking into a store and escaping with cargo through the jungle and over mountains on commandeered heavy construction equipment pursued by the raskol police. Though it did involve a coherent narrative sequence, his discourse was characterized by extreme hyperbole and delightful images of power, much like those of the cinematic Kung Fu heroes which Rawa-speakers, like other Papua New Guinea nationals, find fascinating. Exaggerated images of power so governed his discourse that the metaphoric or metalinguistic substitutions which might lend some conceptual or explanatory coherence to the narrative were missing. The story was not at all believable because of the highly exaggerated scenes of driving over mountain ranges at unrealistic speeds, outrunning police vehicles in the process. The storyline had an ending: what began with taking ended with profuse sharing as Tapa gave the goods to those he had enlisted in the deed.

So exaggerated were his hyperbolic evocations of power that at first I did not believe the tale, thinking it some strange fantasy taken directly from the cinema. However, some time later, a couple of his compatriots told me that he had indeed given them the things they had obtained in order to persuade me that he is not a bad character, as they supposed I might have judged him to be, perhaps fearing that I might report him. Now I suppose that his story must have been a very grandiose account of a relatively small incident.

I could not see in Tapa any genocidal capacity fostered by emotional numbness and the banal violence that inheres in passive conformity to state institutions. Rather, he was actively participating in violence and thus unmasking the violence that inheres in colonial apartheid systems. He is the one that bourgeois citizens typically fear. Nevertheless he is not so unlike the Western children who play with modern superhero dolls (Allison, chapter 4). In Tapa's mind he morphed from ordinary to superhuman; however, it would be impossible to see him as having at the same time assumed a phallic hegemonic ideal, for he had disrupted the bourgeois state rather than internalized it. But this was not mere fantasy: he had actually achieved power in a most direct and violent way.

Tapa was quite the opposite of Meyango. Meyango's discourse and behavior were governed by the fact that what he did not have was precisely power, which he imagined to reside secretively elsewhere in such a way that it could be given, as from whitemen's mothers. Tapa, on the other hand, went to the source of white people's material wealth in the most direct way possible and actually expropriated the wealth, albeit temporarily, that Meyango could only imagine. Tapa had something like a mini "cargo cult" in which the goods actually came and were freely shared, but soon were all gone and the illusory prosperity vanished. Tapa's and Meyango's discourses were also complementary in ways that parallel their strategies. Tapa's narrative had virtually no metaphorical or lexical substitutions, but was instead constituted almost entirely of singular, self-referential exaggeration, hyperbole, and power imagery. Meyango's discourse was characterized by virtually no coherent narrative but instead a series of random, unfettered metaphoric and lexical substitutions. And Tapa's discourse also lacked the loose orchestration of Western and Melanesian voices that characterized Meyango's.

The difference between these discourses can also be described in terms of two linguistic disorders that Jakobson (1971) thought were the product of the two logical mental capabilities necessary for language production. The first mental capacity is the ability to create contiguous elements in a logical grammatical sequence – the ability to freely combine words into larger contexts and syntactic relations. The second capacity is the ability to freely select and substitute words within those sequences. Jakobson identified two types of linguistic aphasia based on these two abilities, supposing that one may become impaired and cause patients to rely entirely on the other to express themselves. It is of course problematic to pathologize people, who might otherwise be considered religious leaders or petty thieves, as having types of mental disorder. This is what, after all, states do to de-legitimize opposition. However I accept that these two sorts of linguistic disorder are quite common and can be used to characterize many "normal" types of speech. I invoke Jakobson because he helps me to understand some of the peculiarities of these two men's discourses and relate them to their strategies of obtaining power.

Meyango's strategy was to create a direct contiguous relation with the source of power whitemen are supposed to have. Yet it is exactly the contiguous element that was missing from his discourse. Instead of a logical grammatical narrative his discourse consisted of a set of allusions or metaphoric substitutions for that relation he sought. The idiosyncrasy of his disquisition thus takes the form of what Jakobson called a "continuity disorder" – lacking narrative sequence to achieve the maximum expansion of metaphoric possibilities. Tapa, on the other hand, actually did create the contiguous relation that Meyango sought, and his discourse had a logical narrative, but was most characterized by a singular hyperbolic imagery of power achieved. What it lacked was a set of substitutions that would have provided some variety and add some suspense, triumph, tragedy, or other uneven up-and-down quality that would have helped to make better sense of the narrative sequence. It thus takes the form of a "substitution disorder" – lacking metaphors for the singularity of contiguously achieved power.

Tapa's strategy was more successful in getting the goods. The relative success or lack of success of these complementary strategies should indicate how Rawa-speakers experience the trajectory of modern world history. Perhaps the most salient factor distinguishing these strategies and discourses is the absence of women in Tapa's contiguous achievement of power and their presence among

Meyango's many metaphoric substitutions. Perhaps Tapa's power is in this way as phallic as the imaginary superhero after all; however, this power was not, in the end, hegemonic, for he managed to transform it into another kind of power altogether by using it to produce sharing and sociality in his own community. Since Melanesian power is achieved through gender difference, comprehending the complementary strategies of Meyango and Tapa and how they construct "selves" in the modern colonial contexts requires understanding Rawa notions of "self" and gender. For Rawa the "self" is pulled in opposite directions related to cosmic gendered forces and toward different sorts of social activities, which are inimical yet necessary to one another – activities whose relation can also be seen to have shifted historically.

Rawa human spirits

My analysis of the gendered, embodied Rawa self in terms of human spirits is facilitated by the fact that, like a great many animistic peoples and Papua New Guinea cultures,[3] Rawa-speakers distinguish two different types of human souls or spirits: the first I call the "breath spirit," and the second the "spirit double." (1) The Rawa *yuka*, "breath" spirit, gives life to a newborn infant when it draws its first breath and departs with a dying person's last gasp. It is spoken of as having "good" (*metemi*) productive and "bad" (*piyomi*) destructive potentials. It provides the energy for productive activity, but may also be either too powerful or too weak and ineffectual. Yuka may thereby be outwardly destructive toward or too reliant upon others. The yuka is related to Rawa ancestral beliefs according to which, at the death of a local leader who had been initiated, this spirit would "go ontop" to reside in the place of the dead. The initiation consisted of, among other things, having a bone nose piece passed through her or his pierced nasal septum. Without initiation the yuka might become one of a variety of terrestrial ghosts or spirits. (2) The spirit double, *kapokapoyi*, transliterates as "dream," "reflection," "shadow," and "picture," which includes noises and other signs made by the living and the dead alike. It may be thought of as the "image spirit" and as embodiments. Thus the skin is conceived of as a shadow or image aspect of the self. The *kapokapoyi* can be stolen and ruined, as well as pollute others through metonymic contagion.

Relating the breath spirit and the spirit double is an organic metabolic life process whereby the inward animating life force of the breath spirit generates the outward image of the spirit double, which in turn serves as its embodying container. Rawa-speakers often designate someone who has been enervated through old age, pollution, or sorcery, for example, as "skin nothing" – an outward image without an inner animating life force or breath spirit. These two forces produce life. If either is somehow stolen, goes missing, or is for some reason lacking, the result is illness and death. Any major imbalance between them causes the breath spirit to be dependent upon or destructive toward others. People produce many spirit doubles which are not easily distinguished. Indeed, the breath spirit exhausts itself in producing spirit doubles and is conceived of as a continual life-enervating process of producing them. This life-enervating process is also reflected in the Rawa ethic of giving and expenditure.

Against the grain of Western urban capitalist colonial culture, Rawa-speakers cultivate and define themselves in terms of sharing and giving to others. As with many other Melanesians,[4] it is thought that as one procreates, produces, feeds, and passes on one's life energies to others one grows old and dies – a process that effects a meaningful death. The attempt to take and keep for oneself, on the other hand, is considered tantamount to sorcery.[5] As in Mauss' (1967) "spirit of the gift," Rawa-speakers suppose that the gift compels its return. They may interpret inexplicably missing bridewealth money or unusual noises, for example, as "shadows" (*kapokapoyi*) of a bride's parents' "anger." Attempts to magically invoke empathetic sorrow are aimed at "pulling" money from others. Magical acts and emotions compel gifts, continual giving, and thus also returns. It is important to emphasize, however, that what is primarily required here is continual giving rather than returns. While return implies the priority of human relationship, it also entails the construction of closed systems of human relationship. Continuous giving, by contrast, is a persistent process of expenditure. Inasmuch as giving draws upon external sources of energy, it is open to history and disallows the metaphysical construction of closed ahistorical cultural systems.[6]

Rawa-speakers see productive life force as animating a person's corporeal embodiments. This force appears when the traditional Rawa sorcerer exposes his internal energy, denuded of its outward-containing embodiment – removing his spirit double through the use of "hot" allergenic vines and leaves while fasting in a completely darkened room. He becomes temporarily a terrifying glowing fire which can destroy the spirit doubles of others. The breath spirit is in all appearances much like the sun; it is the major emanation of the creator spirit – origin and source of life-productive energies in the earthly realm of embodied existence. Other Rawa ghosts who have died by violent means seem to consist of these hot breath spirits, roaming the jungle at night in the form of horrifying hot and destructive fires, like that of Coleman lanterns. Both the embodiment-denuded sorcerer and the lantern-like ghosts are male, for the proclivity to be "hot" and all that it entails is a masculine trait in the thinking of Rawa-speakers.

Gender, power, and self

The Rawa "breath" and "shadow" spirits are also gendered, particularly as reflected in the pollution beliefs and concerns which underlie and motivate many ongoing everyday considerations and behaviors. Unlike most Papua New Guinea cultures,[7] Rawa-speakers suppose that men can pollute women as well as women pollute men. Men might pollute women whenever they achieve ritually powerful states or endeavor to practice magic, classically after initiation into adulthood. After initiation, young men present themselves in their bright shining splendor, often using love magic in the form of a fleck of red paint on the temple or neck. Initiates affect women simply by being seen, and pollute women especially by allowing their breath, typically in the form of cigarette smoke, to pass over their victims. They may also give intended victims cigarettes or food that will cause these women to experience dysmenorrhea and menorrhagia.

Menstruation is normally seen as a debilitating excess loss of blood as a result of "the moon viewing women" (neo-Melanesian *mun lukim meri* or Rawa *kombo pareyi kenote*). The moon is another emanation of the creator spirit – archetypally the sun. A ritually empowered man presented before a woman is like her being viewed by the moon or sun. Women may pollute men by preparing or allowing their shadow (*kapokapoyi*) to pass over men's food while menstruating, causing men to experience shortness of breath, symptoms of emphysema, and respiratory infections (neo-Melanesian *sotwin* or *kus*).

In these gender-pollution scenarios, women's excess production causes the enervation of men's creative energy, while men's overabundance of uncontainable energy overpowers and compromises women's containing productive embodiments. The breath spirit is the life energy of the sun and is the source of productivity. It may be destructive if not corporeally contained and is associated with male efficacy. Feminine efficacy, on the other hand, is associated with the spirit double – the outward embodiment of productivity. In Rawa gender aesthetics, women are supposed to consume much and be fat and procreative, while powerful men supposedly consume little and are thin, with the capacity to fight and destroy external threats.

Rawa-speakers say that the productive procreative blood of men (semen) is "hot" (*kokingo*) while that of women is "cold" (*kingo,* or *kio,* "nothing"). Because of this, men are prone to aggressive anger while women are given to empathetic sorrow. Yet men and women have both these emotional proclivities to different degrees. The ideal man is supposed to be easy-going, but also quick to anger when provoked and to act aggressively when needed. Men's anger must be tempered with sorrow to not be destructive; otherwise they act as sorcerers. Women are supposed to be compassionate, nurturing, and sympathetic, but these capacities must be bolstered by assertiveness. Women chide men for wanton destructive aggression and useless competition in card games and physically attack men who take their wives' money to gamble.

These gendered emotional proclivities are not, however, dialectically balanced. Compassionate sorrow is thought of as both mood and motivation, cause and effect, of giving among kin and is, therefore, given priority. Giving and dependency is the primal state of human relations in the family, and able to encompass anger. The unmarked feminine category "cold" (*kingo*) encompasses the marked masculine "hot" (*kokingo*). Sorrow is both inspired by and the impetus for productive albeit enervating expenditures of life energy in the domestic household, and Rawa-speakers claim it to be central to their distinctive identity in counterdistinction to the modern urban capitalist world. If Ortner (1990) is correct in asserting that females tend to be associated with the encompassed context where genders are coded in this way, Rawa-speakers are an obvious exception to this observation. I suspect, however, that the Rawa case can be generalized to much of Melanesia, because Melanesians generally find the existential gravity of giving in their home villages inescapable no matter where they live, and feel it necessary to bury loved ones who die elsewhere in their natal territory.

Anger and aggressiveness, on the other hand, are provoked externally by the failure to give or by limits on giving: where giving fails to be answered by return and resources are at stake, anger and aggressiveness are and should be the result. Otherwise, one becomes the victim of external competition for resources. Anger and aggressiveness are perceived to be appropriate to the urban capitalist world. Thus different emotional states are directly related to, if not actually the defining criteria of, different spheres of human activity and of economic exchange: external to, versus internal among, kin – that is among those who share blood, substance, and resources (Dalton 1996a, 1999).

These Rawa exchange spheres might seem to parallel the separation of work and home under capitalism in which the feminine came to be seen as the heart of a heartless world and women were assigned the unremunerated social labor of nurturing and giving (Lutz, chapter 9). While there may be a historical relation between capitalist expansion and the development of Rawa exchange spheres, like other Melanesians, Rawa-speakers do not distinguish between public and private realm (Strathern 1980, 1981). Rather than being seen as a refuge, the Rawa domestic household is understood as a process of giving that constitutes the very condition of existence in which both genders necessarily participate. Yet Rawa also find it necessary to forgo these expenditures to obtain power in the external world.

Each of these gendered proclivities can be said to entail a different mode of magical efficacy and power. Empathetic sorrow involves the power to obtain expenditures within family, household, kin, and clan. It is a moral imperative and is seen as the effect and cause of the nurturing and giving that takes place in the household. Yet Rawa-speakers also employ their most culturally significant and prominent magical forms to produce sorrow so as to obtain gifts, alliances, and favors from others. This sorrow-creating behavior, not biological ties, defines Rawa kinship. The Rawa marriage system as well as Rawa identity in opposition to the "whiteman" are predicated upon a magical efficacy that produces compassionate sorrow and, therefore, giving from others. It involves a productive form of loss – productive of children and social bonding. Aggressive anger, on the other hand, involves the power to obtain and keep resources which are contested or threatened through force and violence. It deals with the accursed share of expenditures without return – with absolute rather than productive loss.

While women and men both attempt to elicit empathetic sorrow in others, they do not endeavor to become sorrowful themselves. As with love magic among the Trobrianders (Weiner 1988), the Rawa elicitation of sorrow in others is a means whereby the autonomy of others is breached and control is thereby gained over them. When women and men attempt to practice magic, rather than make themselves "cold" they endeavor to make themselves "hot" and efficacious in a masculine manner. Men forgo eating "cold" foods and intercourse, while women do the same and also employ herbs and magic to stop menstruation. Men also bleed their penises during initiation and some at specific times during the rest of their lives to shed the "cold" red blood of their mothers and wives.

In endeavoring to make others "cold" (compassionate), one attempts to incorporate outsiders within the sphere of giving and kin and, one might say, to make them into what is, in the "New Melanesian Ethnography,"[8] called "dividual" or "partible" persons – defined through their relations with others. Endeavoring to make oneself "hot" and powerful outside of this sphere by obviating domestic life expenditure, on the other hand, is akin to the construction of an ego. I suppose, as does Mageo (1996), that there is a continuum between egocentric and sociocentric societies and orientations. In other words, societies foster the relative construction of more individually oriented autonomous egos or of more socially oriented partible persons along a continuum. People in egocentric societies nevertheless define themselves in terms of their position in a social group or in terms of their perception by others of their kin or peer groups. People in sociocentric societies nevertheless have a sense of themselves as distinct from others. In Papua New Guinea this is clearly the case because, despite being sociocentric societies inhabited by people who are defined primarily by their relations, people in these societies endeavor to make individual names for themselves. They attempt to outperform one another and to gain power by innovating upon established cultural symbolic orders.[9] The interplay between these qualities of power-laden "hot" and "cold" emotional temperatures mirrors the entanglements between the constructed and "unconstructed," integrated and fragmented selves that Obeyesekere elucidates in his comments in this volume. But here I wish, not to point out how individual selves may be undone through different power constellations, including especially modern nation-states which seem to me to valorize the individual versus the state, but rather, to show how normally partible persons are constructed as Cartesian-like integrated egos through the attempted achievement of "hot" masculine power in the external world. Yet these attempts always to some degree fail and so punctuate the otherwise contextually disjointed Rawa person. This makes "hot" masculine power, the Cartesian ego, and the Western obsession with it all illusions of power, whether archetypally morphed in the form of phallic cyborg-heroes or precariously constructed by institutionalized individuals under state-approved professional guidance and care. The partibility of the Rawa person makes that person normatively divided and incoherent and is therefore an example of the idea that self-fashioning may entail a conflict or a stitching together of disparate heterological aspects.

I also suggest, as does Knauft (1989), that the tendency to act in more a sociocentric or egocentric manner, as well as the tendency to innovate upon conventional symbolic constructs rather than identify with and conform to them (Wagner 1981), varies directly with levels of political organization. When levels of political integration are lower, local leaders act in a more sociocentric manner, and individuals tend to innovate upon rather than conform to symbolic orders. Rawa culture, furthermore, delimits one context in which people operate more as group members and another context in which they operate individualistically. As discussed above, Rawa-speakers distinguish between two spheres of human activity and economic exchange: within kin and community (as defined by sharing substance and resources), and external to this group. The first of these is more sociocentric and the second is more egocentric.

The mortal expenditure of life energy through procreation and productive giving in the domestic sphere is inevitable and largely unavoidable. The attempt to make oneself powerful in the external world by avoiding or halting personal expenditure, no matter how temporary, is equally necessary and irreducible. However, it is also willed and practiced consciously as a magical technique for this type of empowerment. This power is always and only justified as necessary to maintain and protect the economy of giving and expenditure among kin. In this way, the psychic economy of egocentric and sociocentric orientations is intimately intertwined. Egocentrism among the Rawa is the impossible but necessary attempt to halt temporarily the expenditure of energy that otherwise takes place through productive sharing in the domestic household; it is the impossible attempt to halt giving and the expenditure of life energy – the otherwise normal and inevitable productive life processes of sharing and giving to kin.

Rawa self and social history

The compulsion to empower people to compete outside the sphere of giving, moreover, is historically situated. In previous generations, each Rawa hamlet kept a practicing sorcerer to deal with enemies during times of vicious internecine warfare. However, it is not clear that this indigenous practice antedates the colonization of New Guinea: the fighting that is known to have taken

place during the time of the ancestors was the result of territorial disputes stem-
ming from the displacement of populations from the north coast by German
colonial expeditions. After pacification, traditional Rawa sorcerers were done
away with, but leaders of the large nucleated villages formed after pacification
are purported to have sorcery magic that they purchased from elsewhere. Now
as then, however, lineage groups commonly raise a young man to be a physically
powerful and fierce warrior to intimidate and fight external adversaries. Today
these adversaries include Western society: one such young man in the village
where I worked so hated "whitemen," for example, that when a headman gave
me permission to live in his village, he also sent this man to live at the mission
station a long way from the village.

Rawa-speakers tell of the institution, in a mythical time, of the bridewealth
exchange whereby "lines" or lineages were established by being separated
from each other and thereby set in competition with one another. Populations
displaced from the Rai Coast by German colonial punitive expeditions then
appeared over the mountains and set off a brutal series of internecine struggles
over territory. With Australian colonial rule and state-building came pacification and the demise of traditional Rawa sorcerers, but also an exploitative
competitive capitalist market economy and political system. Independence and
development have left Rawa-speakers competing for monetary resources in a
national arena and among themselves in trade store and other business ven-
tures. Local competition takes place in ceremonial pig and beer markets, and
in extensive and passionate card-game gambling. A common complaint these
days among Rawa-speakers concerns men who obtain employment in urban
centers and lose touch with their relatives in the village. Prehistorically up to
the present one may trace a historical increase in competition and fighting for
resources that correlates to colonial intrusion. This increase has exacerbated
the paradox whereby losses and expenditures that are retained by kin and clan
are predicated upon external loss and irretrievable expenditure. It has made the
Rawa sphere of domestic giving and sharing ever more dependent upon the
sphere of anger and aggression. This paradox is deeply felt. Although the spirit
double side of the Rawa psyche is fundamentally motivated to merge with kin
and clan in the economy of the domestic group, this proclivity is increasingly
undercut by an egocentric economy, motivated to forgo this expenditure and
empower people in an external world.

Wagner (1981) offers a model of the tribal Papua New Guinea self based
on an *irresolvable* paradox reminiscent of existential and phenomenological
anti-psychiatric writers (Laing 1959, 1972; Lacan 1980; Deleuze and Guattari
1983). This self is experienced as the innate resistance to the normal behavioral
mode of continual improvisation and achievements of power in relation to the
conventional symbolic system. The patterning of relations in terms of gifts and
debts likewise poses paradoxes placing people in a position of having, but being

unable to pay off, their "ontological debts."[10] Whenever a bridewealth payment or ceremonial exchange transpires, there is always a surplus of unsubstantiated social debts and relations that remain after all the wealth has been given away, leading many Melanesians to speculate on so-called "cargo cults."

Rawa-speakers live within a related paradox involving the necessary expenditure of life energies that are kept within the domestic group and the equal necessity of obtaining and engaging in expenditures that are not retained. This is the way that Rawa-speakers articulate the dilemma facing a person in any gift economy in which one has the obligations to both give and to receive. Giving is the source of honor, status, and value, but dependency and interdependence are nevertheless fostered.[11] That puts the Rawa moral person seeking honor and status in a position of having to innovate upon convention to try to achieve power by forestalling the expenditure of life energy, but nonetheless to expend the energy thus obtained on behalf of kin, community, and others. Rawa-speakers organize this paradox in terms of the relation between an internal sphere of "sharing" and an external one of "buying" or "exchanging." External "exchange," however, has been historically inflated.

In its colonially amplified form, this contradiction between giving and taking can be thought of as creating a double bind (Bateson 1972).[12] In this context, the "double bind" consists of being forcefully held strictly accountable for being or doing something one cannot or is not allowed to be or do. Bateson tied this bind to the inability to employ metalanguage, which Laing (1972) viewed as the type of hypnosis normally operating in families and societies. My argument here is that the double bind in which Rawa-speakers are placed is both indigenous and exogenous: in their own culture, Rawa-speakers are put in the position of having to pay back their "ontological debts" or of substantiating all their relations with gifts – an impossible task because there is always a surplus of relations left over after a person's goods have been expended. There are never enough goods to substantiate all one's relations. This requires Rawa-speakers to attempt to obtain more goods in the external competitive arena, which obviates the domestic giving it also serves. In addition, the colonial state puts Rawa-speakers in the position of having to become like "whitemen" (which would potentially allow enough wealth to substantiate all one's relations and pay off one's ontological debts) without really allowing them to do so. In colonial Papua New Guinea, Rawa-speakers were told that they were not civilized enough to share what whitemen have but that they must nevertheless endeavor to obtain it, and that they could not rebel without having what little power they had forcibly taken away from them.

Rawa villagers told me that missionaries and government agents had persuaded them that if they believed in the Christian God, participated in economic and social development, and worked hard, they would "live materially the same as whitemen." Western emissaries also told them that the backward beliefs and customs of their ancestors accounted for their lack of material wealth. Yet a great many government and missionary figures also encouraged them not to entirely abdicate their "traditional customs." Development schemes were then predicated on the supposition that rural villagers are no longer "primitive" but not yet Westernized, and Rawa-speakers were therefore put to work supplying raw materials to the global capitalist economy through smallholder coffee cash-cropping. The laborious production of dried coffee has only impoverished them, yielding an average village household income of less than 200 kina (dollars) per year. Local business enterprises built on this level of income only pit villagers against each other to, they say, "pull money from others." Villagers complained to me that they are not paid fairly for their coffee: what little is given back to them for the work they do does not allow them to better their lives. When villagers endeavor to circumvent this supposed path to economic development through card-game gambling, local stealing from trade stores, urban raskol activities, and occasional cargo cults, they do so with the full knowledge that these activities are illegal and that they may be and sometimes are prosecuted for them, if not worse.

   In my view, this colonial double bind dovetails with and exacerbates the indigenous Rawa double bind. Local Rawa culture and external colonial process must be thought through together, without imagining Rawa culture as pure – that is as an isolated, functionally integrated, self-regulating whole operating outside of world history. Rawa culture is neither steam-rollered over by nor valiantly resisting an external historically changing world capitalist system.

Conclusions: Rawa selves and discourses of modernity

To Rawa-speakers, Western bourgeois people seem to have a quality that enables them to have much without the conflict Rawa-speakers feel between domestic giving and external competition. They presume that blessed by god and the rational ability bestowed upon them to control nature whitemen can have much without taking from others. The Rawa persona is an enervating process of giving and expenditure – as the breath spirit produces spirit doubles. The increasing historical need for an egocentric empowerment in the external world, however, obviates this process and produces greater psychic conflict. This colonial double bind exacerbates the discord between domestic giving and external competition. Higher levels of political integration in the state and competitive world economic system mean less flexible, more authoritative conventional symbolic orders, and greater difficulty for individuals to innovate power in the external world. It also makes it more necessary than ever for them to arrest the expenditure and act in a modern egocentric fashion.

   Among the Rawa the double bind is not a pattern of interaction among individuals in a family situation, as Bateson conceived it; rather, it is culturally patterned and institutionalized. Institutionalized double binds result in a state of mind I call "normative schizophrenia." I define normative schizophrenia as a pattern of behavior which results from a consciousness that is governed by conflicting emotions produced by an institutionalized double bind. I further argue that normative schizophrenia results in certain discourse disorders that can shed light on cargo cults and raskol gangs in contemporary New Guinea.

Because Bateson's double binds entail an inability to use metalanguage, it can be related to the type of linguistic aphasia discussed earlier, which Jakobson (1971) identified as "substitution disorder." Remember that this disorder entails the inability freely to select and substitute words within contiguous elements in a logical grammatical sequence. Jakobson says that these sorts of substitutions are necessary to employ metaphor and metalanguage. According to Bateson, the use of metalanguage is necessary to confront and expose the logic of double binds and by extension the illusions that power employs. It is just these metalinguistic and metaphorical allusions that filled the cargo cult leader Meyango's discourse and that were absent from the raskol incident leader Tapa's. This, I have argued, is because Tapa had actually achieved, albeit temporarily, a contiguous relation with power, whereas Meyango was only able to construct allusions to power.

It would appear that Tapa had done a better job of directly confronting power, and of stripping its illusions, than had Meyango. However, it can also be supposed that because Tapa's power was so fleeting, and because his discourse emphasized having and giving rather than taking, it actually fell prey, for a time, to the illusion of power actually obtained, as could be seen in his hyperbolic exaggerations. By obtaining power through mere force, Tapa actually failed to uncover and understand how it is actually maintained through cultural illusions. Meyango, on the other hand, was managing a confrontation with power in his discourse and clearly understood that whitemen's power is predicated on a secret or trick. His confrontation with power took the form of trying to get the whiteman to share his secret – to get him to give. Given that whitemen suppose that they have unlimited wealth because of the rational capacity bestowed upon them by their creator rather than colonial exploitation, his demand that the whiteman share this unlimited power was a direct assault on this Western illusion. Logically, if whitemen actually do have the technological or spiritual secret of wealth, there would be no reason for them not to share or give it to those who they actually instead exploit.

While Tapa's short-lived illusion of having power was more successful in getting the goods, Meyango's unsuccessful strategy appreciated power as an elicited effect. Tapa's discourse was therefore characterized by exaggeration whereas Meyango's was characterized by a lack of contiguity. Unlike the victims of double binds, the purveyors of double binds have to construct ideologies which also avoid the logic of the double bind. This leads them into a type of "contiguity disorder" that Freud called "tea kettle logic." This is a logic whereby a series of logically inconsistent explanations are offered, all of which aim toward the same empirically and logically false conclusion. "The tea kettle is not broken." "It was already broken when you gave it to me." "You broke it after you got it back." "You never loaned me a tea kettle," and so forth. I believe that Western discourse about the underdevelopment of the Other is characterized by just this sort of contiguity disorder.[13] Meyango's discourse was also characterized by such random substitutions and he thus acted more like the purveyor of a double bind – trying to get the whiteman to give – while Tapa was more the victim of whitemen's double bind, which he expressed in a burst of violent activity.

I do not know if Tapa practiced magic before undertaking raskol activities, as he had previously to prepare for card gambling, for example. But he clearly forestalled the expenditure of life energies long enough to take with impunity from others rather than give. Yet this episode ended quickly with giving and sharing. Meyango's complaint, on the other hand, was that he could not practice magic and forgo giving because of his attachment to his wife, yet he saw mothers as the origin of the power he sought. The fundamental way that Rawa-speakers obtain power is, paradoxically, through giving, and this remains not only the moral center of their world, but their understanding of the basic condition of human existence. Stealing or taking is only a transitory and unrealistic means of obtaining power, although often a more effective way of getting goods in the modern world, as many rich colonialists and Tapa well know.

Rawa "self," consisting in breath spirits and spirit doubles, is not only processual and historical but also paradoxical. It is predicated particularly on the notion that the person is a process of life-expenditure, existentially caught between birth and death. This "self" entails means of obtaining magical power through the temporary cessation of life-energy expenditure, which has gendered emotional attributes involving methods of controlling others and pollution dangers. This attempt to gain power is egocentric, resembling selfhood schemata in Western egocentric societies, but the Rawa "self" is fundamentally sociocentric, consisting of "partible" people defined by relations of giving.

The Rawa "self" is a cultural actor of both assertion and dependency – of having to both give and take in a culture in which honor and status are gained through giving, and of never being able to pay back or materially substantiate all of the debts incurred through life. Rawa-speakers articulate this conundrum in terms of a contrast between inside domestic society, which is defined through acts of sharing, and the external exchange that takes place outside of this realm. Within the sphere of sharing, expenditures of life energy are made and required on behalf of progeny and kin who obtain and keep them, which thereby have meaning within that realm. Beyond the sphere of sharing, however, expenditures of life energy cannot be said to have the same or perhaps any meaning, for they represent losses that are not retained by kin. They thus entail the absolute loss of meaning. This loss is the subject of the peculiar modernist discourses of cargo cults and of raskol gang-leaders who live by a cargo cult logic. This discourse's syntax is the product of the impossible double binds in which the Rawa are placed by the a colonial global apartheid system.

Historically, the realm outside of family and kin has expanded in importance: Rawa-speakers increasingly depend upon outside markets for their transactions and are ever increasingly engaged in the national economy and global capitalist system. The Rawa invention of "self" entails the difference between giving and expenditures that have meaning, on the one hand and, on the other, those that enjoin the increasing absolute loss of meaning in the modern world. The Rawa self is all about power – gained primarily and paradoxically through giving and enervating expenditures of life energy. Yet, increasingly, power entails meaningless expenditure without return in the modern capitalist world system.

NOTES

Acknowledgements. I would like to thank Jeannette Marie Mageo for her great editorial care, for her support in the completion of this article, and for her intellectual encouragement, engagement, and sensitivity.

1. The terms "person" and "self" have been used inconsistently in the literature. In this chapter I follow Mageo's usage (1996, 1998), which is: "self," an encompassing word for the range of phenomenological experiences used to construct identity cross-culturally, as well as an encompassing word for these constructions; "persona," the sociocentric self; "ego," the egocentric self.
2. I have elaborated this elsewhere (Dalton 1996a, 1999).
3. This pattern was noted long ago by Tylor (1899) and Frazier (1922). While many Papua New Guinea cultures distinguish these same spirits others do not, sometimes subsuming both ideas in one belief, or do so in a manner which highlights their relation. A quick comparison of a few of the sources employed in this chapter shows that, among Papua New Guinea cultures, many apparently combine the ideas of the "breath" spirit and "shadow" spirit in the same term: Huli (Glasse 1965:30); Sambia (Herdt 1989:106; Salisbury 1965:56); east coast South Pentecost (Lane 1965:255, 279 fn.3) while others make the same, Ngaing (Lawrence 1965:207); west coast South Pentecost (Lane 1965:255, 279 fn.3) or apparently similar distinctions, Kwoma (Williamson 1983:15–16); Lusi (Counts and Counts 1983:53); Mae (Meggitt 1965:110), while yet others seem to recognize only or primarily either the "shadow," Lakalai (Valentine 1965:166–167); Mekeo (Stephen 1989:227); Kunimaipa (McArthur 1971:177) or "breath" spirits, Daribi (Wagner 1977:146); Telefolmin (Jorgensen 1980:360–362).
4. Counts and Counts (1983:51) make this point clearly and cite other examples in the literature.
5. Burridge (1969) finds a similar parallel between Tangu perceptions of white people and of local sorcerers.

6. This point about the notion of "expenditure" is argued cogently by Bataille (1985, 1991a, 1991b) and Derrida (1978).
7. But see Faithorn (1975) and Counts and Counts (1983:50) for examples of Melanesian cultures where men pollute women.
8. The term "New Melanesian Ethnography" is coined by Josephides (1991) and employed critically by Foster (1995) to indicate currently theoretical trends in Melanesian anthropology, including the social persona, but these ideas have their ancestors in Leenhardt (1979) and, before him, Mauss (1985).
9. Examples and discussions of individual innovation as basic modes of behavior in Melanesian societies include Read (1955), Stewart and Strathern (1988), Strathern (1979), and Wagner (1981).
10. This succinct and illuminating expression in relation to Melanesian cultures is taken from Errington and Gewertz (1987).
11. Dependency versus interdependence is the central paradox of Kaluli cultural performance (Schieffelin 1976).
12. Bateson's formulation is nearly identical to Laing (1972). Lyotard (1988) applies the double bind to structures of colonial experience.
13. Taken collectively, Western theorists have wrongly explained so-called "cargo cults" in terms of just these sorts of logically inconsistent explanations (Dalton 1996b).

REFERENCES

Bataille, Georges. 1985. The Notion of Expenditure (Allan Stoekl, trans.). In *Visions of Excess, Selected Writings* (Allan Stoekl (ed.), pp. 116–129, Minneapolis: University of Minnesota Press.
    1991a. *The Accursed Share*, Vol. 1 (Robert Hurley, trans.). New York: Zone Books.
    1991b. *The Accursed Share*, Vols. 2–3. (Robert Hurley, trans.). New York: Zone Books.
Bateson, Gregory. 1972. *Steps to an Ecology of Mind: Collected Essays in Anthropology, Psychiatry, Evolution, and Epistemology*. Northvale: Jason Aronson Inc.
Burridge, Kenelm. 1969. *Tangu Traditions: a Study of the Way of Life, Mythology, and Developing Experience of a New Guinea People*. Oxford: Clarendon Press.
Counts, Dorothy Ayers and David R. 1983. Father's Water Equals Mother's Milk: The Conception of Parentage in Kaliai, West New Britain. *Mankind* 14(1): 46–56.
Dalton, Douglas. 1996a. Cargo, Cards, and Excess: The Articulation of Economies in Papua New Guinea. *Research in Economic Anthropology* 17:83–147.
    1996b. "Cargo Cults" and Discursive Madness. American Anthropological Association Annual Meeting. San Francisco.
    1999. Meaning, Contingency, and Colonialism: Reflections on a Papua New Guinea Shell Gift. In *Money and Modernity: State and Local Currencies in Melanesia* (David Akin and Joel Robbins, eds.). Pittsburgh: University of Pittsburgh Press.
Deleuze, Gilles and Félix Guattari. 1983. *Anti-Oedipus: Capitalism and Schizophrenia* (Robert Hurley, Mark Seem, and Helen R. Lane, trans.). Minneapolis: University of Minnesota Press.
Derrida, Jacques. 1978. From Restricted to General Economy: A Hegelianism Without Reserve. In *Writing and Difference* (Alan Bass, trans.), pp. 251–277. Chicago: University of Chicago Press.
    1992. *Given Time I: Counterfeit Money* (Peggy Kamuf, trans.). Chicago: University of Chicago Press.

1995. Archive Fever: A Freudian Impression. *Diacritics* 25(2):9–63.

Errington, Frederick and Deborah Gewertz. 1987. *Cultural Alternatives and a Feminist Anthropology: An Analysis of Culturally Constructed Gender Interests.* Cambridge: Cambridge University Press.

Faithorn, Elizabeth. 1975. The Concept of Pollution among the Kafe of the Papua New Guinea Highlands. In R. Reiter, ed., *Toward an Anthropology of Women* (R. Reiter, ed.), pp. 127–140. New York: Monthly Review Press.

Fanon, Frantz. 1967. *Black Skin. White Mask* (Charles L. Markmann, trans.). New York: Grove Press.

Foster, Robert J. 1995. *Social Production and History in Melanesia.* Cambridge: Cambridge University Press.

Frazier, Sir James George. 1922. *The Golden Bough.* New York: MacMillan Publishing Co., Inc.

Glasse, Robert M. 1965. The Huli of the Southern Highlands. In *Gods, Ghosts, and Men in Melanesia: Some Religions of Australian New Guinea and the New Hebrides* (Peter Lawrence and Mervyn Meggitt, eds.), pp. 27–49. Melbourne: Oxford University Press.

Herdt, Gilbert. 1989. Spirit Familiars in the Religious Imagination of Sambia Shamans. In *The Religious Imagination in New Guinea* (Michele Stephen and Gilbert Herdt, eds.), pp. 99–121. New Brunswick: Rutgers University Press.

Hymes, Dell. 1962. The Ethnography of Speaking. In *Anthropology and Human Behavior* (Thomas Gladwin and William C. Sturtevant, eds.) pp. 13–53. Washington, DC: Anthropological Society of Washington.

Jakobson, Roman. 1971. *Selected Writings II: Word and Language.* The Hague: Mouton.

Jorgensen, Dan. 1980. What's in a Name: The Meaning of Meaninglessness in Telefolmin. *Ethos* 8(4):349–366.

Josephides, Lisette. 1991. Metaphors, Metonyms, and the Construction of Sociality. *Man* NS 26:146–161.

Knauft, Bruce. 1989. Imagery, Pronouncement, and the Aesthetics of Reception in Gebusi Spirit Mediumship. In *The Religious Imagination in New Guinea* (Michele Stephen and Gilbert Herdt, eds.), pp. 67–98. New Brunswick: Rutgers University Press.

Lacan, Jacques. 1980. *Écrits: A Selection* (Alan Sheridan, trans.). London: Tavistock Publications.

Laing, Ronald D. 1959. *The Divided Self: An Existential Study in Sanity and Madness.* New York: Penguin Books.

1972. *The Politics of the Family and Other Essays.* New York: Random House.

Lane, R. B. 1965. The Melanesians of South Pentecost, New Hebrides. In *Gods, Ghosts, and Men in Melanesia: Some Religions of Australian New Guinea and the New Hebrides* (Peter Lawrence and Mervyn Meggitt, eds.) pp. 250–279. Melbourne: Oxford University Press.

Lawrence, Peter. 1965. The Ngaing of the Rai Coast. In *Gods, Ghosts, and Men in Melanesia: Some Religions of Australian New Guinea and the New Hebrides* (Peter Lawrence and Mervyn Meggitt, eds.), pp. 198–3–223. Melbourne: Oxford University Press.

Lawrence, Peter and Mervyn J. Meggitt. 1965. Introduction. In *Gods, Ghosts, and Men in Melanesia: Some Religions of Australian New Guinea and the New Hebrides* (Peter Lawrence and Mervyn J. Meggitt, eds.), pp. 1–26. Melbourne: Oxford University Press.

Leenhardt, Maurice. 1979. *Do Kamo: Person and Myth in the Melanesian World* (Basia Miller Guilati, trans.). Chicago: The University of Chicago Press.

Lyotard, Jean-François. 1988. *The Differend: Phrases in Dispute* (Georges van den Abbele, trans.). Minneapolis: University of Minnesota Press.

McArthur, Margaret. 1971. Men and Spirits in the Kunimaipa Valley. In *Anthropology in Oceania: Essays Presented to Ian Hogbin* (L. R. Hiatt and C. Jayawardena, eds.), pp. 155–189. Sydney: Angus and Robertson.

Mageo, Jeannette. 1996. The Reconfiguring Self. *American Anthropologist* 97(2): 282–296.

1998. *Theorizing Self in Samoa.* Ann Arbor: University of Michigan Press.

n.d. Continuums of Self: Beyond Binary Cultural Relativism. Unpublished MS.

Mauss, Marcel. 1925/1990. *The Gift: The Form and Reason for Exchange in Archaic Society.* London: Routledge.

1967. *The Gift: Forms and Functions of Exchange in Archaic Societies* (Ian Cunnison, trans.). New York: W. W. Norton.

1985. A Category of the Human Mind: The Notion of Person; the Notion of Self. In *The Category of the Person: Anthropology, Philosophy, History* (Michael Carrithers, Steven Collins, and Steven Lukes, eds.), pp. 1–25. Cambridge: Cambridge University Press.

Meggitt, Mervyn J. 1965. The Mae Enga of the Western Highlands. In *Gods, Ghosts, and Men in Melanesia: Some Religions of Australian New Guinea and the New Hebrides* (Peter Lawrence and Mervyn Meggitt, eds.), pp. 105–131. Melbourne: Oxford University Press.

Ortner, Sherry B. 1989–1990. Gender Hegemonies. *Cultural Critique*, Winter:35–80.

Read, Kenneth E. 1955. Morality and the Concept of the Person Among the Gahuku-Gama. *Oceania* 25:231–282.

Salisbury, Richard F. 1965. The Siane of the Eastern Highlands. In *Gods, Ghosts, and Men in Melanesia: Some Religions of Australian New Guinea and the New Hebrides* (Peter Lawrence and Mervyn Meggitt, eds.), pp. 50–77. Melbourne: Oxford University Press.

Schieffelin, Edward L. 1976. *The Sorrow of the Lonely and the Burning of the Dancers.* New York: St. Martin's Press.

Silverstein, Michael. 1976. Shifters, Linguistic Categories, and Cultural Description. In *Meaning in Anthropology* (Keith Basso and Henry A. Selby, eds.), pp. 11–55. Albuquerque: University of New Mexico Press.

Stephen, Michele. 1989. Constructing Sacred Worlds and Autonomous Imagining in New Guinea. In *The Religious Imagination in New Guinea* (Michele Stephen and Gilbert Herdt, eds.), pp. 211–236. New Brunswick, NJ: Rutgers University Press.

Stewart, Pamela J. and Andrew Strathern. 1988. Seeking Personhood: Anthropological Accounts and Local Concepts in Mount Hagen, Papua New Guinea. *Oceania* 68:170–188.

Strathern, Marilyn. 1979. The Self in Self Decoration. *Oceania* 49:241–257.

1980. No Nature No Culture: The Hagen Case. In *Nature, Culture and Gender* (C. MacCormack and M. Strathern, eds.) pp. 174–222. Cambridge: Cambridge University Press.

1981. Self-interest and the Social Good: Some Implication of Hagen Gender Imagery. In *Sexual Meanings: The Cultural Construction of Gender and Sexuality* (Sherry B. Ortner and Harriet Whitehead, eds.) pp. 166–191. Cambridge: Cambridge University Press.

1988. *The Gender of the Gift*. Berkeley: University of California Press.

Sykes, Karen. 1999. After the *Raskol* Feast: Excessive Consumption and Youths' Alienation in Papua New Guinea. *Critique of Anthropology* 19(2): forthcoming.

Tylor, Sir Edward Burnett. 1899. *Primitive Culture: Researches into the Development of Mythology, Philosophy, Religion, Language, Arts, and Custom*. New York: Holt.

Valentine, C. A. 1965. The Lakalai of New Britain. In *Gods, Ghosts, and Men in Melanesia: Some Religions of Australian New Guinea and the New Hebrides* (Peter Lawrence and Mervyn Meggitt, eds.), pp. 162–197. Melbourne: Oxford University Press.

Wagner, Roy. 1974. Are There Social Groups in the New Guinea Highlands? In *Frontiers of Anthropology: an Introduction to Anthropological Thinking* (M. J. Leaf, ed.), pp. 95–122. New York: D. Van Nostrand.

1977. Speaking for Others: Power and Identity as Factors in Daribi Mediumistic Hysteria. *Journal de la Société des Océanists* 56–57, Vol. 33:145–152.

1981. *The Invention of Culture*. Chicago: The University of Chicago Press.

1986. *Asiwinarong: Ethos, Image, and Social Power among the Usen Barok of New Ireland*. Princeton: Princeton University Press.

Weiner, Annette B. 1988. *The Trobrianders of Papua New Guinea*. New York: Holt, Rinehardt, and Winston.

Williamson, Margaret H. 1983. Sex Relations and Gender Relations: Understanding Kwoma Conception. *Mankind* 14(1):13–23.

7 Self models and sexual agency

Jeannette Marie Mageo

Jeannette Mageo's "Self Models and Sexual Agency" begins with the self, deconstructing simplistic dichotomies between egocentric and sociocentric cultures that seem particularly ill-suited to colonized societies.[1] In developing a more complex model of identity variations between cultures, she suggests how these variations articulate with social and epistemic power. These articulations help to explain not only deprecatory models of race and gender but also restrictive models for sexual behavior. Mageo illustrates these relations through the historical collision of Samoan culture with radically different cultures of self, namely nineteenth-century Victorian mission culture and twentieth-century American culture. Prior to missionization, Samoan women's sexual agency was epistemically sanctioned. Through this form of agency, furthermore, social power could be (genealogically) negotiated. By the mid-twentieth century, however, female sexual agency had become a route to male abandonment and disparaged children, and it was clouded by an increasing sense of shame. Samoan men then took up formerly female discourses and sex roles in effeminate joking and theatrical transvestism, which became mediums in which to think through a colonial de-stabilization of male gender identity.

Mageo's analysis shows how the persistence of gendered idioms of experience can have radically different and in some ways almost opposite pragmatic outcomes in the same society at different points in time. In one respect she pushes open and expands full circle Marshall Sahlins' notion that the practicality of results can change all the more, not in spite of cultural continuities, but because of them (1981, 1985). In another respect she problematizes this type of continuity. Though gendered idioms of female sexual agency may persist, men rather than women become the actual agents of exposition, and this agency is thereby transformed as if beyond practical recognition. Understanding of selfhood as a lived and practical experience emerges not as a function of either epistemic or social power, but through their interplay in social and cultural history. Mageo reveals power relations as well as selves to be constituted in the flux of temporal changes that occur in dynamic relation to competing cultural force fields. As was the case in Allison's chapter and also Ewing's, gendered dimensions of modernity emerge as key to the projections and identifications

of contemporary social personhood. The way that Samoan self–power relations are neither reducible to Western imposition nor to indigenous persistence
underscores the fluid and hybrid relationship of power to the self.

The spirit possession stories with which Mageo's essay concludes address
questions as to whether possession is an ineffectual cry of protest or part of a
more active form of gendered agency that links to ongoing social efficacy. Rather
than crediting a sharp and real distinction between personal fantasy life and
public political life, Mageo shows how they flow continually into one another.
As in Allison's essay, issues of psychic power are raised through sexuality. Here
sexuality can be read as more generally implicating bodily life and personal
experience, their differential organization, and their privileging or repression
for certain groups via constellations of social and epistemic power.

Jeannette Mageo and Bruce Knauft

In 1842, writing London from his South Seas post, the missionary Drummond
remarks of the Samoans,

A great number of both sexes are clothed on the Sabbath particularly with something
European, although not always very tastily put on. . . . I have seen a good old grey headed
man coming to chapel with a woman's gown on and I have seen a female coming to the
same place clothed in a gentleman's morning coat.

This tableau – gray headed men showing off ladies' gowns and "females"
flaunting gentlemen's jackets – is a colonial genre tale meant to demonstrate
the amusing naiveté of the "natives." Genre aside, the problem Drummond
stumbled upon here ran much deeper than a lack of familiarity with "civilized"
conventions of dress. More than 130 years after Samoa had become a South Seas
watering hole for European missionaries, whalers, traders, consuls, planters,
and others who sported Western dress, long after the Samoans' royal Hawaiian
cousins had mortgaged the proverbial ranch to clothe themselves very tastily
with something European (Sahlins 1985) – Schoeffel describes Samoans in
much the same terms as Drummond:

A W.H.O. Leprosy Consultant told me with some perplexity that he had been invited
to attend the annual White Sunday service at Magiagi village and noticed that several
children whom he had examined physically a few days previously were attired in the
clothing of the opposite sex. . . . Families with relatives overseas often receive parcels of
new children's clothing for White Sunday and a family in possession of a surplus . . . [of]
expensive girls dresses may put them on a small boy to publicly demonstrate their
affluence (1979:110).

In face of this tendency to blithely overlook Western dress distinctions one
might rightly assume that Samoans draw gender boundaries differently than

Westerners do. One might further assume Samoan ways of gendering were untouched by "contact"; this truly would be naiveté. Although the Samoan self/sex/gender system has proved remarkably tenacious, my purpose is to trace colonial and postcolonial amendments to this system. In Samoa the colonial encounter was punctuated by two tidal waves. The first was a wave of nineteenth-century missionaries, who were avatars of English conceptions of self/sex/gender. The second wave was of American World War II servicemen, who furthered the cultural erosion missionaries began.

This ethnohistorical project will allow me to illustrate a theory of the self and power. I argue that cross-culturally self systems carry identifiable psychological attributions by dominant groups to less empowered groups. These attributions operate as judgments of capacity and as judgments of propriety. The group is deemed capable only of that which it is attributed; if group members engage in activities beyond this level, they are deemed to be acting inappropriately – against nature, against morality, and so forth. These attributions, furthermore, are rooted in models of the self and presuppose varying degrees of agency in a general sense and varying kinds of sexual agency. I begin with a presentation of this self theory, going on to trace its rootedness in power relations and from there turning back to trace transformations of self and power in Samoan ethnohistory.[1]

Self models and power

There are multiple folk models of the self in all cultures; however, I believe that cross-culturally these models are organized as a tiered ensemble in which the tiers can be distinguished by differing degrees of reflexivity. This ensemble consists in four kinds of self models: natural, moral, performance, and creative models. Natural models are models *of* being – that is, of the essential or constitutive dimension of personhood. Moral models are models *for* what people should and should not do. Performance models are models *for* how people should act in specific cultural domains. In creative models, approaches to being and action developed in other kinds of models are freely combined to suit real-life contingencies.

Natural models

We all have experiences of self that are grounded in individual and in social experience – those experiences that G. H. Mead called the "I" and the "Me" respectively (1934). Yet people in culture tend to emphasize either subjective or social experience.[2] These emphases are matters of degree, suggesting that self models vary along a continuum. The poles of this continuum are, on one end, that people are individuals and, on the other, that they are role players in social groups. We will soon see that these self models are: embedded at the lexical level via the terms and phrases through which people are referenced in a culture; unreflectively regarded as tantamount to universal "human nature."

In more sociocentric cultures, words that signify role playing or characteristic social behavior are used to reference the self. Thus in Samoa *aga* translates as "nature" in the sense of essential character, but also means "persona" – that is, a social mask, face, or role.[3] Linguistically-embedded models are hegemonic; they privilege and they marginalize – not political factions, as in Gramsci's understanding of hegemony (1992) but experiences. To the extent that a small-scale culture is sociocentric, the marginalized quality of inner subjective experience is often indicated by a lack of distinctions made among these experiences, namely, between feelings or thoughts, desires or volitions.[4] In Samoan there is one word for all these events – *loto*. The marginalized character of these events is evident in Samoans' tendency to deny that describing inner experience is even possible (Gerber 1985:133).

A. Lakoff tells us that evident in the American phrase "I'm not my*self* today" is a metaphorical folk model of the person as having "a single way . . . we *really* are," this way being that of inner self (1996:102, 107: my emphasis). This phraseology assumes a "divided self," one part of which is unitary and constant, the other fluctuating. In this American folk model Lakoff claims that the former is identified with the person as a subject, is equated with consciousness and rationality, and is perceived as "the true self," while the latter is a composite of body, emotions, desires, and social role. Folk understandings of passion suggest that in more sociocentric cultures subjectivity (rather than social role) tends to be conflated with the body, emotion, and desire. In other words, whatever aspect of the self is marginalized in natural models is thus conflated.

The Samoan *loto* best translates as "subjectivity" but is also a quasi-organ that Samoan ethnomedicine locates in the chest and which is not the heart (Mageo 1989). When a girl runs off with a boy without thought for her family's honor, she is said to feel a yearning in her *loto* (*momo'o i loto*): she is swept away by passion beyond all reason.[5] Freud, an excellent analyst of Euro-American cultures, associates that reservoir of passion, the id, with an "oceanic sense"; this is a sense "of being one with the external world," which Freud believes is normally dormant in people (1961:12). Yet when passion is awakened the lover feels "that 'I' and 'you' are one" (Freud 1961:13). In states of passion, Samoans tend to be overwhelmed by subjectivity, which they experience as passionate (i.e. highly embodied and emotional), while Euro-Americans tend to be overwhelmed by their connectedness with another.

Moral models

Inasmuch as passionate feeling is alloyed with the marginalized form of experience, it contradicts cultural assumptions about human nature. People's response is to shift from models *of* the self to models *for* the self – the first of which are "moral models." Although people may admit that human *nature* does not conform to their folk model, they are apt to say that human *behavior* should. To the extent that natural models are egocentric, virtuous behavior is perceived as tantamount to responsible individualism. To the extent that natural models are sociocentric, virtuous behavior is perceived as tantamount to responsible role playing. Contrarily, vice is equated with what natural models elide.[6] In sociocentric Samoa, for example, respect for status is a paramount virtue, while vice is seen as likely to be sourced in the "I." One demonstrates respect by serving superiors, which Samoans say is "to stand at one's post," meaning to play one's assigned role. Elders often say to disobedient children "Don't *fai loto* to me!" *Fai* means "to make." "To make *loto*" is to be individualistically willful rather than respectfully compliant.

Whatever one's moral models, when comparing them to human behavior it is apparent that people are prone to act in the manner they proscribe. Foucault shows that proscriptions, by aiming at the control of a suspect form of experience, call attention to this experience and produce knowledge about it (1990). This knowledge awakens people to the insuppressible character of behavior at odds with moral models – as saints and prophets in many societies have ruefully declared, and as children's inclination towards individual willfulness reminds Samoans daily. Moral models, then, reflect on human nature in a judgmental mode. This new reflectivity provokes a bifurcation in models *for* behavior.

Performance models

Cultural life is segmented into formal and informal domains: in formal domains all are expected to act out cultural virtue. In informal domains, behavior proscribed in moral models is prescribed. This prescription is possible because in performance models virtue and vice turn rhetorical – by which I mean they assume an "as if" character. Samoan moral models, for example, demand respect for superiors, but when Samoans are behaving formally towards a male they greet him as "High Chief" (*ali'i*), irrespective of his actual status, a habit Robert Louis Stevenson noted even among little boys playing marbles on the streets of Apia (1892:2). When being informal, Samoans deprecate one another's status, but this is joking behavior not literally meant. I married a Samoan, Sanele. When Sanele was growing up an uncle embarked late on an election campaign. His slogan was "Never Too Late." For weeks after his uncle lost "Too-Late" was Sanele's nickname among his chums.

American moral models valorize self-reliance and disparage dependence (Hsu 1961:219). But, according to Quinn's informants on American marriage, in the domain of private life one is supposed to act with "emotional commitment" (1992:105). Since the Enlightenment, the individual's independence has been founded on "his" reasoning capacity, but one of Quinn's informants (Nan) defines commitment as "kind of losing yourself... surrendering your [independent] judgment and perspective and stuff like that." Nan adds, however, while total emotional commitment is an "ideal," it does not correspond to her actual feelings, which are conflicted. Inasmuch as conflicted feelings often lead to divorce, one might say that "emotional commitment" is rhetorical. Emotional commitment is part of the poetics of American private life rehearsed nightly on practically every television network; Nan is describing a performance prescribed in American private life.

Performance models are those that Goffman explores in *The Presentation of Self in Everyday Life* (1956). They carry with them a dawning realization of the conventional nature of self models along with their affiliated modes of acting and talking. American romance is full of extravagant expressions of "endless love" that to one degree or another people realize are tropic (Holland and Eisenhart 1990). I do not mean that performance models are cynical. Formal and informal performances often feature cultural ideals that people like Nan believe in more fervently than they do in moral rules. It is just that people notice that these performances are situationally cued and neither realistically mirror human nature nor consistently mirror human sentiment and behavior.

Public/private is that domain distinction typical of more individualistic cultures, the distinguishing criterion being how intimate the individual is with others. When an individual is with intimately related others, the domain is private (informal). When an individual is with others to whom he or she is not personally tied, that domain is public (formal). Feminist anthropologists argue that public/private is not always a culturally salient domain distinction.[7] Their critique of the Western tendency to read this split into every culture has been taken as an argument against "a domain split period" (Ortner 1990:52). Performance models, I believe, pivot on formal/informal domain splits, but the binary divide is not always between public/private. In sociocentric Samoan society, formal domains are those in which people of differing status are present; informal domains are those in which people of the same status are present.[8]

Performance models underwrite prestige systems and aim at social achievement. Thus, acting as an individual distinct from others is quintessential not only to American moral individualism but also in the professional (formal) domain. There, to gain prestige, one demonstrates individual initiative and enterprise. From Orwell's *Citizen Kane* to *The Godfather, Part II*, this performative individualism has been the measure of success, even when morality is dubious. In their internalized forms, performance models comprise what Marcuse would call the "performance principles" of various societies (1955:35–40). They shape compelling interior dialogues that channel people's energy into achievements supportive to a given sociocultural order rather than towards alternative forms of satisfaction, symbolized in *Citizen Kane* by the polysemous "Rosebud."[9]

Achievement needs are found in all societies (Markus and Kitayama 1991:241), although what constitutes achievement and what sorts of achievements are most recognized differs wildly from economic, to political, to intellectual, to artistic, to spiritual, and to combinations thereof.[10]

Creative models

The attempt to divide cultural life into formal and informal domains draws attention to the real variety of cultural contexts. People's response is to freely combine preexisting models of how to be a person to address the novel contingencies of real situations. Creative models are those described by Bourdieu in which, rather than merely replicating cultural schemata, one improvises (1977; see also Quinn and Strauss 1997). Dreyfus uses game playing as a metaphor for the cognitive processes involved in improvisation. When beginning to learn a game, one typically conforms to rules. Experts, however, freely combine models drawn from previous experience to create new moves (Dreyfus 1984:30). So too, people with creative models draw upon all available patterns to reinvent their culture's ways of being a person.

People with creative models do not necessarily philosophize about them. Thus Dreyfus argues that experts are seldom skilled at telling others abstractly what they do. Bourdieu likewise locates these models in practice rather than in talk. Nonetheless, a creative relation to self models suggests fuller reflectivity: one can make new models only insofar as one recognizes at some level that existing cultural models do not reflect a necessary human or social reality. I leave illustrating creative models to the conclusion of this chapter where we will consider an actual case (but see also Holland *et al.* 1998). People have access to all these varieties of self models and may move back and forth among them. While I have implied a temporal sequence, I am merely using temporality as a trope for a logical unfolding.

Self systems and agency

These tiered self models predicate not only progressive degrees of reflectivity but also progressive degrees of agency – and this is where they connect to power relations. Creative models represent the fullest form of human agency but natural, moral, and performance models indicate progressive degrees of agency and are implicated in ideological doctrines about developmental levels. I am *not* saying that different groups in any sense reside at different developmental levels. Rather, the natural-moral-performative series is often indirectly invoked in the *evolutionary folk theories* of many societies.

Analyzing British colonialism in India, Chatterjee says an evolutionary folk theory was used to justify depriving colonial subjects of political agency (1993).

The colonized were posited to occupy (temporarily) a lower developmental level than the colonizing group, therefore requiring governmental parenting by the more evolved group. In the westerly Samoas, likewise, the colonial German Governor Solf wrote "the natives are . . . all big children in need of education and loving guidance" (1907:1–2 quoted in Meleiseā 1987:3). Somewhat later the colonial New Zealand administration declared that the typical Samoan

has all the faults natural to his imperfect development . . . he is still a child, well mannered and attractive when pleased, but at times capricious and wayward, with primitive passions easily aroused (*Handbook of Western Samoa* 1925:41–42).

Developmental narratives about the path of a gradual historical development or alternatively about intrinsic developmental differences are not only invoked by colonists. They are also used within a society as a way of legitimating the unequal treatment of cultural subgroups. Thus the Comaroffs show that the same atavistic attributions colonists used to describe Africans were also used to describe lower-class Londoners (1992:265–298). Doctrines about developmental levels ground relations of power in the self by suggesting that: (1) certain types of people (typically those of a given class, caste, race, ethnic group, or sex) are more or less realized in their selfhood and (2) more or less capable of becoming so and, for these reasons, (3) lesser types of agency are appropriate for them.[11]

A *natural level* is attributed to everyone who is regarded as human.[12] In more egocentric societies even slaves will be seen in a limited sense as individuals, accountable for their own actions; however, they tend to be deemed capable only of *physical agency* – labor.[13] The type of accountability held to be appropriate for them, therefore, is labor for those with higher capacities. When a *moral level* is attributed to a group, members are considered capable of *moral agency,* but as lacking the ability to channel their energies into culturally defined achievement modes. The type of accountability held to be appropriate for them is moral: their behavior is judged on how well they keep moral rules, personify moral ideals, and contribute to the achievements of superiors by offering both physical labor and moral support. When a *performative level* is attributed to a group, that group is deemed capable of *agency for achievement* and life is about what one accomplishes.

A debate on woman's nature that raged in nineteenth-century English society provides an illuminating example of natural-versus-moral attribution types. The conservative wing of this debate attributed to women a natural developmental level, crediting them only with a capacity for physical agency. Females were equated with their reproductive physiology. Menses served as a organizing trope and alibi for this equation: menstruation was seen as the analogue of rut in animals and the menstrual cycle as dooming women to nervous over-excitement, instability, and morbid psychology (Laqueur 1990:218–219; McClintock 1995:39).[14] The liberal wing regarded women as society's moral barometers and their moral sensibility as indexical of humanity's progress (Millar 1806; Thompson and Wheeler 1825).

In all known societies men are attributed achievement needs (Mead 1949: 296–324). We saw that performance models aim at achievement, suggesting that dominant male groups are attributed these self models. In societies where women are attributed moral models and men performance models, women are expected to play a supporting role to male achievement rather than taking starring parts themselves. This male/female gender dimorphism is often rehearsed in contrastive dress conventions. Male dress will then be more action-oriented or will display badges of office – gold braids on shoulders, medals on chests, the silk robes of judges or academics and so forth. Female dress will display an aestheticized moral ideal tied to sexuality – as illustrated by Victorian fashions that displayed delicacy but also a curvilinear shape, which symbolized sexuality and covered the curves as well.

Developmental levels and sexuality

Attributed developmental levels have entailments for sexual agency. When a group is attributed a natural level their style of sexual agency is presumed to be *animalistic*. Immoralities such as incest and prostitution are expected of them, the latter particularly of females (see for example Trawick 1990; Kelly 1991). "Impulse" is a concept that holds, problematically, that there is a part of the self that exists apart from culture and is pure biology. There is probably no part of the self uncontaminated by cultural patterning, but we saw that cultures tend to *conceptualize* some part of the self as passionate – that is, as intrinsically unconstrained and in need of moral tethering. Morality is often framed as the restraint of impulse in this sense of the word. When a moral developmental level is attributed to a group their sexuality is expected to be largely an exercise in restraint – as it is in virginity cults for women in many cultures. I call this sexual agency *in the negative tense*. When a group is attributed a performative level, renunciation is still expected but it is part of a course of action directed towards achievement rather than being an end in itself. People are expected to act with discretion and appropriateness, forgoing or indulging in sex depending upon the situation; they exercise a *situational* style of sexual agency.[15] For them cannons of sexuality morality are tempered and relativized, as they are for men in many cultures. This, of course, is the legendary "double standard."

When women are attributed a moral developmental level, sexuality is considered agentive for them in the negative tense: they are presumed capable of restraining sexuality for higher purposes. In cultures where people make this attribution, nineteenth-century Victorian England, for example, women tend to be seen as innately sexually reluctant. Then women will be perceived as sexually acted upon rather than as exercising sexual agency in a positive sense even in circumstances in which bodily wants need less bridling (marriage for example).

Just as colonizing cultures used evolutionary folk theories to argue that political agency was inappropriate for colonial subjects, so also Western scientists have used evolutionary reasoning to argue that full sexual agency was unnatural to women. Early evolutionary theory held that there was natural selection for "modesty" in females and "prowess" in males (Ellis 1900). These beliefs were projected even onto the egg and sperm (Martin 1991). Contemporary evolutionists still hypothesize that female sexual choice is more weighted to restraint than male choice (Buss 1994; Pinker 1997:460–493), even though non-human primate studies fail to bear out this hypothesis (Hrdy 1986; Small 1993:117–184; Zihlman 1995). The relative dates of these citations bespeak the tenacity of the sexual-restraint attribution.

Evolutionary folk theories may also be used backhandedly to explain the behavior of those who do not conform to social attributions. In Victorian society, women who failed to show sexual reluctance were regarded as having slipped back to a lower evolutionary level near to animality and were often thought of and referred to as whores (McClintock 1995:53, 54). Amazingly this "whore" designation is still common in Western evolutionary treatise on women who do not evince moral sexual reluctance (Fisher 1992:94; Pinker 1997:480; Wright 1994:85). The Samoan case, however, belies the universality of these attributions.

Precontact Samoa and nineteenth-century England

Precolonial Samoan society did not organize gender around a moral/performative dimorphism. All members of the extended family and village were enlisted in the sociocentric project of achieving status for their group. In Samoa status was crystallized in titles and captured through what one might call "genealogical work." This gender homogeneity was visible in dress conventions. Males and females alike wore skirts of leaves, or tapa or a mat tied at the waist. To dress up for a dance, rainbow-bright flowers, leaves, and berries were hung around the neck and strewn through the hair, which might be bleached white for effect in both sexes.[16]

If both men and women were attributed an achievement orientation, they were offered different achievement avenues, avenues that were tied to formal and informal performances. In old Samoa, men specialized in formal performances which reached their zenith at ceremonies; the refinement and lavishness of ceremonial speeches and prestations was one of the principal measures of the participating groups' status. There, through an esoteric rhetoric, men made implicit genealogical arguments about their groups' rights to high titles.[17] They also forged political alliances through which they might later assert those rights in wars, which were also understood as male performances. Women would come to battlefields without fear of molestation, visiting and gossiping with the rival party on the periphery as they witnessed the fray (Churchward 1887:47; Pritchard 1886:61–62).

Women specialized in informal performances, which reached their zenith at entertainments called "Joking Nights." Girls came to these occasions "redolent and glistening with perfumed oil," wearing only "a leaf girdle . . . so scant and high that a part of their tattooed upper thigh is visible . . ." (Churchward 1887:229; Krämer [1902] 1995:374). There they performed hilarious, sexy choreographic jests, which itinerant Britons generally found far more "unfeminine" than the gentlemen's morning coats these girls sometimes donned for Sunday services. The British consul Churchward remarks, "Alas for such a man's feelings should he . . . remain too long, and witness the very extravagant performance of these . . . damsels, when . . . hounded into delirium by the approving shouts of the audience" (1887:229–30). Joking Nights' ribald choreography gave girls the excuse "to flaunt their charms" (Krämer [1902] 1995:374). But this display was not mere vanity.

Women sought to achieve status for their groups by bearing children who were *gafata i luma*, "genealogic steps forward" (Hjarnø 1979/1980:91–93). This aim dictated divergent courses of action to high-status girls and to ordinary girls. High-status girls were to remain virginal but also to display their beauty and talent to attract as many highly titled suitors as possible.[18] The point was to capture the best of these titles in the next generation for one's family and village. Titles were awarded on the strength of maternal and paternal lines. When a high-status girl had a child with a high title, that child combined two elevated genealogies and had an arguable warrant for that title after the bearer's death. The prototype for high-status girls was the *tāupōu* – a chief's daughter temporarily appointed as his village's premier girl for the purpose of marrying her to an exalted title. Virginity was a veritable synonym for the *tāupōu*: when the nineteenth-century missionary lexicographer, Pratt, asked Samoans the word for virgin, *tāupōu* was the word they gave him ([1862–1911] 1977:152).

Because genealogy was charted through maternal and paternal lines, a common girl could not bear a child whose significance was equal to a *tāupōu's* child. Nevertheless, she could raise her family's status by bearing the child of a high-status male. Over generational time, this child's descendants might be incorporated in the higher-status family's title system, opening their resources to the lower-status family. Failing this, the child might someday bear the title of the girl's own family (all extended families had a head-of-family title) adding luster to that title's genealogy.[19] To this end common girls displayed themselves. The missionary Williams ([1830–1832] 1984:117) notes their refusal to cover their breasts (of which he says they were "exceedingly proud"). Girls would dress

in a finely woven mat wrapped at the waist and split up the left side "to expose the whole front side of their left thigh," powder themselves with turmeric,
string blue beads round their neck and then "walk about to shew themselves"
(fa'alialia). The purpose was, they told Williams, to attract the sons of chiefs.
Joking Nights were staged when an entourage from one village visited another
and were a likely occasion for common girls to encounter high-status boys who
might be induced to sire "genealogic steps forward."[20] As counter-intuitive as
it seems from the perspective of Anglo-American Calvinism, sexy dressing and
night dancing were in line with what Marcuse (1955) would call the "performance principle" of Samoan society, channeling human energy towards the
achievement of status.

Missionaries to Samoa were embroiled in a debate in their home society about
a similar performance principle. This debate began as one about the propriety
of sociocentric versus individualistic marriages and is illustrated by female
heroines throughout late-eighteenth and nineteenth-century English novels. In
the early Western novel, Samuel Richardson's Clarissa for example, the heroine
is expected by her parents to marry much as Samoan girls did, for the betterment
of family fortunes ([1748] 1985). To avoid such a match Clarissa runs away.
Her own belief is that marriage should be undertaken on the basis of sincere
personal feeling. Clarissa's subsequent death makes her a martyr in the cause of
a new sexual ethic. Likewise Charlotte Brontë's Jane Eyre is a testament against
marriage for family fortunes (which in this case binds the hero, Mr. Rochester,
to a destructive union). This sociocentric–individualistic debate was sufficiently
unresolved throughout the nineteenth century that novels with a happy ending
perforce reconciled the need for marriage to a higher-status partner with a
serendipitous love match. Like her Samoan counterparts, Jane Eyre practices
hypergamy by marrying far above her station.[21]

This English debate was not simply about individualistic versus sociocentric
marrying but also, within the individualistic camp, between moral versus situational sexual ethics. On the one side were those who believed in romantic love.
Their position was eloquently expressed in the poetry of Lord George Byron,
one of the most popular of British nineteenth-century writers.[22] Byron recognized that deep personal sentiment did not always correspond with moral rules
(suggesting situational sexual agency). On the other side of this debate were
those who believed evangelical religion, which became broadly popular during
the same period (Davies 1961). Evangelicals also preached an individualistic
relation to sexual sentiments: one was to choose a spouse with whom one was
"spiritually compatible" (Davidoff and Hall 1987:219–221, 323, 437). But this
choice featured sexual agency in the negative tense expressed by premarital
virginity and lifelong fidelity. Both camps advocated "free choice" marriages
hinging on the personal values and feelings of its parties because they shared
a model of the self as grounded in subjectivity. Their contrapuntal positions

around a common cause made romantics and evangelicals interlocutors who regularly appeared in one another's texts.

Romantics, albeit in a negative guise, appeared in evangelical preaching – sometimes in interdictions against reading novels, but also in sermons on motives for marriage (Davidoff and Hall 1987:90, 437; Davies 1961:156). Evangelicals often appeared in popular novels. In *Jane Eyre* one meets the stern and loveless evangelical minister, Mr. Brocklehurst, who runs the boarding school in which Jane grows up. (Mr. Brocklehurst, incidentally, was noted for the dress code he imposed on girls: uncurled short hair and plain wrappers.) Superficially incompatible, romantics and evangelicals conspired to privilege individuality just as they conspired in Jane Eyre. Jane fully achieves romantic love by virtue of her character and intellect, which was cultivated at Mr. Brocklehurst's boarding school.

In England, this transition in sexual ethics (from sociocentric family considerations to individualistic personal justifications) ran parallel to a new definition of formal and informal domains along sex lines. Many Victorian men

deliberately excluded middling women from the clubs and taverns, from Masonic lodges and financial organizations, from the commercial rooms of pubs, from political rallies, and Town Hall meetings, from the chamber of Manufacturers, from parliamentary and council elections and from the universities; in short, from all the institutions of public, commercial power, which were henceforth defined as exclusively male spaces. (McClintock 1995:160)

The eighteenth-century parlor had often been the office of an adjacent factory. Women were involved in factory business along with their husbands. When middle-class women were evicted from "male spaces," the effect was to forefront a domain split between public and private life (Hall 1979:15; Davidoff and Hall 1987; Rosaldo 1980:401–402).

The first wave: Christian colonization

English Protestant missionary societies derived from the Evangelism movement (Gunson 1978). Their belief in women's capacity to be preeminently moral beings who should specialize in private life but who should also exercise a deeply personal sexual agency in the negative sense traveled to Samoa with the London Missionary Society *circa* 1830. Missionaries founded boarding schools for girls, just as their colleagues (like Mr. Brocklehurst) were doing at home. Samoan girls' age-old jocular habits, their "lewd manners" in missionary terms, sometimes "rendered immediate expulsion necessary" (Bullen 1847). Nonetheless, girls showed an enthusiasm and an aptitude for education. "[M]ore are seeking admission than can be accommodated," one missionary says of his wife's school for girls; "In Reading, Writing, Arithmetic, Geography, Sewing . . . they make respectable progress, but the great advantage of such an Institution is the Moral and Religions Education," which profited particularly "by them being . . . apart from the corrupting influence of other Natives" (Mills 1844). In other words, girls who boarded were more likely to maintain their virginity.

One cannot but wonder: why would girls abandon their vernacular freedoms for missionary cloistering? The answers were various, but one was that Christian education opened new avenues to status. The premarital virginity that missionaries preached was in local terms that of the *tāupōu*, a word that colonial visitors translated as "village princess." This association was reinforced by the church weddings that missionaries promoted for all girls; prior to missionization only high-status marriages involved ritual fanfare prior to cohabitation.[23] Similitude to the village princess also came to be emblemized by a Christian education, denoted by a speech style.

In Samoan one can use *tautala lelei*, "Good Speech" or *tautala leaga*, "Bad Speech" (Shore 1982:272; Ochs 1988:54–58). Good Speech employs the /t/, /n/, and /r/ sounds, in preference to the /k/, /ng/, and /l/ sounds employed in Bad Speech. Bad Speech is the contemporary pronunciation style. If Bad Speech is now the standard style, why should it be pejoratively named? Good Speech is Samoan as it was first recorded by missionaries; later the language drifted towards the /k/, /ng/ and /l/ sounds (Shore 1982:267–276). Through the nineteenth and early-twentieth centuries mission organizations dominated the Samoa printing industry (Huebner 1986). As a result, a missionary version of the Samoan language became the literary standard and this standard the gauge of linguistic propriety. Bad Speech, Shore argues, is an unwritten "ideology of ethnic integrity" (1982:271). Good Speech, I suggest, became a colonial context marker: it was used in written language and in church (both missionary imports) but also in speaking with foreigners, fencing out colonial others. Even when I was studying Samoan in the 1980s, Samoans would reprimand me if I used Bad Speech; it was not consonant with my dignity as a *pālagi* (white Westerner).

Dignity was a vernacular concept (*mamalu*), indeed an age-old bodily badge of status. But during colonial times Good Speech became a verbal equivalent of dignity. To borrow Fanon's metaphor (1967), *mamalu* acquired a colonial dusting. So did respectable girls. Good Speech became so identifying an aspect of girls' style that transvestites mimicking girls would affect it (Ochs 1988:57). This language shift was indexical of changing ideas about sexual agency, which we will soon see were supported by a redefinition of formal/informal domains.

Our stereotype of missionaries to the South Seas is that they sought to banish permissive sexual practice, but in Samoa they also undermined the sexual restrictions entailed in sociocentrism just as their brethren at home were doing in English society.[24] Although in pre-Christian Samoa lower-status girls exercised sexual agency in a positive sense, situational restraint was expected of them. They were *not* to elope "on the will of the girl" but with family status in mind (Schultz [1911 n.d.] 22–23). Samoan lore intimates that girls often resisted these pre-Christian Samoan family values (Moyle 1981; Muse and Muse 1982:12–13). Missionaries supported their resistance, counseling parents that girls should chose their husbands in accord with sincere inner sentiments (Mead [1928]1961:101). Although missionaries drew conclusions from this principle about sexual agency in the negative tense, Samoan girls seemed to read the romantic texts against which evangelicals preached between the lines. By the late-nineteenth and early-twentieth century even high-status girls began eloping based on their personal inclinations (Willis 1889; Keesing 1937).

Moreover, English missionaries' public/private domain distinction undermined girls' genealogic mode of achievement. Public/private implies a divide between intercourse, a private event, and marriage, a public event, the latter having legal entailments that the former does not.[25] In pre-Christian Samoa, bearing "genealogic steps forward" relied on the absence of the private domain and with it any absolute contrast between intercourse and marriage. While there had been some differentiation between serious and casual unions (Schultz 1911:22–25), males referred to females with whom they had sexual congress as "wives."[26] Little distinction was made between legitimate and illegitimate children. Many of Samoa's highest families still trace their lineage to the daughter of Salamāsina, Western Samoa's first paramount, born prior to this paramount's formal marriage (Schoeffel 1987).

Samoan girls flocked to mission schools but, according to forlorn missionary, Bullen, they "come when they please," remained "as long as they please," did "very much as they please," and then would "leave again when they please" (1847). Missionaries told girls' parents to make them stay but girls would then "sigh for liberty to range at large with their idle companions" (Bullen 1847). The parents, Bullen continues, "After twice correcting" a girl would "say *in her hearing*, 'Well if this does not suffice, I suppose she must have her own way.'" But gradually there came to be new moral models: models of good Christian girls who were virginal, like village princesses, and models of bad girls who would "range at large" and "walk about to shew themselves" – temptresses like the Biblical Eve. Eve, *Eva* in Samoan, became a term for "ranging at large." When a girl was given to ranging, people would say "Look at Eve" ("*Se va'ai ia Eva*").

The second wave: World War II

Sahlins (1985) says that Hawaiian girls who swam to Cook's ship to mate with sailors were applying an old hypergamy to new circumstances. American GIs appeared to be high-status and provoked a similar response from Samoan girls.[27] Like mission schools, military boyfriends were associated with language training. Saying "I love you" became a Samoan euphemism for speaking a foreign language – probably because GIs taught their prospective girlfriends a little English, along with the romantic rhetoric of American private life, the better to seduce them. Rather than becoming members of important households or enjoying "endless love," girls were deserted by their military boyfriends after the war, ending up with children everyone considered illegitimate and who, therefore, turned out to be status-steps backwards.

A wartime song describes girls dressing up in high heels, no gentleman's-morning-coat mistakes here, and wearing lipstick to show off "next to a military boy" but adds that these "stupid" girls "end with no status whatsoever."[28] At Joking Nights showing off one's charms was a status-acquisition avenue. This World War II song derides girls who used flaunting as a way to acquire status. What had once been an accepted mode of achievement came to be seen as hollow presumption. Still there is a saying, "She wants to decorate her lips": it means "She wants to act above her proper status." Note that in both the wartime song and the saying, the old-style hypergamy has come to be symbolized by flaunting, in Samoan *fā'alialia*.

After the war the Christian ideal of female premarital virginity became ever more the vogue and girls' levity was censured. Samoans still complain of a girl who laughs too much that she is "looking for a mate." But girls did not trade their pre-Christian specialty in joking performances for a new specialty in ceremonial performances. Men retained those titles that gave one a voice in ceremonies. This change in girls' performance models muted them in all public domains. In pre-Christian Samoa girls had bantered at Joking Nights, which were probably staged in the village center (Shore 1977:318). Over the early decades of the twentieth century Joking Nights moved out of the increasingly Christian center of Samoan life to secret occasions in the bush.[29] Within the village girls might continue their old jocular habitus in private with one another but not elsewhere. Here again an imported public/private domain split intruded on Samoan social reality. Like their English sisters, Samoan girls came to be excluded from the public domain and were swallowed up by the private domain. Traces of the pre-Christian past remained, however, for married women were notorious for their ribald joking – so much so that unmarried girls were often warned away from them.[30]

The shift in self models was also evident in (un)dress. Describing the dressing customs of Samoan children, one of Shore's informants says, "boys . . . run around naked. The girl, however, should be covered up" (1982:228). This circumspection is not shed after childhood, for the girl's dignity, Shore explains, "lies in her control over her body, in what she does *not* do" (1982:228). Once Samoan girls had engaged in informal performances, walking about or dancing to show off their splendidly decorated bodies; they practiced a situational sexual agency in which restraint was not an end in itself but an ingredient in the achievement of status. In Christian Samoa girls covered up their bodies and were attributed sexual agency in the negative tense.

Joking Nights had taken place in the meeting house of the village's women's organization, which for that occasion was called a "spirit house": performers were understood to be taking on the shape-shifting nature of spirits.[31] When missionaries banned Joking Nights, there arose a new comedy theater called Spirit House; the skits likewise reveled in sexual joking, but starred boys rather than girls. And so it might seem that, in Western terms, Samoans finally got the sexes and their vestments right. In fact, what was once probably no more than a casual attitude towards Western conventions of dress and sex became a thoroughly ironic attitude. Typically in this theater the only performer in costume was the lead comedian. Like the "good gray-headed man" who attended Drummond's 1842 Sabbath, he was often clothed in something European, such as the brightly flowered imported dresses Samoan women began to wear in colonial times.[32] Indeed some plays were a Western-dressing ritual. In one skit a male comic dresses to go to church, instructing "her" son to gather up her makeup and with it a fragmented gender identity: "go to the safe and get me my *mascara* . . . . Then go on behind our pigsty and get me my *lipstick* . . . . then go to the chest and get us the *Camay*" (Sinavaiana 1992a:110).

Linking feminine sexuality with excrement – rouged lips with pigsties – seems a designation of girls as sites of intercultural pollution. Remember that in the wartime song we just heard "decorating one's lips" (expressing inappropriate status aspirations) was part of showing off "next to a military boy." The song is performed in the male persona. One of my older informants told me that it was authored by Samoan boys whose girlfriends deserted them during the war; then foreign dressing customs became an anchor for the bitterness of rejected lovers. In Spirit House, however, boys' misogynist reactions became a critique of colonial sex roles, entertaining to girls and boys alike. This critique revolved around the village princess. When not clothed in an imported dress the lead comedian was likely to wear the ceremonial headdress and leaf skirt that in colonial times became the village princess's signature costume.[33]

In the choreographic idiom of an earlier age Joking Night girls had once flaunted their sexuality. The new transvestite "village princesses" of Samoan comedy theater waggled their hips, smiled flirtatiously, their gestures representing an intentional confusion of colonial conventions of dress, sex, gender, and more. By conflating the image of the virginal village princesses with sexy Joking Night girls these new comedians not only made ironic commentary on the Christian sex/gender conventions inscribed in nineteenth-century ladies' gowns and gentlemen's morning coats, but also on Samoan affectations of these conventions.

Thus the informal joking that girls had once performed and through which they had achieved was turned to counter-colonial ends. But girls themselves went from being agents of these performances to audience; in this Samoans affected a Western-style gender dimorphism that would not have left English missionaries so nonplused at Sabbaths long ago. Girls' agent-to-audience transit iterated their reduction from performance models to moral models, and from situational sexual agency to sexual agency exercised via restraint. Spirit possession offered an alternative stage upon which Samoan girls dramatized a conflict between the old performance models and Christian teachings. Throughout the early part of the twentieth century a reinvented form of spirit possession was developing; girls were the principal victims.[34] Possession episodes layered elements of traditional mediumship with folk explanations of ailments as spirit-induced and with Christian-colonial images. These possessions reached epidemic proportions in the decades following World War II.

In recounting the lore that surrounds spirit-possession episodes, Samoans depicted spirit girls in a manner that resembled pre-Christian Joking Night girls: spirit girls flaunted their bodily charms and followed boys back to their dwellings.[35] In old Samoa, when girls commonly married by elopement, elopement had been understood as following after a boy (Schultz [1911]n.d.:22; Moyle 1981:122–123). Likewise, spirit girls' dress evoked scantily clad Joking Night girls: spirit girls were often seen in a state of partial or complete nudity and inspired the girls they possessed to shed their clothes.[36] One might say girls' old informal performances had gone, but not entirely: they had gone into the realm of spirits – call it a cultural unconscious, a twilight area where diminished lifeways linger on in fantasy form.

Spirit possession also expressed a conflict between girls' pre-Christian performance models, which entailed *fā'alialia* (flaunting), and Samoan-Christian moral models. Samoans referred to spirit possession as being "hit" and as a "punishment." The girl's infraction often had to do with flaunting. Perhaps she had worn a red flower in her hair, or worn her hair down. Perhaps she had been ranging at large alone in the bush. These were standard pretexts for possession.[37] Sometimes the cause of possession was less obvious but still symbolically tied to Samoan-Christian moral models and girls' resistance to them – as illustrated in the two spirit stories to follow. They were told to me in one long interview in English by a former sister-in-law. I call her Easter, a typical Samoan name, many of which lack gender tags.

The spirit grandmother

Maybe [it was] when I was 13 . . . that was the time I was attending high school . . . Well actually I don't think I know much about it. I know I was lying there . . . I think she [Easter's mother, Forest] was scolding me . . . I was so scared . . . I was just staring out . . . They couldn't tell if it was my voice . . . She [Forest] said . . . when I was back again . . . it was her mother . . . [I] was telling about things that were happening long ago... It was really my grandmother that was talking out. My mom was scolding me while I was outside... picking rubbish... and then she said I was just blanked out... the next thing, I was in the middle of the house... She [the grandmother] was really telling my mother not to treat us like that.... She [Forest] gets angry... usually pulls our hair and gives us spanks... To me, I didn't think it was *ma'i aitu* [spirit possession]... but to them, they said... my grandma was really in me and talking about those things my mom... has to do. She [Forest] must of smacked me... with something that really hurt me.

By making Forest appear unreasonable, this story raises a question: why does Forest really punish Easter? Respect is the foundation of the Samoan moral system. Children are most frequently punished for being disrespectful, *tautalaitiiti*. *Tautalaitiiti* literally means "to talk above one's age." It is a primary Samoan category for juvenile misbehavior, usually glossed as "cheeky." Children are commonly perceived to act out disrespect through disobedience but, particularly for girls, any form of sexual precocity – flaunting for example – is also *tautalaitiiti* (Mead [1928]1961:33, 137, 140; Shore 1981:200). When a child is cheeky in the disobedient sense, she is scolded or hit. When she is cheeky in the sexual sense, her hair may be pulled and cut. The above incident occurs when Easter is carrying out her mother's orders. Forest scolds/smacks Easter. So, disobedience seems to be at issue. But this account's details tell a counternarrative. Easter dates her possession to her thirteenth year. Her grandmother actually died when Easter was 17. By dating the episode to the beginning of puberty, Easter intimates that she tells *her* truth, not *the* truth and that sexuality may be at issue. This intimation is confirmed by Forest's actions.

My mom... really tells us what to do... Even if you don't know where you put your hair ribbons, the only thing she has to do is cut your hair. For example, 'cause every day you go to school [we] have to plait our hair in two... On Monday you have to wear white ribbons, on Tuesday blue ribbons, Wednesday white ribbons...' cause we have long hair, me and Octopus [one of Easter's younger sisters]. So during those days, when you come back on Monday, you have to put your blue ribbon or your white ribbon so that you'll be able to get it on Wednesday... Some days we might forget where we put the ribbon or we put it in a misplace... or else somebody must have grabbed it... one of my brothers... and then in the morning my mom was going to plait our hair... she just got the scissors and cut it short 'cause we just couldn't find the ribbon...

Apparently Easter's offense is again a cheeky failure to obey: Forest acts as if Easter lost or hid the ribbons. This appearance is belied by the sexual significance of hair.[38] In pre-Christian Samoa a girl's head was partially shaved at puberty to denote the subordination of her sexuality to group interests, but a long tuff and tail (*tutagita*) was left dangling down as well. It signified that sexual flaunting that was a part of hypergamous practices.[39] When Christianity reformed girls' roles, girls grew their hair long and bound it in a bun. Should a girl be caught in a sexual indiscretion, however, her hair was cut. Spirit girls wore their hair streaming down; people who saw them sometimes saw only this streaming hair.[40] By cutting off Easter's hair (which once hung down to her knees), Forest implies that Easter lost the ribbons because she wanted to let her hair stream down, which in Samoan-Christian terms would be "flaunting." Easter's own view further affirms this sexual subtext.

It must have been because my father ... was always drunk ... He was out of the family for a couple of days. ... Maybe because I was the elder of the girls ... When they ... quarreled ... it was only me and my dad, he just had to grab [me] and we go and stay somewhere else for a week ... Twice I remember ... we left, only my dad and myself, and went and stayed with my dad's family ....

Easter infers that the reason why Forest was angry with her was sexual jealousy. I do not mean to imply any actual impropriety. Here Oedipal sentiments symbolize illicit sexuality. Like all Christian-Samoan girls, Easter was supposed to be a virgin, so any sexuality but that in a negative tense would have been illicit for her. It is Easter's sexuality that puts her in conflict with Forest, who personifies a punitive Christian-Samoan moral code. Easter's unbound hair, rippling down her shoulders rather than tied in ribbons, is a trace of pre-Christian informal performances and of the corresponding genealogic stepping-stone mode of achievement that missionaries saw as the antinomy of ethical sexual agency.

The spirit grandfather

I argued at the beginning of this chapter that creative models are combinatory: one draws upon all available models for being and action to maximally exercise agency in face of real-life contingencies. Just as creative models draw upon other kinds of models, so also the combinatory practices they entail can be used to revise other self models. It is from their most reflective tier that self systems are rewritten, as is illustrated by this second spirit story.

In the westerly Samoas where Easter grew up primary schools are usually in villages but high schools tend to be in more urban areas. People with high-school-age children may migrate back and forth between a town and a village residence. Easter's family migrated between Apia and Forest's home village on the shore of a vast, remote, mountain-ringed bay. There, Easter's uncle held the extended family title. During high school recesses village Protestant ministers revived the Bible classes with which Samoan schooling first began. So it was in Easter's village. Classes concluded with a celebration at which prizes were awarded to those with high scores on the final exam. Easter always scored high on exams but her family was Catholic so she was not allowed to attend the Bible school. Being forbidden to sit for exams was terribly disappointing for her and she still recalls one awards day when she longed to see who was getting the prizes.

That morning Easter was assigned the task of weeding her grandfather's grave near their house. She did so weeping. Her brothers, she complained to me, were sent to gather wood on the other side of the village which took them right past the awards ceremony. Next, Easter was sent up into the mountains behind the house to get fresh drinking water. Finding the spring and filling her pails, Easter began to return when she heard a old man behind her calling.

"Hey, where are you taking that water?... I could help you." Easter shouldered a long pole at the two ends of which sat her pails. The old man took the pole, lagging slightly behind her as they began to chat.

"Where are you going?" Easter asked.
"To the prize giving."
"Do you have any sons or daughters attending the prize giving?"
"Two," the man answered.
"My mom said no one of us should go. I really want to go to see who's getting the prizes." [Her mom and uncle, she said] "make bad rules for children."

When their paths diverged, Easter turned to take back her pole. "You look at his face," she told me, "and couldn't tell who that person is," but his voice was strangely familiar. Everyone in the village came from one of two extended families. Easter knew them all. Strangeness of visage is an identifying mark of spirits. Recognition of voice is the method healers use to identify possessing spirits. Later that day Forest told Easter the old man was her deceased grandfather whose grave she had weeded, the previous holder of the family title. Spirits in Samoa, *aitu*, allude to the pre-Christian past. Missionaries called them "demons" and saw them as the irremediably heathen residues of Samoan culture. Symbolically, by entering into commerce with her grandfather spirit, Easter forsook the present-day village and with it the normal rules and roles of Samoan-Christian society.

In her relations with spirits Easter's agency progressively expands. In the first story, Forest acts as an agent, scolding Easter for unspecified moral infractions. Easter is mute, but her spirit grandmother acts as an agent, scolding Forest through Easter's mouth. In this second story, rather than being an innocent who is saved by *deux ex machina*, Easter (unknowingly) employs a method by which precontact Samoans solicited spirit help: they prayed on graves (Turner [1884] 1984:151). Easter weeps on her grandfather's grave. He promptly appears in the guise of a kindly old man, yet one who far outranks her mother and uncle. In old Samoa the deceased holders of high titles became minor gods, *tupua* (Stair 1897:211). Easter complains to him that her uncle and Forest make "bad rules for children." Samoans define respect as a deferential attitude in which one silently hides personal sentiments before all those of higher status. Here Easter resists respect relations and discovers her voice in the spirit realm. This discovery is followed by a recitation of her achievements: Easter begins telling me about her high school days when she was "the most talented student in the whole school" and won a nursing scholarship to New Zealand.

Ever since the missionaries arrived, Samoans have been fervent believers in schooling.[41] The first schools, like Mrs. Mills', were attached to missions. Today the holiday, with which this chapter opened, known as White Sunday, carries on biblical education for children. It is called "White" because children get new white clothes that flaunt family wealth. What is surprising about White Sundays is not the cross-dressing they sometimes inspire but their resemblance, admittedly limited, to Joking Nights: White Sundays are also occasions on which youngsters display their talents and thereby contribute to family status. On White Sundays, children recite a biblical text from memory and are applauded by elders. Schooling is modeled on these performances: students regard it as a text-memorization project and as an occasion on which to achieve status.

Remember that in school and church (White Sunday combines both these occasions) one uses Good Speech, Samoan language as first recorded by missionaries. Most consistently Good Speech was associated with colonists. Colonists were attributed status and, therefore, evoked the formal domain. Those venues created by the colonial experience, however, are mixed domains. Samoan formal performances are polite to a ceremonial degree and participants are deferential, crediting all others with high status. Informal Samoan performances playfully and competitively discredit others' status. Village celebrations in old Samoa featured playful status competitions: there were Joking Nights in which jesters besmirched one another's dignity and sports in which competitors represented their villages (Stair 1897:236–237). School is a domain associated with church-going ceremonies and Good Speech, yet in school peer competition is appropriate.[42] Easter's increasing agency coincides with her identification of a mixed domain, school, in which she can display her talents and achieve. This identification is paralleled by her mixture in fantasy of the pre-Christian past and the Christian present in the personage of her grandfather spirit. He is an *aitu* but sends his children to Bible school. This fusion anticipates Easter's resolution to the opposition between a pre-Christian ethos that encouraged girls to exercise agency in the pursuit of status and Christian ethics that confined girls to moral roles.

Easter's father stopped her from taking the nursing scholarship, telling the scholarship committee that she fainted at the sight of blood. She acquiesced because she believed that his real reason for intervening was to keep her close by. Like the sons of whom Obeyesekere writes in describing the Gaṇeśa complex (1990), Easter appears to let her father(s) disempower her. In the Samoan generational kinship system the word for father and uncle are the same. Easter's uncle keeps her from attending Bible School and from attending the awards ceremony. Her father keeps her from accepting an award she later wins. These two figures represent two sides of protective parenting – one is overly strict, one overly fond. But it all comes down to a gender dimorphism in which boys are allowed scope to range but girls are limited in their achievements.

Samoans disapprove of family members directly expressing care (Gerber 1975:51, 53). Parents express it indirectly by protective rules and children by obedience; it is through obedience that Samoan children learn to care. Easter stands up to her strict father better than she does to her fond father; fondness seems to trap her in a bind in which to exercise agency is to fail to care. Or does it? One of her brothers claims that Easter did not go to New Zealand because there was a man she wanted to marry. She did marry. Their parents were angry about it. By raising the marriage question, this brother implicitly asks: did Easter reject her scholarship out of deference or was it elopement in the will of the girl? There is a third possibility: taking the scholarship and elopement were symbolic equivalents for Easter.

Symbolically going to nursing school and getting married both hinge upon shedding blood/fainting. Bloody deflorations were the signature event of high-status marriages in precolonial Samoa.[43] During colonial times (to a lesser extent even today), when a boy wished to marry a girl but her parents objected, he might catch her alone and strike her in the solar plexus, inducing a faint. Then he deflowered her and often she would elope with him to avoid disgrace.[44] Easter defers in regard to nursing school while asserting her own desires in regard to marriage, exercising a situational agency rather than allowing her self to be consistently obstructed by the moral demand for deference.

Easter's father was a catechist. After marriage, Easter went to a seminary school and became a catechist. Her husband followed her in this vocation. Here is the fulfillment of her long-sustained ambition: to sit for religious school exams and, in Samoan terms, to get first prize – high status. Chief Tuiteleleapaga (1980:45) tells us that after Samoan boys were trained as native pastors unmarried girls came to envy their "wives sitting with their husbands on the dais with deacons during church services and receiving the first and best of everything." These wives were called by the same title as the chief's wife, *faletua*. "In an assembly in church or any other place," Tuiteleleapaga continues, the pastor's *faletua* "not only receives the first and best share, but priority in salutatory remarks." Easter reclaims sexual agency and agency for achievement – taking a husband when her parents object and identifying a domain in which she can perform and achieve (church/school). She articulates a new performance model and mode of achievement – albeit a model and a mode discovered by many Samoan girls and that reach all the way back to Jane Eyre and the evangelical Mr. Brocklehurst. Like Nergis, in chapter 5, Easter does so by creatively combining the self models of impinging cultures, strategically negotiating for herself expanded scope, straining but sustaining her bonds with loved ones.

Self and power implications

The pivot between power and the self is agency. My theory interrogates agency, asking how people like Easter can realize it with or against the grain of their societies. The intimate tie between agency and sexuality highlights an interplay between epistemic power and the self, showing that while effective social agency may be strategic, it engages fantasy as well as reason and is rooted in emotion and the body. For Samoan girls the body is a site of struggle and for the transformation of culture – not merely for its expression.

Self models also shed light on a feminist debate on gendered selves and power. Earlier feminists argued that patriarchal social orders relegated women to private domesticity; this was constitutive to their domination (Rosaldo and Lamphere 1974). Later, ethnographers demonstrated that women were far from always so confined (Lamphere 1993; Rosaldo 1980). Women cannot be so confined because not every culture makes a strong public/private domain split. But the association of women with informal domains, as those are locally defined, is cross-culturally common.[45] Gender roles often turn upon culturally diverse domain splits, public/private in nineteenth-century England, hierarchical/peer in precolonial Samoa. What this means is that gender roles do not have natural correlatives in other cultures. A "good gray-headed man" coming to chapel in a woman's gown and a "female" wearing a "gentleman's morning coat" are metaphors for this comparison problem.

I suggest a historical parallel, however, between a salient public/private domain divide and moral models for women – models that limit their sexual agency and agency for achievement. In Victorian England, a public/private domain split was coterminous with the attribution of moral models to middle-class women and of sexual agency in the negative tense, as well as to a shrinking scope for achievement. In colonial Samoa, when domains began to be reshuffled, these variables – a public/private domain split, along with decreased sexual agency and contracted achievement avenues for women – again changed in tandem with one another.

When social orders that moralize women's roles arise, women themselves often promote these orders because they deem it to their advantage, as did Victorian feminists who defined themselves as specialists in morality, and nineteenth-century Samoan girls who matriculated at missionary boarding schools. In patriarchal and colonized societies, such apparent advantages may have circumscribing implications, but women do not rest with circumscription. This is why Samoan girls went on wearing red flowers in their hair, even under threat of spirit possession, and why, when possessed, they shed their clothes and girdling Christian roles with them. This is why women, like Easter, go on creatively concatenating self models, thereby opening new avenues for achievement for themselves and for all who follow after them.[46]

NOTES

Preface Note

1. The dynamic tension between egocentric and sociocentric processes explored here is one that is general to many erstwhile "indigenous" world areas in the contemporary world (e.g. Knauft 1997).

Acknowledgments: I thank Linda Stone and Kathey-Lee Galvin for their editorial comments on earlier drafts of this chapter, and the volume reviewers for the excellent comments. Some of this material draws upon my previous book, *Theorizing Self in Samoa* (University of Michigan Press, 1998).

1. So as not to inordinately burden this chapter, in the text I present only a few examples of my theory's cross-cultural relevance, relegating other supporting cross-cultural data to the notes. Three of the self models presented here have lexical and/or discursive components (moral, performative, and creative) that I have explored in prior work (1995, 1998). However, these are models for acting in the world. Discourse, therefore, is not an adequately encompassing term for them. For a discussion of the biases and advantages of my historical sources on pre-Christian Samoa see further Mageo 1998:xi–xiii.

2. On egocentric and sociocentric self models see further Dumont 1970, Shweder and Bourne 1984, Mauss [1938] 1985, Fogelson 1982, Levy 1983, Rosaldo 1984, Sampson 1988, Harris 1989, Markus and Kitayama 1991, and Hollan 1992. While I treat egocentrism and sociocentrism as a continuum, these authors do not.

3. For examples of other cultures in which people's nature is identified with their persona see Geertz 1984:128–29; Mauss 1990:39; Tedlock 1992:110, 115.

4. For other examples of cultures where thoughts, feelings, volitions, and desires are conflated in very general terms for subjectivity and in which people deny the possibility of knowing very much about inner experience see Wikan 1990:35–37; Tedlock 1992:109, 112; Selby 1974:62–63; Ochs and Schieffelin 1984:290.

5. Likewise, when subjective sentiments appear in Bali, they are apt to take the form either of passionate love believed to be caused by black magic or of passionate anger resulting from personal offense that often leads to sorcery on the part of the person offended (Wikan 1987, 1990).

6. For examples of other cultures where individualism is regarded as a source of vice see Tada 1991:265–267. The highly sociocentric Balinese describe inner life as turbulent and this turbulence as inspiring all manner of inappropriate and evil actions (Wikan 1987, 1990).

7. For examples see Nelson 1974, Leacock 1978, Rosaldo 1980, Sudarkasa 1986, Yanagisako 1987, Collier 1988, and Lamphere 1997.

8. Another important domain split may be between sacred and secular. Domains, like egocentric or sociocentric orientations, are a matter of emphasis; sacred/secular, hierarchical/peer and public/private are arguably domain splits present in every society, but they are not equally salient in every society.

9. On these interior dialogs see further Mageo 1998:81–101.

10. In traditional Hindu society, for example, spiritual achievements like those of Brahmin religious specialists were considered more important than military or economic achievements (Carmody and Carmody 1992).

11. The Confucian philosophy of ancient China, for example, was forever comparing the state to the family: the ruler must "treat the common people as his own children," says *The Doctrine of the Mean* (Chan 1963:105). In Bedouin societies, as in those inspired by the Enlightenment, rational sense (*'agl*) is a valorized social principle; *ágl* characterizes males who should, therefore, direct women and children (Abu-Lughod 1986).

12. People are not, however, always regarded as human; sometimes they are seen as pollutants – trash, rubbish, and so forth (see Scheper-Hughes, chapter 2).

13. In the ante-bellum South, blacks were thought human but incapable of moral agency; slavery was touted as the means of their development (Fitzhugh 1854 and Harper *et al.* 1852). Ante-bellum slave-holders, however, more or less infinitely deferred the point at which slaves would reach moral adulthood, just as Chatterjee's British colonials did in India (1993).

14. For other societies that see women as having a very limited capacity for moral reasoning see Foucault on the Greeks (1986) and Abu-Lughod on Bedouins (1986). Even in societies that attribute women a moral level, this level may be gradated with the highest grade being the preserve of men. Such has probably been the case in American society until recently (Gilligan 1982). Traditionally Hindus believed women were capable of moral development but they had to be reincarnated as men to reach the highest levels of spiritual realization (Carmody and Carmody 1982).

15. Nineteenth-century American women were expected to be morality specialists and were confined to the domestic sphere (Branagan 1807:277, 278; Greenwood 1850: 311; Welter 1966). When women began leaving private life for public life during the twentieth century, they also began eroding the American domain distinction between public and private: feminists, for example, argued that the personal was political. Formerly American private life was associated with women and with moral standards of sexual agency. Public life was associated with men and with performative standards. As the public/private domain split continues to erode, people debate which standard should apply. President Clinton's Monica Lewinski affair can be analyzed in terms of moral versus performative attributions. Many of Clinton's supporters alleged that although he acted "inappropriately," he should not have been judged on his sexual conduct *per se*. Rather, Clinton's achievements and the relevancy of his conduct to his performance as president was the issue.

16. Male and female also wore tattoos. Male tattoos were fairly solid from waist to knees and mandatory for participation in ceremonial life; females' were lace-like on thighs and voluntary (Stair 1897:116–117; Krämer [1902]1995:68–94). Hairstyles also differed for the two sexes (Stair 1897:117–121). On bleaching hair see Stair 1897:132. The significance of contrastive decorations on, versus with, the body (tattoos or hairdos as opposed to clothes) is intriguing, but I lack space here to explore it.

17. On this rhetoric and the negotiation of title claims see Keesing 1934:48, Meleiseā 1987:2, and Mageo 1998:110–114.

18. See further Keesing 1937, Freeman 1983:227–231 and Krämer [1902]1994:34–36.

19. A famous example of a child with an elevated genealogy augmenting a previously lackluster title is that of Salamāsina's son, Tapumānaia, who was kidnapped by a lower-status village so that the village could award the child its highest title, so greatly increasing the title's prestige (Krämer [1923] 1949:78–79).

20. On visiting males taking new consorts particularly at evening entertainments see Pritchard 1866:134–135; Krämer [1902]1995:377 and Tuiteleleapaga 1980:63, 68–69.

21. For other examples see Austen's *Sense and Sensibility, Persuasion*, or *Pride and Prejudice*. On the more sociocentric orientations towards human sexuality that had prevailed in England prior to the nineteenth century see Marcus 1966.

22. On Byron's popularity see Davidoff and Hall 1987:159–160. Here I use the term "romantic" in a limited sense to refer to those who valorized romantic love. Evangelicalism too was born of the Romantic Movement (Davidoff and Hall 1987:27, 158, 160; Davies 1961:247, 256, 277).

23. See further Schultz [1911] n.d. Common girls began to effect other stylistic resemblances to the village princess, for example taking up her dignified dance style (Mageo 1998:197–201). On the *tāupōu* as a symbol of the Samoan-Christian ideal for girls see further Mageo 1996a:67, 1998:164–217.

24. See Williams [1830–32] 1984:77–79, 84, 130. Other colonial visitors also objected to marriages undertaken for reasons of wealth and status. See for example Wilkes 1845:148–49.

25. On missionary redefinitions of marriage see Mageo 1996a:67–70 and 1998:148–151. On colonialism accenting a public/private domain split in a colonized culture see also Comaroff and Comaroff 1992.

26. On sexual partners as wives see Pritchard 1866:134–135, Schoeffel 1979:185–186, Shore 1981:199, 204, and Freeman 1983:247–248.

27. On Americans in the two Samoas during World War II see further Franco 1989, Stanner 1953 and Mageo 1996a:70–72, 1998:148–151. On illegitimate children during the period see Stanner 1953:327.

28. For the full song text see Mageo 1998:256–257.

29. On the relocation of Joking Nights see Sloan 1940:106 and Mageo 1998:160.

30. On the jocularity of older women see Krämer [1902] 1995:374; Schoeffel 1979: 215–221; Sinavaiana 1992a:213.

31. On the place-name of Joking Nights see Shore 1977:318. On Joking Night performers and shape-shifting see Mageo 1996b:36–38.

32. On transvestite dress and joking in Spirit House see Shore 1977:318–333, 1978:178, Mageo 1992, 1996c, Sinavaiana 1992a, 1992b:197.

33. On comedians dressing like village princesses see Sinavaiana 1992b:197.

34. On the possession epidemic see further Mageo 1994, 1996a, 1996b and 1998: 164–190.

35. On the behavior of spirit girls see Cain 1971, Goodman 1971:470–471, Stuebel 1976:94–95, Schoeffel 1979:381–421, and Mageo 1996a, 1996b.

36. See further Goodman 1971:178, Mageo 1991:363–364, 1998:172, 179–183.

37. On these possession pretexts see Goodman 1971:469 and Mageo 1991:363, 1994: 420, 1996a, 1998:177–181.

38. On hair and sexuality see Leach 1958, Hershman 1974, Mageo 1994.

39. On these pre-Christian hairdos and their relation to pre-Christian sexual practice see Turner [1884]1984:122, Stair 1897:121, Krämer [1902]1994:34 and Mageo 1994:408–17.

40. On the hair of spirit girls see Goodman 1971:470, Stuebel 1976:94–95, Schoeffel 1979:406–408, Mageo 1991:94–95, 1998:172–174, 180–181.

41. On Samoans' enthusiasm for schooling see Turner [1861] 1986:18–19, 27, 61–78, Holmes 1974:61, and Huebner 1986:399. Willis 1889:52, Gilson 1970:102 and Garrett 1982:125. References to mission schools and to Samoans' enthusiasm for them are so thick in the missionary record as to make citation impractical. See the letters from Samoa to London in the London Missionary Archives, now called

the Council of World Missions Archives, held at the main library in the School for Oriental and African Studies at the University of London.

42. See further Sutter (1980) on school as competitive (as opposed to home life). Sutter wrongly believes that competitiveness is non-traditional for Samoans. For other instances of domains complicated by transnational experience see Moran 1990; Ewing, chapter 5, and Dalton, chapter 6, this volume.

43. On traditional deflorations see Tuiteleleapaga 1980:69 and Freeman 1983:231. On Samoan blood symbolism see Shore 1981.

44. On rape and elopement in Samoa see Schoeffel 1979:184, Goodman 1983, and Freeman 1983:245–248.

45. *Women, Culture and Society* (Rosaldo and Lamphere 1974) was probably the most noteworthy early attempt to make such generalizations. Two important critiques were MacCormack and Strathern, 1980, and Lamphere, 1993 (see also Rosaldo 1980). MacCormack and Strathern argued that nature/culture was not a universal opposition; therefore, neither was the association of men with culture and women with nature (or with nature/culture mediation). Lamphere argued that women were not always confined to private space in a public/domestic opposition. Ortner has countered the first critique (1996). This chapter argues that the absence of a private/females association is no barrier to valid cross-cultural theorizing about gender.

46. Gailey (1987) argues that colonialism results in a status descent for women. The Samoan case suggests a more complex result. For a Tongan parallel see Gorden 1992.

REFERENCES

Abu-Lughod, Lila 1986. *Veiled Sentiments*. Berkeley: University of California Press.
Bourdieu, Pierre. 1977. *Outline of a Theory of Practice* (Richard Nice, trans.). Cambridge: Cambridge University Press.
Branagan, Thomas. 1807. *Excellency of the Female Character Vindicated*. New York: Samuel Wood.
Brontë, Charlotte. [1847] 1977. *Jane Eyre*. New York: New York University Press.
Bullen, T. 1847. June 12 letter to London Missionary Society Headquarters from Leone, Council of World Missions Archives [20/5/6], School of Oriental and African Studies, University of London.
Buss, David M. 1994. *The Evolution of Desire*. New York: Basic Books.
Cain, Horst. 1971. The Sacred Child and the Origins of Spirits in Samoa. *Anthropos* 66:173–181.
Carmody, Denise and John T. Carmody. 1982. *Eastern Ways to the Center*. Belmont, CA.: Wadsworth.
Chan, Wing-Tsit, ed. and trans. 1963. *A Source Book in Chinese Philosophy*. Princeton: Princeton University Press.
Chatterjee, Partha. 1993. *The Nation and Its Fragments: Colonial and Postcolonial Histories*. Princeton: Princeton University Press.
Churchward, William B. 1887. *My Consulate in Samoa*. London: Richard Bentley & Son.
Collier, Jane. 1988. *Marriage and Inequality in Classless Societies*. Stanford: Stanford University Press.

Comaroff, John and Jean Comaroff. 1992. Homemade Hegemony. In *Ethnography and the Historical Imagination*, pp. 265–296. Boulder: Westview Press.

Davidoff, Leonore & Catherine Hall. 1987. *Family Fortunes*. Chicago: University of Chicago Press.

Davies, Horton. 1961. *Worship and Theology in England from Watts and Wesley to Maurice, 1690–1850*. Princeton: Princeton University Press.

Drummond, G. 1842. October 26 letter to London Missionary Society Headquarters from Savai'i, Council of World Missions Archives (CWM, 15/5/D), School of Oriental and African Studies (SOAS), University of London.

Dumont, Louis. 1966. *Homo Hierarchicus*. Mark Sainsbury trans. Chicago: University of Chicago Press.

Duranti, Alessandro. 1981. *The Samoan Fono, a Sociolinguistic Study*. Canberra: Research School of Pacific Studies, Australian National University.

1983. Samoan Speechmaking Across Social Events. *Language and Society* 12:1–22.

1984. Lauga and Talanoaga. In *Dangerous Words* (D. Brenneis and F. Meyers eds.), pp. 217–237. New York: New York University Press.

1994. *From Grammar to Politics*. Berkeley: University of California Press.

Ellis, Havelock. [1900] 1940. The Evolution of Modesty. In *Studies in the Psychology of Sex*, Part 1, V. 1. New York: Random House.

Ellis, S. 1842. *Daughters of England*. London: Fisher.

Enright, John. 1997. Change on the Winds of War. *Samoa News*, May 19th, page 6.

Fanon, Frantz. 1967. *Black Skin, White Mask* (Charles L. Markmann, trans.). New York: Grove Press.

Fisher, Helen E. 1992. *Anatomy of Love: The Natural History of Monogamy, Adultery and Divorce*. New York: W.W. Norton.

Fitzhugh, George. [1854] 1965. *Sociology for the South, or the Failure of Free Society*. New York: Burt Franklin.

Fogelson, Raymond D. 1982. Person, Self, and Identity: Some Anthropological Retrospects, Circumspects, and Prospects. In *Psychosocial Theories of the Self* (Benjamin Lee ed.), pp. 67–109. New York: Plenum Press.

Foucault, Michel. 1986. *The History of Sexuality, Vol. 2: The Use of Pleasure*. (Robert Hurley trans.). New York: Pantheon.

1990. *The History of Sexuality, Vol. 1: An Introduction* (Robert Hurley trans.). New York: Random House.

Franco, Robert W. 1989. Samoan Representations of World War II and Military Work. In *The Pacific Theater* (G. M. White and L. Lindstrom, eds.). Honolulu: University of Hawai'i Press.

Freeman, Derek. 1983. *Margaret Mead and Samoa*. Cambridge, MA: Harvard University Press.

Freud, Sigmund. 1961. *Civilization and Its Discontents* (James Strachey, trans.). New York: W.W. Norton.

Gailey, Christine W. 1987. *Kinship to Kingship*. Austin: University of Texas Press.

Garrett, John. 1982. *To Live Among the Stars: Christian Origins in Oceania*. Geneva: World Council of Churches in association with the Institute of Pacific Studies.

Geertz, Clifford. 1984. "From the Natives' Point of View": On the Nature of Anthropological Understanding. In *Culture Theory* (Richard A. Shweder and Robert A. LeVine, eds.), pp. 123–136. Cambridge, MA: Cambridge University Press.

Gilligan, Carol. 1982. *In a Different Voice*. Cambridge, MA: Harvard University Press.

Gilson, R. P. 1970. *Samoa 1830 to 1900*. Melbourne: Oxford University Press.

Goffman, Erving. 1956. *The Presentation of Self in Everyday Life*. Edinburgh: University of Edinburgh University Press.

Goodman, Richard A. 1971. Some Aitu Beliefs of Modern Samoans. *Journal of the Polynesian Society* 80:463–479.

1983. *Mead's Coming of Age in Samoa: A Dissenting View*. Oakland: Pipeline.

Gorden, Tamar. 1992. Review of Kinship to Kingship. *American Ethnologist* 19: 601–604.

Gramsci, Antonio. 1992. *The Prison Notebooks* (Joseph A. Buttigieg and Antonio Callari, trans.). New York: Colombia University Press.

Greenwood, Grace. 1850. Letter "To an Unrecognized Poetess, June, 1846." In *Greenwood Leaves*. Boston: Ticknor, Reed and Fields.

Gunson, Niel. 1978. *Messengers of Grace*. Melbourne: Oxford University Press.

Hall, Catherine. 1979. The Early Formation of Victorian Domestic Ideology. In *Fit Work for Women* (Sandra Burman, ed.), pp. 15–33. Canberra: Australian National University.

Handbook of Western Samoa. 1925. Wellington: Government Printer.

Harris, G. 1989. Concepts of Individual, Self, and Person in Description and Analysis. *American Anthropologist* 91(3):599–612.

Hershman, P. 1974. Hair, Sex, and Dirt. *Man* (NS) 9: 274–298.

Hjarnø, J. 1979/1980. Social Reproduction: Towards an Understanding of Aboriginal Samoa. *Folk* 21–22:72–123.

Hollan, Douglas. 1992. Cross-Cultural Differences in Self. *Journal of Anthropological Research* 48:283–300.

Holland, Dorothy C. and Margaret A. Eisenhart. 1990. *Educated in Romance*. Chicago: Chicago University Press.

Holland, Dorothy, William Lachicotte Jr., Debra Skinner, Carole Cain. 1998. *Identity and Agency in Cultural Worlds*. Cambridge, MA: Harvard University Press.

Holmes, Lowell D. 1969. Samoan Oratory. *Journal of American Folklore* 82: 342–345.

1974. *Samoan Village*. Stanford: Stanford University Press.

Hrdy, Sarah B. 1986. "Empathy, Polyandry, and the Myth of the Coy Female." In *Feminist Approaches to Science* (R. Bleier, ed.), pp. 118–146. New York: Pergamon Press.

Huebner, Thom. 1986. Vernacular Literacy: English as a Language of Wider Communication and Language Shift in American Samoa. *Journal of Multi-Lingual and Multi-Cultural Development* 7(5):393–411.

Hsu, Francis L. K. 1961. American Core Value and National Character. In *Psychological Anthropology* (Francis L. K. Hsu ed.), pp. 209–230. Homewood, IL: Dorsey.

Keesing, Felix M. 1934. *Modern Samoa: Its Government and Changing Life*. London: Allen and Unwin.

1937. The Taupo System of Samoa. *Oceania* 8:1–14.

Knauft, Bruce M. 1997. Gender Identity. Political Economy and Modernity in Melanesia and Amazonia. Journal of the Royal Anthropological Institute 3:233–260.

Krämer, Augustin. [1902] 1994. *The Samoan Islands* (Theodore Verhaaren trans.). Vol. 1. Honolulu: University of Hawai'i Press.

[1902] 1995. *The Samoan Islands* (Theodore Verhaaren trans.). Vol. 2 Honolulu: University of Hawai'i Press.

[1923] 1949. Salamāsina. Unpublished manuscript (trans. unknown). American Samoa Community College Pacific Collection.

Lakoff, Andrew. 1996. Sorry, I'm Not Myself Today. In *Spaces, Worlds and Grammar* (Gilles Fauconnier and Eve Sweetser, eds.), pp. 91–123. Chicago: Chicago University Press.

Lamphere, Louise. 1993. The Domestic Sphere of Women and the Public World of Men. In *Gender in Cross-Cultural Perspective* (C. B. Brettell and C. F. Sargent eds.), pp. 67–77. Englewood Cliffs, NJ: Prentice Hall.

1997. The Domestic Sphere of Women and the Public World of Men. In *Gender in Cross-Cultural Perspective* (Caroline B. Brettell and Carolyn F. Sargent, eds.), pp. 82–91. Atlanta: Prentice Hall.

Laqueur, Thomas. 1990. *Making Sex*. Cambridge, MA: Harvard University Press.

Leach, Edmund R. 1958. Magical Hair. *Journal of the Royal Anthropological Institute* 88:147–164.

Leacock, Eleanor. 1978. Women's Status in Egalitarian Societies. *Current Anthropology* 19(2): 247–275.

McClintock, Anne. 1995. *Imperial Leather*. New York: Routledge.

MacCormack, Carol P. and Marilyn Strathern. 1980. *Nature, Culture, and Gender*. Cambridge: Cambridge University Press.

Mageo, Jeannette Marie. 1989. *Āmio/Aga* and *Loto*: Perspectives on the Structure of the Self in Samoa. *Oceania* 59:181–199.

1991. *Ma'i Aitu*: The Cultural Logic of Possession in Samoa. *Ethos* 19:352–383.

1992. Male Transvestism and Culture Change in Samoa. *American Ethnologist* 19(3):443–459.

1994. Hairdos and Don'ts: Hair Symbolism and Sexual History in Samoa. *Man* 29:407–432.

1995. The Reconfiguring Self. *American Anthropologist*. 97(2):282–296.

1996a. Spirit Girls and Marines. *American Ethnologist* 23:61–82.

1996b. Continuity and Shape Shifting: Samoan Spirits in Culture History. In *Spirits in Culture, History, and Mind* (J. Mageo and A. Howard, eds.), pp. 29–54. New York: Routledge.

1996c. Samoa, on the Wilde Side: Male Transvestism, Oscar Wilde, and Liminality in Making Gender. *Ethos* 24(4):1–40.

1998. *Theorizing Self in Samoa*. Ann Arbor: University of Michigan Press.

Marcus, S. 1966. *The Other Victorians*. New York: Basic Books.

Marcuse, Herbert. 1955. *Eros and Civilization*. Boston: Beacon.

Markus, Hazel R. and Shinobu Kitayama. 1991. Culture and the Self. Implications for Cognition, Emotion and Motivation. *Psychological Review* 98:224–53.

Martin, Emily. 1991. "The Egg and the Sperm." *Signs* 16(3):485–501.

Mauss, Marcel. [1938] 1985. A Category of the Human Mind: The Notion of Person; the Notion of Self (W. D. Halls, trans.). *In The Category of the Person* (S. Collins and S. Lukes eds.), pp. 1–25. Cambridge: Cambridge University Press.

Mead, G. H. 1934. *Mind, Self and Society* (C. W. Norris, ed.). Chicago: Chicago University Press.

Mead, Margaret. [1928] 1961. *Coming of Age in Samoa*. New York: Morrow Quill.

1949. *Male and Female*. New York: William Morrow.

Meleiseā, Malama. 1987. *The Making of Modern Samoa*. Suva: Institute of Pacific Studies, USP.

Millar, John. 1806. *Origins of the Distinction of Ranks*. Edinburgh: William Blackwood.

Mills, W. 1844. March 19, Letter to London Missionary Society Headquarters from 'Upolu, Council of World Mission Archives (17/6/B), School of Oriental and African Studies, University of London.

Moran, Mary. 1990. *Civilized Women*. Ithaca, NY: Cornell University Press.

Moyle, Richard. 1981. *Fagōgo*. Oxford University Press for Auckland University Press.

Muse, C. and S. Muse. 1982. *The Birds and Birdlore of Samoa*. Walla Walla, WA: Pioneer.

Nelson, Cynthia. 1974. Public and Private Politics: Women in the Middle Eastern World. *American Ethnologist* 1:551–565.

Obeyesekere, Gananath. 1990. *The Work of Culture: Symbolic Transformations in Psychoanalysis and Anthropology*. Chicago: University of Chicago Press.

Ochs, Elinor. 1988. *Culture and Language Development*. Cambridge University Press.

Ochs, Elinor and Bambi B. Schieffelin. 1984. Language Acquisiion and Socialization. In *Culture Theory* (Richard A. Shweder and Robert LeVine eds.), pp. 276–322. Cambridge: Cambridge University Press.

Ortner, Sherry B. 1996. "So, *Is* Female to Male as Nature is to Culture?" In *Making Gender*, pp. 173–180. Boston: Beacon Press.

Pinker, Steven. 1997. *How the Mind Works*. New York: Norton.

Pratt, George. [1862/1911] 1977. *Pratt's Grammar and Dictionary of the Samoan Language*. Apia: Malua.

Pritchard, William T. 1866. *Polynesian Reminiscences*. London: Chapman and Hall.

Quinn, Naomi. 1992. The Motivational Force of Self-Understanding: Evidence from Wives' Inner Conflicts. In *Human Motives and Cultural Models* (Roy D'Andrade and Claudia Strauss, eds.), pp. 90–126. Cambridge: Cambridge University Press.

Quinn, Naomi and Claudia Strauss. 1997. *A Cognitive Theory of Cultural Meanings*. Cambridge: Cambridge University Press.

Richardson, Samuel. [1748] 1985. *Clarissa*. Harmondsworth, UK: Penguin.

Rosaldo, Michelle Z. 1980. The Use and Abuse of Anthropology: Reflections of Feminism and Cross-Cultural Understanding. *Signs* 5(3):389–417.

1988. Towards an Anghropology of Self and Feeling. In *Culture Theory* (R.A. Shweder and R.S. Levine eds.), pp. 137–157. Cambridge: Cambridge University Press.

Rosaldo, Michelle Z. and Louise Lamphere, eds. 1974. *Woman, Culture and Society*. Stanford: Stanford University Press.

Sahlins, Marshall. 1981. *Historical Metaphors and Mythical Realities*. Ann Arbor: University of Michigan Press.

1985. *Islands of History*. Chicago: University of Chicago Press.

Sampson, Edward E. 1988. The Debate on Individualism: Indigenous Psychologies of Self and Their Role in Personal Societal Functioning. *American Psychologist* 43(1): 15–22.

Schoeffel, Penelope. 1979. Daughters of Sina. Doctoral Dissertation. Australian National University.

Schultz, Dr. E. [1911] n.d. Samoan Laws Concerning the Family, Real Estate and Succession (Rev. E Bellward and R.C. Hisaioa trans.). Housed in the University of Hawai'i Pacific Collection.

Selby, H.A. 1974. *Zaptec Deviance*. Austin: University of Texas Press.

Shore, Bradd. 1977. A Samoan Theory of Action. Doctoral Dissertation. University of Chicago.

1978. Ghosts and Government. *Man* 13:175–199.

1981. Sexuality and Gender in Samoa. In *Sexual Meanings* (S. B. Ortner and H. Whitehead eds.), pp. 192–215. Cambridge: Cambridge University Press.

1982. Sala'ilua: *A Samoan Mystery*. New York: Columbia University Press.

Shweder, Richard A. and Edmund J. Bourne. 1984. Does the Concept of the Person Vary Cross-culturally? In *Cultural Conceptions of Mental Health and Therapy* (A. J. Marsella and G.M. White eds.), pp. 97–137. Dordrecht: D. Reidel.

Sinavaiana, Caroline. 1992a. Traditional Comic Theater in Samoa. Doctoral Dissertation. American Studies. University of Hawai'i at Manoa.

1992b. Where the Spirits Laugh Last: Comic Theater in Samoa. In *Clowning as Critical Practice* (W. E. Mitchell ed.), pp. 192–219. Pittsburgh: University of Pittsburgh Press.

Sloan, Donald. 1940. *The Shadow Catcher*. New York: The Book League of America.

Small, Meredith. 1993. *Female Choices*. Ithaca, NY: Cornell University Press.

Stair, Rev. John B. 1897. *Old Samoa*. London: The Religious Tract Society.

Stanner, W. E. H. 1953. *The South Seas in Transition*. Sydney: Australian Publishing Company.

Stevenson, Robert Louis. 1892. *A Footnote to History*. London: Cassell.

Stuebel, C. 1976. *Myths and Legends of Samoa*. Wellington and Apia: A. H. and A. W. Reed and Wesley Productions.

Sudarkasa, Niara. 1986. The Status of Women in Indigenous African Socities. *Feminist Studies* 12:91–104.

Sutter, Frederic K. 1980. Communal versus Individual Socialization at Home and in School in Rural and Urban Samoa. Doctoral Dissertation. University of Hawai'i.

Tedlock, Barbara 1992. *Dreaming*. Santa Fe: School of American Research.

Tuiteleleapaga, Napoleone A. 1980. *Samoa Yesterday, Today and Tomorrow*. New York: Todd and Honeywell.

Turner, George.[1861] 1986. *Selections from Nineteen Years in Polynesia: Missionary Life, Travel and Researches*. Apia: Western Samoa Historical and Cultural Trust. [reprint].

[1884] 1984. *Samoa*. London: Macmillan.

Welter, Barbara. 1966. The Cult of True Womanhood. *American Quarterly* 18:151–174 (Summer).

Wheeler, A. and W. Thompson. 1825. *An Appeal of One-Half the Human Race, Women, Against the Pretensions of the Other Half, Men, to Retain Them in Political and Thence in Civil and Domestic Slavery*. London: Longman, Hurst, Rees, Orme, Brown, and Green, R. Taylor.

Wikan, Unni. 1987. Public Grace and Private Fears: Gaiety, Offense, and Sorcery in Northern Bali. *Ethos* 15(4): 337:365.

1990. *Managing Turbulent Hearts: A Balinese Formula for Living*. Chicago: Chicago University Press.

Wilkes, Charles. 1845. *Narrative of the United States Exploring Expedition During the Years 1838, 1839, 1840, 1841, 1842*. Philadelphia: Lea and Blanchard.

Williams, John. [1830–1832] 1984. *The Samoan Journals of John Williams* (Richard M. Moyle, ed.). Canberra: Australian National University Press.

Willis, Laulii. 1889. *The Story of Laulii* (W. H. Barnes ed.). San Francisco: Jos. Winterburn.

Wright, Robert. 1994. *The Moral Animal: The New Science of Evolutionary Psychology.* New York: Pantheon Books.

Yanagisako, Sylvia J. Mixed Metaphors: Native and Anthropological Models of Gender and Kinship Domains. In *Gender and Kinship* (Jane F. Collier and Sylvia J.Yanagisako, eds.), pp. 86–119. Stanford: Stanford University Press.

Zihlman, Adrienne L. 1995. Misreading Darwin on Reproduction. In *Conceiving the New World Order* (Faye D. Ginsburg and Rayna Rapp, eds.), pp. 425–443. Berkeley: University of California Press.

Part IV

Reading power against the grain

8   Eager subjects, reluctant powers: the irrelevance of ideology in a secret New Guinea Male Cult

Harriet Whitehead

Harriet Whitehead's "Eager Subjects, Reluctant Powers" asks: do individuals universally desire power as our Western presuppositions suggest? Correlatively, is holding power over others necessarily a pleasurable prerogative? Her study of a male cult in the Mountain Ok area of Papua New Guinea exposes the tension between possessing the symbolic capital of ritual knowledge and the onerousness of actually having to hold authority. While the secrecy of ritual augments its power as a form of knowledge, this supreme power/knowledge saddles the leader with controlling a wide range of social and material phenomenon – who gets sick or stays well, how well crops and people grow, and so on. This expectation makes the social accountability and personal cost of such power quite high.

In a brief but wonderful parallel, Whitehead suggests a similarity between the recruitment of Seltaman ritual elders and the way that Chairs of Anthropology Departments must be recruited – usually most reluctantly. In both cases, the position is all the more onerous because its ostensible symbolic power carries little social clout. And in both cases, the position becomes a lightning rod for discontent. Suspicions abound that the leader is dealing darkly in administrative sorcery. Holding only a fleeting symbolic authority, the person becomes responsible for social and material misfortune that occurs during his or her tenure. Among the Seltaman, it is only when potential leaders have already borne such suspicion anyway, sometimes by simple virtue of seniority, that they are worn down and assent to assume the role, much to the relief of their cohort. In roles of both ritual and academic eminence, one also finds an ultimate lack of leaderly self-confidence that is all the more difficult to bear for the inability to publicly acknowledge it.

Again, however, such dysphoria needs to be viewed vis-à-vis the potential realpolitik of these orientations as tactical strategies among adults. If the purview of symbolic authority is coupled with unrealistic social responsibility, then its position is more likely to be shunned. However, if the duty is only to make sure that it rains eventually (perhaps for an African chief) or only to imagine some kind of nirvanic self-reincarnation (perhaps for an Indian Brahmin), then the symbolic authority of leadership is far less taxing. These are but quick and blunt comparisons. But they do suggest it is material to consider the recursive and interactional effects of social with epistemic power, and to see how these may inform a more nuanced anthropology of motivation.

More deeply, Whitehead forces us to examine what it is about the shadow as opposed to the high profile of power that makes it especially appealing. Indeed, the attractions of subordination are one of the issues that a simplistic reading of power hegemonies consistently leave out. This undermines our critical understanding of topics ranging from discipleship to anorexia, to military obedience, to a sense of academic perfectionism that can be self-defeating. It is here that psychic power most intricately reengages with power in its social and epistemic dimensions. As Frantz Fanon exposed so poignantly in *Black Skin, White Masks* (1967), there is an obvious recursive relationship between social subordination and psychic oppression. This includes the self-subordination, if not self-hate, that alternates with resistance through the humiliations of early childhood or adolescence, racism, sexism, or sexual abuse, and class or ethnic or religious castigation.

This recursive relationship between power and subordination has been productively emphasized by postcolonial scholars (e.g., Nandy 1983, 1995; Karkar 1996) and in important anthropological analyses such as that of Indian Parsi by Luhrmann (1996) or of Samoans by Jeannette Mageo (1998). It has not yet been sufficiently appreciated in mainstream psychological anthropology. This more critical awareness raises further questions about the traumas of Seltaman's own primary socialization and ritual initiation. Is their apparent pleasure in being dominated only the fruit of comfortable dependency relations in early life, as Whitehead suggests, or does it connect to earlier forms of social and psychic subordination? Further, what do ritualized desires to inflict pain in manic triumph or to endure pain as reparation/purification have to do with reproducing satisfying early dependencies? Are these desires an unavoidable by-product of that most primary dependency relationship with our mothers, as Klein argued (1984) and as Stephen demonstrates in her work on mortuary ceremonies (1998, 2000)? And what do pain, secrecy, and dependency have to do with wanting to cordon off the sexes, placing power (however empty) and knowledge (however fanciful) on one side of the gender line and not on the other?

Jeannette Mageo and Bruce Knauft

I want to discuss some potential misunderstandings concerning the power implications of cosmological notions in the Mountain Ok cultures of Papua New Guinea. I begin with the secret parts of the cosmology. Anthropologists in the Mountain Ok culture area have a tendency to become quite focused on the content of the secret myths and magic associated with the male cult in these groups (Barth 1975, 1987; Brumbaugh 1980; Jorgensen 1980, 1981, 1990), whereas I will suggest that the content is rather secondary. What deserves our focus is the character of the relationships in which these secrets are learned. The relationship of cosmology to power is the larger issue, though as we shall see power and the self become implicated quite rapidly.

The Mountain Ok culture that I studied is that of the Seltaman people, a collection of about 225 souls occupying two villages in the mid-montane rain forests of the Western Province of Papua New Guinea. They were formerly tribal; they now enjoy a mixed economy but earlier relied solely on their own horticulture, pig-raising, and foraging. They are neighbors and close kin to the Baktaman made famous by Fredrik Barth in his 1975 work, *Ritual and Knowledge among the Baktaman*. The Seltaman and Baktaman and their regional neighbors traditionally maintained a multi-leveled male initiatory cult that centered on sacrifice to the ancestors.

My starting point here is a common misunderstanding concerning the role of cosmology. This is the idea that concepts of the true – in a word, 'cosmology' – function as 'ideology,' that is as justification for social inequality in the eyes of those who might object to it ("justification" here meaning any representations that move people toward acceptance). The notion of cosmology as ideology is particularly ill-fitted to the situation of the Mountain Ok cultures, at least it is if we consider their male cult lore to be the essence of their cosmology. This is because in Seltaman and throughout the Mountain Ok area, the social inferiors in the system – youths, women, outsiders – do not know the cult oral tradition. The genealogies, the creator-being stories, the procedures for keeping and sacrificing to an ancestral bone, the recipes for truly effective sorcery, indeed virtually all higher spiritual knowledge is kept secret from the uninitiated and imparted with a surprising haphazardness even to the initiated (cf. Barth 1987). The more secret levels of cult tradition are obtained largely through apprenticeships of junior initiate to senior initiate and these relationships are quite private. There is seldom any way for the new apprentice to check his knowledge against that of diverse other men in a face-to-face situation, even should he want to, and since elders merely scoff at the reputed knowledge of their local peers, there is not much reason for him to be curious about the knowledge of anyone but his own mentor (Whitehead 1994).

To the apprentice-recipient of sacred knowledge and sacred objects, the particulars of the knowledge and the details of the sacred objects appear as scraps of a collage, the other scraps of which may remain forever the possession of someone else. A recipient of sacred knowledge will often make no effort to gain further elucidation, either in relation to his own scrap or the scraps of others. Highly initiated elders among Seltaman (three of my informants fell into this category) felt as though they themselves lacked full understanding of the tradition, that the key to the whole must be in the possession of a someone more senior than they, perhaps some elder in a different Mountain Ok community. Brumbaugh reports a comparable situation among the neighboring Feramin (Brumbaugh 1990, pers. comm.).

What is not at issue is that there is efficacious power operating in the world and that someone somewhere knows more about it than oneself. This must be the case since others can always be found who are enjoying greater prosperity than oneself. These more prosperous others must have power, or an alliance with power. The only question then is how one may enlist these more powerful other parties to one's own side. The point is not to learn sacred knowledge so that one can enjoy power. The point is to persuade another to take responsibility for the power he is presumed to have, then put oneself under his wing. Neither those who do the persuading nor the powerful parties they attempt to persuade need any cult knowledge in order to bring about the requisite relationship. Cult knowledge enters in primarily after the relationship has been formed, sustaining it, deepening it, sometimes moving it in certain directions in a manner comparable to gift-giving.

Take the matter of selecting a ritual chief, the man who alone may open the communal culthouse and who will lead the performance of all community rituals. Seltaman will look around and see who among the mature householders of advancing age enjoys consistent good fortune – good crops, good pigs, good hunting, a successful family – and deduce that this man's ancestors (*awadik*) are a generous force. This man, in other words, is himself under the wing of power. The issue now becomes how the rest of the community might find room under that same powerful wing.

If the candidate in question gets along well with members of the community, or enough of them at any rate, he will be approached to become a ritual chief and to donate a skull and forearm bone from one of his ancestors to the communal culthouse so that the entire community may benefit from the efficacy of his ancestral power. If he agrees – and many men demur because the honor is a burdensome one – his ancestral bones will be installed in the communal culthouse and the man himself installed in the office of ritual chief, *kinim em* ("sacred man"). The man in question may already keep a personal ancestral bone in a small personal culthouse, or simply hidden in his secular man-house. Or there may be some senior initiate in his extended family who happens to know where a bone can be found that technically qualifies as the "ancestor" of this potential candidate. Either way is acceptable. The point is that first one finds the candidate and gets his consent, and then one worries about hooking him up with the correct ritual and cosmological paraphernalia.

During my first visit to the Seltaman in 1987, a new communal Amyol culthouse was built and a new chief, Gilbert, was installed. Gilbert had hesitated for several weeks but finally, under pressure from an as-yet-uninitiated faction of young men and their relatives, who wanted the Amyol initiation to be performed, he agreed. As it happened, Gilbert had to retrieve previously unused ancestral bones from their hiding-place in the forest and install them in the communal culthouse. He did so at the direction of another senior, Manfred, who had more knowledge of how these things were done. The retrieval of unused bones is not unusual in these circumstances and, according to my informants, it is not unusual for the new chief to turn to greater experts for help in doing it. Finally, Gilbert, the new chief, had to be taught all of the ritual procedures and initiation methods by a different senior, Wangsep, who volunteered to be his assistant, since again Gilbert lacked the requisite know-how. In effect, the empowerment of this ritual chief began in the presumption that he had power already. The rest of the components of his office were assembled collaboratively by those who wished to put themselves under his wing.

We are brought here to a second common misconception concerning ideology. When we note the eagerness of Seltaman to pursue the 'inferior' position in a situation of status inequality, we must ask whether the assumption of the inferior position really requires any persuasion, as theorists of ideology seem to think. Undoubtedly this depends on what sort of inferior position is at issue. In Seltaman, the matter is rather clear: even fully initiated Seltaman men, when considering who should be responsible for communal rituals, tend to prefer to be under the authority of the ritual chief rather than to be chief themselves. This aspect of social inequality, eagerness for the subordinate spot, is not uncommon cross-culturally and is especially prominent in ritual and religious systems. It does not necessarily contradict the notion that people seek power over others and use appeals to an alternate religious reality in order to gain that power; rather it throws into bold relief what is emotionally appealing about the underside of a power difference. Cast in the intimate relationship that may obtain between a ritual chief and his cult membership, this power difference recapitulates the parent–child relationship. The "inferiors," in this case the ritual subjects, are conceived to be indulged and are indulged in their desire for dependency, while their spiritual hierarch – whether seen as the guardian of the ancestor or the ancestor himself – takes responsibility for their well-being and accepts blame should that well-being falter. In these sorts of authority systems, the self is never equal in power to all other parties and would not want to be, for then there would be no one to turn to.

A paradoxical corollary of such systems is that those who willingly submit to power are, by that act, engaged in a relationship of intimacy with power and intimacy with power empowers the intimate. In effect, to be subordinated, in the right way and to the right power, means to become powerful. Thus men are closer than women to the gods of Seltaman life, the ancestors, because they are intimate with the ancestors; and senior initiates for the same reason are closer than juniors. Men are thus relatively more ancestor-like than women in the eyes of the community (including the community of women), and seniors relatively more ancestor-like than juniors. As intimacy with the ancestors increases so too does the empowerment that flows therefrom. In an almost seamless transformation aging ritual seniors, especially those who are keepers of bones, come to be thought of as almost ancestors (*awadik*) themselves.

But as ritual power increases, so too does responsibility and danger. A bone-keeper, including the ritual chief of the communal culthouse, must worry that some slight offense or neglect will cause the ancestor to strike him or his family with illness. He must worry that crop failure or excessive bad weather will be blamed on his ancestor and thus indirectly on him. Many grown men told me that they would not undertake the keeping of a bone, private or communal, at least not anytime soon. "I'm too young," Peter and Mathew each said as I interviewed them on their ideas about becoming bone-keepers. (Both men would be best described as middle-aged.) Peter shrank from the idea of bone-keeping entirely and hastened to assure me that he knew nothing about his aging step-father's ritual business, despite what others might be saying. "I'll look after an ancestor when my hair turns white," Mathew interjected, to indicate that he had not ruled out the possibility entirely, "But if I did it now, I might do something wrong. I don't want the ancestor to kill me."

In a very real sense, the ultimate authority in the Seltaman ritual system is *relegated* to those cornered into being unable in good conscience to refuse it rather than seized by those eager to control their fellow man. Ritual leadership in Seltaman is rather like the chairmanship in academic departments; it is the thankless job that someone has to do, the bad banana that only mother will eat. The life cycle of the community removes one generation of seniors from a man's horizon, decreasing his opportunities for dependency on a living person senior to himself and simultaneously rotating him into the position of one of those toward whom younger men turn. Flattered but reluctant, he takes up the burden. Relieved to have found someone, the younger men settle back into the hopeful contentment of ritual subordination.

Their contentment is the positive side of an ambivalence, however. There is a negative side. Blame for misfortune seeks its outlet and the usual target in the Seltaman system are the ritual seniors. As stated, there may be community misfortunes, such as widespread crop failure, and a ritual chief may be deposed along with his ancestor if such misfortunes occur. Moreover any senior, but especially the seniors who keep bones, stands liable to the rumored accusation of *biis* or *kimon* sorcery whenever a family is stricken by a death or a crippling chronic illness. In these cases there is no public ritual recourse such as deposing the man from office because the identity of a sorcerer can never be definitively proven in the Seltaman system.

Yet rumor is a powerful force. The potential stigma of sorcery is perhaps the major reason mature men initially shrink from becoming bone-keepers. Some shrink from it until the day arrives when they learn that their name has been mentioned in connection with a sorcery-death *anyway*, something that will tend to happen if a mature man engages too often in conflict with others. Hurt and resentful, an accused mature man may then seek solace in the power of a personal ancestor and take up the guardianship of his bones. Unlike the Etoro or the Gebusi of the Papuan Plateau, who actively root out and execute their alleged death-dealers (Kelly 1994; Knauft 1985), Seltaman continue to live – uneasily – with their rumored *biis* and *kimon* practitioners. Moreover, a certain synergy operates between the attribution of sorcery and the attribution of power and knowledge, though not as much as in some New Guinea systems where men actively cultivate a sorcery reputation in order to gain respect. In Seltaman the stigma of sorcery, reaching a certain level, begins to undercut a man's position. Until it reaches that level, however, it contributes a certain sinister élan to a senior's profile in the community. Among Seltaman seniors, the evil walk among the good and one can never be quite sure who is which. Some seniors, such as Gilbert, are trusted completely. Others, such as the two men who instructed Gilbert, are both trusted and feared. A few, like Peter's step-father, are simply feared.

The larger point of all this is that ritually articulated power differences are embraced by both subordinate and superordinate with ambivalence, but nonetheless are embraced quite fiercely. For juniors the craving for guardianship, which never seriously questions that there is efficacious power in the world, continuously and fitfully seeks its resting-place in specific seniors. A 'good one' is out there somewhere, or so it is thought. For seniors, there is often in the end nowhere else to go than to the position being attributed to them, that of the authoritative, the knowledgeable, and the lethal.

Exposition of cult lore is not essential in order for us to glimpse the psychological dynamics that underlie this authority structure. These dynamics spring into action in our own and many other cultures where conditions are right. One of the most intense forms of emotional/spiritual experience, in any culture, is this bonding of self to a presumed greater Other. In his comprehensive treatise on psychologically universal dimensions of social relationality, Alan Fiske has proposed that authority-ranking is one of four basic innate cognitive schemata underlying human social life. Because the schema is in some important sense innate, the cultural forms that the schema comes to invest will be experienced as compelling, gratifying, and sensible by those raised in or willingly converted to that cultural form. At the same time, expressions of the authority schema embedded in a *different* cultural form may appear offensive to those same individuals (Fiske 1991).

Where Seltaman culture and our culture seem most discrepant in regard to relations of authority is that Western (US) culture seems, at this point in history, to have a button marked "Question Authority" whereas Seltaman culture, as yet, does not: question particular authorities, yes, but question authority in general, no. It would be misguided to pathologize this stance – as Westerners are wont to do – by comparing it to masochism or by suggesting hidden destructive family dynamics, rife throughout the population, to account for it. Except for the experience of illness, or the loss of a parent through illness, Seltaman children enjoy loving, secure, and largely unstressful childhoods. The fosterage of orphans, too, is immediate and virtually seamless. Indeed, if we wish to speculate on the psychodynamic roots of an authority-trusting people, we would be surprised to uncover widespread family dysfunction. On the contrary, it is likely that the very security and reliability of adult–child bonds in the Seltaman world "lowers the bar," so to speak, for the establishment of trusted hierarchy.

To return to our point about ideology: an exposition of Seltaman secret cult lore is not essential for us to glimpse the deep premises underlying the Seltaman authority structure, for these premises appear in Seltaman life widely and publicly. The idea that there is efficacious power in the world is bound up with the perception that some people prosper while others do not. An ineluctable power is never far away from those who are prospering. Over the course of the decade of my visits to Seltaman much of the perceived power shifted from village seniors to a younger generation of prosperous mine-workers living in the mining town of Tabubil. Power gravitated as well to the two literate villagers who served as liaisons between the town-dwelling mineworkers and village life. This cohort of men were initially not more knowledgeable in sacred lore than their seniors, they had simply become astoundingly well off! But sacredness followed on the heels of this. Some of these newly empowered men had reputed vision experiences.

Thomas, for instance, had lain in a coma for days following a mining accident and word spread that he had visited *sapkal am*, the land of the dead, during that time. A "modernized" version of *sapkal am* – complete with roads, cars, and money-filled banks – emerged from his and his contemporaries visions. When he eventually invited an elderly uncle to move into town and live with him, bringing traditional ritual paraphernalia with him, it became obvious to others that a discipleship was in progress and that some merger of old and new forms of sacredness was afoot. Another mine-worker, Tom, had a workplace buddy who had experienced repeated visions telling the location of gold deposits in the Tabubil area. Tom and his visionary companion eventually launched an ambitious gold-mining cargo-cult movement that was in full cry at the time of my last visit. In effect, the visions and dreams of this cohort of men have been putting into circulation new imaginings of sacredness and spiritual efficacy. Along with this, these newly influential men also had begun to attract attributions of sorcery. Specifically, the Tabubil mine-workers together with the two educated village leaders were collectively blamed for a rash of deaths (mainly among the elderly) that occurred around the time of the completion of the Seltaman airstrip. With this defining sorcery moment, these new men became, as village seniors to a great extent still are, the objects of a wide-ranging ambivalence. Both an awestruck vulnerable trust and an insidious paranoia characterized villagers relations toward them.

The premise that power flows from a relationship with death and with the dead is also understood widely by all Seltaman. Coarse versions of this premise, such as the idea that overseas companies that manufacture "tin fish" (canned mackerel) sometimes carelessly let human body parts, the source of their power, get into the tins, circulate as urban legends in the mining town. I was occasionally asked to confirm the conviction most already held that whiteskins know how to use human bones or the skin of dead men to make powerful medicines. (I didn't confirm it but that didn't seem to matter.) Less trivially, the rash of Seltaman deaths near the time of airstrip completion was explained as arising from the accused cohort's need for the flesh and bones of dead men to make medicine for effecting the completion. In these formulations we see a literalistic interpretation of the powers of the dead, namely, one needs their body parts to make efficacious magic. We see too the inference that prosperity goes to those who are willing to create body parts – that is, to kill.

But the dead work in other ways as well, as beneficent spiritual alters. In Seltaman dreams and visionary experiences, big portions of which are not secret, the power of the dead is portrayed as the bounty of the known deceased who have gone to dwell in *sapkal am* ("ghost place"), the world of the dead. Visits, in dream or vision, to *sapkal am* are occasions for meeting deceased loved ones, particularly fathers, who inevitably heap cash upon the visitor, cash that he is, through some quirk of fate, unable to bring back to the world of the living (*amal am*). A common cargo-cult theme throughout the Min area is that the ancestors have been trying for years to mail gifts to their descendants through the post, but outsiders – people in the Port Moresby post office and expatriate residents – systematically divert the packages.

The traditional secret cult lore of the Seltaman, most of which will not be recounted here, can be seen as a pre-contemporary version of these same themes. Sacred lore has, I am hypothesizing, always played upon ideas that were already in earnest circulation. It plays upon them by asserting that there is indeed a world of the dead and that world has special names and a specific geography; munificent spiritual alters who can be entreated for wealth and they too have special names and require particular procedures; and that one key to wealth is an apprenticeship in death-dealing sorcery using specific techniques. It is the specificity of the secret lore, against the background of general belief, that gives it its frisson. That, and a few surprises: death itself and much of ritual was given to men by a woman, the Ancestress, Afek. She, in turn, has her secret names and her specific geography and history.

In other words, there *is* an alternate reality. Some people know it in very specific detail. They may have been taught it; they may have received bits of it in visions. Either way, there is no question in anybody's mind that it is there. Through initiation men become eligible to learn tidbits of the lore and by doing so experience the thrill of the specificity of this alternate reality. A deeper emotional involvement in this world becomes available to them, although they need not take it up.

Another ethnographic case from a Western culture may help illuminate the situation of a Seltaman sacred learner. The French ethnographer and folklorist Jeanne Favret-Saada discovered a largely hidden (secretly believed sometimes and publicly denied always) system of witchcraft among peasants in the dairy-farming area of France (the Bocage). This was not revealed to Favret-Saada until she confusedly agreed to assume one of the positions within the system, that of the *unwitcher* of a Bocage family undergoing a crisis of misfortune. Had she not inadvertently stepped into this position no one would have spoken to her of witchcraft, for to speak about it is to be, in local parlance, "caught" by it, that is, drawn into real belief with the possibility of suffering bewitchment. As Bocage residents put it, "The less one talks the less one is caught" (Favret-Saada 1980:65–91). No one would want to take the risk of enchantment if they did not conceive themselves to be stricken already and in need of help, and certainly no one would want to take the risk for a disinterested party, such as a researcher, but only for a potential helper. Finally, then, to be talking about witchcraft at all was to be engaging with people in a victim–supporter relationship based on shared agreements and evolving shared fantasies. To be chosen as someone's unwitcher during a moment of crisis was comparable in a way to being chosen as a secret paramour: a world of joint fantasy and fear was engaged and this was entirely screened from the view of outsiders. The actual content of the shared secrets could be, within certain constraints of genre, anything that fit the situation. Favret-Saada writes:

> The content of the secret (the utterance) is for the most part neither here nor there: it does not matter whether one is told to pierce an ox-heart, twist steel nails, or recite misappropriated Christian prayers. Magicians know this when they quietly say: "*to each one his secret*", and show themselves in no hurry to increase their knowledge. For what makes an unwitcher is his "*force*" ... The power of the magician ... places him in the position of recognized avenger ... but on condition that he openly declares his readiness to assume this position. (Favret-Saada 1980:19)

There are many comparisons here with Seltaman men's involvement with cult secrets. Seltaman elders also seem to adopt the attitude "to each one his secret" and show themselves in no hurry to increase their knowledge. For the secret of the Seltaman revealer of cult secrets is his willingness to assume the authoritative role. Further, learning of sacred secrets cannot be separated from the relationship in which the transmission of secrets unfolds, that is, a junior's discipleship to a senior who has solicited this engagement. This is a relationship in which the junior is implicitly expected to support the senior in mundane affairs, from construction tasks to village factional disputes, while the senior, at his leisure, hands over bit by bit stories, magical procedures, and ancestral relics. Stephen C. Leavitt has written about secret sharing among another Papua New Guinea group: "The sharing of the secret suggests a deep and unspoken communication; it conveys an ambiance of brotherhood and harmony. The emotional significance of the secret grows with the increased need for such a feeling of solidarity" (Leavitt 1995). So we see that the need for this deeply assuring solidarity is not one-sided, but, rather, springs from the senior's needfulness as surely as from the junior's.

The ideal senior mentor for a man is his own father, but because of the high mortality rate in the Seltaman bush villages many individuals are orphaned before they are adolescent. Consequently this sort of discipleship, when it does occur – and it is entirely voluntary – often springs up between more distantly related partners. Expressed within this discipleship is a combination of paternalism and sporadically frightening dominance. This same emotional–relational combination appears within the ancestral cult at virtually every juncture. It obtains between an individual bone-keeper and his personal ancestor, between the ritual chief and the culthouse ancestor, between men and ancestors generically, and between the senior and junior grades of men. It is the believed-in relational bond in Seltaman male life. If we are to claim that the ideas found in cult lore support this sort of relationship, it is equally the case that this relationship supports the continued meaningfulness of cult lore, and with this the meaningfulness of its continued transmission. A man does not begin to hear cult knowledge at all or eventually have the opportunity to become deeply "caught" by this cult knowledge unless he enters into relationships of this sort – minimally as a junior initiate in relation to the seniors or, additionally, as a disciple in relation to a mentor.

While I was aware of three or four specific mentor–disciple relationships over the course of my visits to the Seltaman, my closest view of the "inside" of such a relationship came when the ritual senior, Walter, who agreed to share some Seltaman secrets with me, elected as his translator one of my assistants, a rather unstable older bachelor, Jerome, who was – by a twist of fate – the only fluent translator available who was also ritually qualifed to hear what Walter had to say. After the first few sessions I began to realize that a relationship had sprung up between Walter and Jerome that had not existed before. Jerome was helping Walter in his gardens, Walter was making hints about giving his daughter in marriage to Jerome. Meanwhile, in our sessions together, Jerome had begun to glow with a new excitement as he saw places where my whiteskin knowledge could be woven together with Walter's traditional knowledge to produce uncanny connections. Jerome suddenly had two mentors – myself and Walter. He had fallen, at least temporarily, into the same spiritual project as the Tabubil mine-workers, one of effecting a tantalizing mediation between the new outside power-knowledge and the revered ancestral power-knowledge. Meanwhile Walter had two disciples – myself and Jerome. Amused by our eagerness, he played his cards cagily. Seeing the drift of our interest, he supplied relevant – or what seemed to him relevant – further tidbits. After especially fruitful sessions he appeared at my house later with fresh demands for smokes, food, cash.

Even though they are aware of and believe in the same general premises as the men, Seltaman women do not get to hear cult secrets or to enter into a mentor–disciple relationship in which these secrets take on hidden life. Moreover, I will suggest – though it is very difficult to prove – that the authority relationship that obtains between Seltaman menfolk and Seltaman womenfolk has a different flavor from that which obtains, within the cult, between men and men. Women seem to experience men's authority on a more matter-of-fact plane and men to exercise this authority over women (and children) more matter-of-factly. While Seltaman women have some fear of men in groups, that is, men in their male exclusive sociality mode, and they have some fear of the ancestors, they are not exposed to the fright lore and the physical intimidation that is poured onto the junior males in initiation. And while women too want responsible persons more knowledgeable than themselves to look out for them, they have no occasion to be seduced, as junior males may be, into the too-good-to-be-true fantasy world of cult power secrets. Both the succour and the dread conjured up by the cult occupy an experiential inner sanctum to which women are never admitted.

The point that introduced this chapter is that Seltaman secret cult lore does not constitute a form of "ideology," a set of ideas that persuade persons toward subordinate relationships within a system of inequality. I would now argue for extending this point to the publically available beliefs to which cult lore attaches itself: that power resides outside the self, ultimately outside the community of the living; that differences in prosperity indicate differential access to these outside forces; and perhaps implicitly that personal relationship is the source of everything. These are ideas that seem to well up from every crevice of Seltaman life even as they saturate it in turn. In no direct way do they spell out a justification for oppressive inequality. On the contrary, they present to all and sundry the seductive possibility that there is no immediate need for power of one's own, as long as one is able to successfully cultivate relationships to those who have access to such powers. This notion of power, embraced by male and female Seltaman alike, bears a rather striking resemblance to the acquiescent doctrines that once surrounded women's role in Western society. A woman's only concern, it was believed, should be to maintain successful bonds with her menfolk. The menfolk then take care of all those functions – necessary to a woman's life – that require greater physical strength, greater worldly education, and greater social influence. There is no particular "love of subordination" expressed in such a stance. Rather, what stands out is a distaste for risk, arduous labor, and social blame.

So too for the crucial status and power divisions in Seltaman life. Senior male power presents itself to both women and junior men as carrying a formidable downside. Access to it entails participation in torturous high-risk ordeals that may lead, after many years, to frightening responsibilities. Several Seltaman women made it clear to me in conversations regarding the male cult that they thanked their lucky stars for their female gender assignment. Of course the majority of persons of both sexes, worldwide, seem to recruit rather easily to their gender assignment, however irrationally, so it is hard to know how much weight to give these claims. Seltaman boys too look forward to fulfilling gender expectations. Nevertheless, when the subject of becoming a man was discussed in relation to initiation, there was no hint of the carefree enthusiasm for one's gender found among the women. Rather, some of my adolescent male acquaintances anticipated the prospect of initiation rather in the way a Westerner might look forward to chemotherapy. They told themselves it was in their best interests, that other men had endured it, and that furthermore it was unavoidable, but they were quietly very frightened. One or two confessed to being on the point of tears just thinking about it.

Yet we cannot dismiss the presence of more positive motives for initiation, separable in some degree from pure gender identity strivings. Some of the Tabubil workmen, for instance, had never passed through Amyol initiation and they resented being left out of a traditonal prestige channel that other men back in the village could claim. The result was that they pressured the villagers into staging the initiation at a time convenient for themselves, though out of phase for the smaller village boys. A second motive, "positive" in a certain perverse way, was revealed by one of my closer village acquaintances, who wanted to progress through the initiation grades in order to learn sorcery. My jaw dropped when he explained this since this was a shocking admission for any Seltaman to make, and the more so from this mild-mannered an well-regarded young man. Yes, he assured me: that was his interest. "Many members of my family have been killed by sorcery [he itemized them, most were long dead], and no one has done anything about it. Well, its time for payback." Another man credited his youthful cousin with similar motives. I am guessing that sorcery ambition is not as rare among Seltaman men as they would have their fellow villagers believe. Below the amiable surface of Seltaman community life lurks a veritable netherworld of sorcery suspicions and sorcery-inspired hatreds. Losses, especially family deaths, let loose the demon of blame in Seltaman society with the result that most families carry a burden of unsatisfied grudges. Rather like the witchcraft beliefs in the Bocage this sorcery-riddled netherworld is one that a Seltaman taps into only when in a certain frame of mind – in other moods, he mocks its breezily – but when it is tapped into this netherworld readily joins up with the hidden world of sacred male knowledge. A man cannot sorcerize effectively, or garden or pig-raise or found a thriving family succesfully, without the help of an ancestor and he cannot acquire the knowledge to enlist an ancestor without the help of a senior mentor; furthermore, initiation is what qualifies a man to hear what a senior mentor has to say.

Thus it would not be inapt to say that in the Seltaman case, and in the Bocage witchcraft situation as well, a sort of frightened eagerness characterizes the way in which many youths seek involvement in the very subordinate relationships one would have thought required persuasion. This is not to suggest that every part of involvement in the male ancestral cult is purely voluntary, or rushed into with frightened eagerness. Coercion is certainly present in the induction of the youngest boys, those between 10 and 12 years old, into the very first stage of male initiation, *daksal*. But once junior males are set on the initiatory path it is often they, as an age cohort, who solicit further stages of initiation from the older age sets rather than their elders imposing these cruel ordeals upon them.

In the end, the cult secrets provide senior and junior with an idiom through which the junior's attachment to an actual person, his mentor, typically a senior kinsman, is gradually transferred to a supernatural guardian, the ancestor. As the senior kinsman teaches his former dependant (often his own son) the rules for tapping into ancestral power, he is erecting a supernatural force in his own stead. All the while he is stepping down from his own position as parent and gradually assuming toward the younger man the position of child. Simultaneously, the junior partner is gradually cutting his emotional ties to his living but fading elder kinsman and directing his dependencies toward that point in imaginary space that his elder partner will soon occupy but that is now occupied by the father's father, the ghostly protector, his *awadik*. The fading elder, as the transmitter of ritual secrets, becomes in effect the gateway to his own transmogrification. The fading elder is no sooner nominated as powerful by a hopeful junior than he begins the slow process of transferring his powers to the junior and grows dependent upon him in turn. In this entire cycle of relationality, power, really effective power, continues to reside outside the self. The self's strivings are predominantly oriented to establishing and maintaining an intimate relationship with this power.

Discussion

This chapter began with the argument that the secret particulars within the Seltaman cosmology are not suitably viewed as a "justification" of an oppressive regime, and by logic could not be, since the oppressed do not learn these particulars. Indeed many of the privileged satisfy themselves with only a sketchy knowledge of these particulars and either await the whim of others for further enlightenment or actually avoid such enlightenment for fear of burdensome consequences. As the argument unfolded, it became possible to add that even those widely held, public ideas into which the secret cosmology taps are not suitably viewed as "justifications" for social inequality. The ideas – that power resides outside the self, ultimately outside the community of the living, that differences in prosperity among the living indicate differential access to these outside powers and, deepest of all, the idea that relationship is the source of everything – are "explanations" of social inequality, perhaps, but with no particular hint of justification. Rather, such notions represent a common and spontaneous wish to the effect that there is no immediate need for power of one's own as long as one is able successfully to cultivate and maintain relationships to others who have access to power.

If we break this position down into its component parts, we see that there are three links in the chain, any of which may be broken and cause the position to – at least in theory – collapse. It will render the Seltaman position less mysterious if we compare the degree of breakage in these links between Seltaman and ourselves. First, there is the component that efficacious power relates itself to individuals who then prosper as a result. Prosperity is not statistically random. And the roots of prosperity are neither complex nor multifactorial. Rather, prosperity has a singular pre-eminent detectable source. Are we Westerners such a contrast to the Seltaman in this regard? I think not. In fact, it is very hard in even the most educated circles of industrially complex cultures to persuade people that prosperity has either a great degree of randomness (indeed social scientists would dispute this point) or that the complexities of achieving it greatly outstrip individual control. Rather, Westerners too favor a singular preeminent detectable source for a person's prosperity: his/her own initiative and hard work. Only when this explanation seems inapt in regard to a particular case do we tend to invoke "connections," but cynically. The lazy but prosperous person must have them, that's all there is to it. It would seem then that the singular pre-eminent source of prosperity argument, entirely intact among Seltaman, is also relatively intact among Westerners.

The second component, which is the location of the source of prosperity, appears hugely different. The pre-eminent source resides in "an Other" for Seltaman, but in "the Self" for Westerners. True, earlier centuries of Westerners considered a bond with a higher Other critical for an individual's success; the various Protestant doctrines even resembled Seltaman thinking inasmuch as the developing relationship between Christian and God was seen as imbuing the Self with qualities necessary for success, which for the Seltaman was sacred knowledge and for the Westerner was types of inner resolve. Moving into contemporary mores, however, Christian reliance on a higher power seems to be articulated more in terms of psychological comfort rather than in terms of worldly prosperity. The contemporary Western inner resources thought necessary for worldly prosperity have a more secular ring: grit, ambition, "motivation," self-starterhood, even a healthy dose of overweening narcissism. Reliance on powerful others indicates weakness. When we do cite a person's "connections" in explaining his or her good fortune, there is a pejorative twist. When the reliance is on a god it amounts to an even more radical breach of the popular consensus by suggesting that the believer is actually a fatalist who accepts the random distribution of fortune, expressed as this god's will.

This dominant cultural difference between Seltaman and Westerners over the location of good fortune's source is all of a piece with the final component: the bonding strategy. Logically, if the source of prosperity is an Other, one must rely on a relationship with that Other to obtain prosperity. Seltaman Other-reliance again contrasts with Western self-reliance. But there is more here than the Self and Other contrast. There is the implied capacity for trusting in relationships, specifically in relationships between non-equals, that seems to pertain in the Seltaman case and not in the Western. There would seem to be a very obvious synergy between this capacity for trusting in non-equal, essentially "authority," relationships and a people's cultural endorsement of such relationships. I would suggest, speculatively, that the Seltaman, historically and collectively, in their childhoods and in their adulthoods, have had better experience in the durability and permanence of close caring relational bonds than have contemporary Western culture-makers, who operate an economy that is extremely corrosive of permanence and tight affiliations of every sort. It is emotionally plausible to Seltaman that help lies in authority relationships. It is a good deal less so to we Westerners. We struggle against our inclinations to hero-worship, follow a guru, and other such follies because our personal histories and collective recent social histories have taught us to culturally discredit, rather than to endorse, these chimeras of hope.

REFERENCES

Barth, Fredrik. 1971. Tribes and Intertribal Relations in the Fly Headwaters. *Oceania* 41:3.
    1975. *Ritual and Knowledge Among the Baktaman*. New Haven, CT: Yale University Press.
    1987. *Cosmologies in the Making: A Generative Approach to Cultural Variation in Inner New Guinea*. Cambridge: Cambridge University Press.
Brumbaugh, Robert. 1980. A Secret Cult in the West Sepik Highlands. Unpublished Ph.D. thesis, SUNY Stony Brook.
Fanon, Frantz. 1967. *Black Skin, White Mask* (Charles L. Markmann, trans.). New York: Grove Press.
Favret-Saada, Jeanne. 1980. *Deadly Words: Witchcraft in the Bocage*. Cambridge: Cambridge University Press.
Fiske, Alan Page. 1991. *Structures of Social Life: The Four Elementary Forms of Human Relations*. New York: The Free Press.

Jorgensen, Dan. 1980. What's in a Name: The Meaning of Meaninglessness in Telefolmin. *Ethos* 8:349–366.

1981. Taro and Arrows: Order, Entropy, and Religion among the Telefolmin. Unpublished Ph.D. thesis, Anthropology and Sociology, University of British Columbia.

1990. Secrecy's Turns. *Canberra Anthropology* 13(1):40–47.

Karkar, Sudhir. 1996. *The Colors of Violence: Cultural Identities, Religion, and Conflict.* Chicago: University of Chicago Press.

Kelly, Raymond C. 1994. *Constructing Inequality: The Fabrication of a Hierarchy of Virtue Among the Etoro.* Ann Arbor: University of Michigan Press.

Klein, Melanie. 1984. *The Psycho-Analysis of Children.* New York: Macmillan.

Knauft, Bruce. 1985. *Good Company and Violence.* Berkeley: University of California Press.

Leavitt, Stephen C. 1995. Political Domination and the Absent Opressor: Images of Europeans in Bombita Arapesh Narratives. *Ethnology* 34:177–189.

Luhrmann, Tanya M. 1996. *The Good Parsi : the Fate of a Colonial Elite in a Postcolonial Society.* Cambridge, MA: Harvard University Press.

Mageo, Jeannette Marie. 1998. *Theorizing Self in Samoa.* Ann Arbor: Michigan University Press.

Nandy, Ashis. 1983. *The Intimate Enemy: Loss and Recovery of Self under Colonialism.* Delhi: Oxford University Press.

1995. *The Savage Freud and Other Essays on Possible and Retrievable Selves.* Oxford: Oxford University Press.

Stephen, Michele. 1998. Consuming the Dead: A Kleinian Perspective on Death Rituals Cross-Culturally. *International Journal of Psychoanalysis* 79:1–21.

2000. Reparation and the Gift. Ethos 28(2): .

Whitehead, Harriet. 1993. Morals, Models and Motives: A Rumination on Alan P. Fiske's *Structures of Social Life. Ethos* 21:3.

1994. The Gender of Birds in a Mountain Ok Culture. In *Naturalizing Power* (Sylvia Yanagisako and Carol Delaney, eds.). New York: Routledge.

9   Feminist emotions

Catherine Lutz

Catherine Lutz's "Feminist Emotions" documents the late-twentieth-century history of feminist scholarly discourse on emotion. This discourse is counter-hegemonic: it shares (problematically) the terms of a dominant discourse that emotionalizes women and femininity. Yet "feminist emotions" have also provoked novel reflections on how self-conceptualization and meaningful agency are narrowed by received wisdom concerning power itself. Do people exercise agency only as self-interested strategists or, potentially, can they exercise agency through what we termed in the introduction "psychic power" – that is, through expansions of the ways our feelings and our bodies cut against the grain of epistemic power? As in Ewing's and Mageo's chapters, but in a more abstract key, feminist discourse on emotion shows how internalized self-constructions can be played back against themselves with surprising repercussions for social and epistemic power.

Feminist identifications of emotion as a source of resistance parallel but are opposed to the American feminization and domesticated disempowerment of women in so-called "family values." This latter form of emotionalizing women/femininity can be seen as a current complement of the affectless phallus-power of the hyper-masculine supervillains in Allison's chapter. Yet feminist discourse on emotion shows how identification with a disempowering attribution can be transformed into an effective medium through which marginalized people, women among them, critique the dominant group.

As Lutz suggests, it is extremely important to consider emotion-discourse reflectively as its own commentary on power relations. It is significant that this discourse of self-awareness and creativity is, in various ways, both Western in various post-James Clifford feminist persuasions *and* ethnographically "indigenous" in different world areas. Lutz argues that our analysis of self and power needs to encourage further dialog that considers how these designations themselves may be re-viewed and critically responded to by other audiences and constituencies. As in Lutz's example, cultural analyses need to deconstruct unexamined forms of power and to conclude by re-opening rather than trying to reach conceptual closure.

At least within anthropology, what used to be the feminist margin is nearer to the center than it used to be.[1] This may not be as dramatic as the irony of Bourdieu's *Homo Academicus* (1988), in which he diagrams his work as at the margins at the same time as he is becoming central in French social science. But there *is* a sense that the "center" Lutz describes is being deeply troubled and re-formed by consideration of feminist critiques even if it is in no way being supplanted by them. Reciprocally, there is a danger that the seeming "success" of gender studies in anthropology and in the academy more generally risks blunting rather than sharpening the edge of gendered and sexual critique. The "mainstreaming" of gender studies, including psychological anthropology, makes all the more necessary the critical self-awareness that Lutz develops.

The different feminist responses identified by Lutz can be seen as addressing various dimensions of power and disempowerment as epistemically encoded in mainstream academic emotion-discourse. Critically understanding women's apparent acceptance of subordination in certain ethnographic locales, for example, speaks to power as subjectivation, whereas asking why women are considered the emotional gender speaks to power in epistemic terms of academic nominalization and the power of category-attribution. In contrast, critically re-gendered analyses of infant/child socialization relate especially to power in its psychic dimensions, whereas viewing power as an epistemic resource articulates especially with social resistance in terms of individual and collective political agency. The same is arguably true of a more critical feminist awareness concerning emotion as life on the social margins. In short, the various feminist responses delineated by Lutz have interesting relations and counter-relations to contemporary conceptualizations of society and the self all along the scales of power.

                                                  Jeannette Mageo and Bruce Knauft

One of the earliest projects of second-wave, mainly white, feminists was to detail and rebel against the use of the power of science and its predecessor experts to construct and deform the self or "personality" of "the woman." This authoritatively pieced-together woman clearly had something other than the capacities of the fully human as normatively construed (Hochschild 1975; Broverman, Broverman, and Clarkson 1970; Ehrenreich and English 1978). Broverman, Broverman, and Clarkson, for example, surveyed clinicians and found that they associated emotionality with normal female functioning and with deficient human (sex unspecified) functioning. Ehrenreich and English (1978) traced the history of expert thought which posited great risks for women who pursued schooling – risks which arose from competition between a woman's uterine and brain functions, expansion of the latter supposedly leading to contraction of the former. When we ask whose emotions have been considered problematic, at least throughout the last century in the US, we find it is the *sine qua non* of many forms of deviance. Havelock Ellis (1929) was one of a long line of commentators who drew on the idea that among women, "as among children, savages, and nervous subjects," the emotions are dominant and inferior reflexes.

With the comparative insight anthropology has afforded into alternative self systems and emotion discourses in societies around the world (e.g. Dalton, chapter 6 and Mageo, chapter 7), its cultural construal in the twentieth-century West has become clearer: emotion has been considered an unfortunate block to rational thought, a link to bodily nature, and a route to certain kinds of social virtue. The power of this idea is multifarious. One of the important aspects of this power is its ability to help position women in unwaged work in the household. This is a key accomplishment of both the positive and the negative valuation of emotion and its association with women: the empathetically emotional woman could be seen as the "angel of the house," quickly transformed into a problem in the workplace where she would react oversensitively to the rough and tumble of commerce and workforce discipline. In line with this, feminists have also homed in on anger as the one emotion exempted from this gender association (Gottlieb 1988), using it as a key index of when or in what contexts women can make claims for respect (Spelman 1989). In this regard Frye (1983) usefully draws attention to what she calls the "uptake" of women's anger, that is, society's recognition of its having occurred and/or having occurred legitimately. This feminist insight places emotions within a fully social view of power.

Feminists have also stepped back from the question of emotion *per se* to build a more fundamental critique of the "non-accidental ideology" of abstract individualism on which psychologizing about women has been based (Scheman 1980), even including most feminist psychology (Fine and Gordon 1991). The notion that the 'personal is political' has been critiqued from this perspective: it has been heard by some people to suggest that emotional change (or personal life) can or should constitute the whole of feminist political work (see Chun 1995 for a contrasting Chinese feminist perspective on this relationship). Therapeutic industries have grown faster than feminist organizing in the West, as newly valorized or politicized emotions are not understood as connected to or subsidiary to organized communities of feminist activism.

Black and Chicana feminists noted that those cultural and scientific definitions were often tacitly descriptions of white womanhood, describing the privileged servitude of a class of white women in wealthy households (Collins 1991; Hull, Scott, and Smith 1982). The distinctive qualities that defined black women under slavery and into the late twentieth century in popular culture are framed less psychologically and more in terms of physical attributes (such as inflated sexuality and 'deviant' morphology [Gilman 1986]) and of moral character (such as an emasculating tendency and a propensity to leisure and/or self-sacrifice [Collins 1991]). Feminist theorizing about emotions has often exercised the power of white privilege to ignore the non-unitary nature of the category "woman" (Spelman 1991). This is evident in the focus on women's love for other women (Smith-Rosenberg 1975) and their orientation toward caring for others (Noddings 1984; Ruddick 1989), to the near-exclusion of attention to women's anger at or dismissive feelings towards other women (Spelman 1991; Burack 1994), often on the basis of race, class, or sexual orientation (Lam 1994). It is also evident in the fuller development of non-individualist frameworks within black feminism (e.g. Collins 1991).

What follows contrasts feminist and normative approaches to the emotions. Feminist approaches are distinguished by their attention to the material, institutional and cultural capillaries of power through which discourses of emotion operate. Normative approaches restrict their questions to the limited power that emotion – as culturally and conventionally defined in Western academic circles – has to shape individual behavior. I go on to discuss the main varieties of feminist definitions and explorations of emotion. While any number of other sortings are possible, the following six types are examined: feminist rereadings of developmental emotion dynamics, emotion as authentic femininity, emotion as epistemic resource, emotion as cultural discourses on power, emotion as social labor, and emotion as life on the social margins. Finally, I speculate about the place of feminist approaches to emotion in the broader context of late twentieth-century knowledge production about emotions.

Feminist and normative approaches to knowledge about emotions

While the approaches taken to emotion by feminists have been varied, they share critical and pragmatic purposes. They are critical in the sense that they redefine what is worth knowing about emotions, asking new questions and questioning the interests served by the old questions. They are pragmatic in the sense of aiming to apply the new questions and their answers to benefit women's (and men's) lives.

Traditional philosophy of science and current normal science argue that all rational persons can imagine and ask any question of nature or social life. Nature, not social context, suggests the questions. In this framework, it matters not at all where a question comes from – only whether the answer is right. Scientific method begins not with how something is discovered, but with how a proposition, once discovered, is tested for its truth value. Scientific questions usually purport to identify some of the most crucial problems requiring investigation. Even those who see themselves as doing basic, non-applied science would usually claim to be working on questions that help to define the essence or central features of a phenomenon like emotion. The work is meant to help to define the object of study in a way that applied or practical science will then want to, even have to, use.

Feminism's challenge to this view has been this: which questions are asked is as constitutive of what we end up knowing as how we test any tentative answers. Harding (1987) has pointed out that the problems that prompt scientific questions do not occur in the abstract. They occur *to* people and they are distributed differentially across social groups. To ask a question, then, is often to identify what the problem looks like from a particular social position. And the questions different social groups have wanted answered about emotion are often different. Oppressed groups, for example, want to know how to change the conditions they live with and how to alleviate the pain they feel on that account.

The questions normative science has asked about emotion in the last several decades have included the following: "How do children become 'improperly attached' to their mothers (but not their fathers)?" "What have mothers done to produce this emotional complex in their children?" "Are women better than men at recognizing facial expressions of emotion?" "Where in or on the body can one identify anger, disgust, fear, etc.?" "How do college students' moods shift around the cycle of the academic year?" "Is disgust universal?" "What are the emotional symptoms of menopause and what drug best treats them?" "What percentage of the female population has angry mood swings as a result of suffering from PMS?" "What emotional disturbances accompany or constitute Late Luteal Phase Dysphoric Disorder (a newly defined disease which constitutes a kind of super-PMS)?"

By the early 1970s feminists were pointing out how many questions about the self had *not* been asked. They were the questions that women would have been asking and some of them were the queries that specifically racial minority women would have been constructing had they been included in the academic debates (they certainly were asking questions privately, in fictional form, and in on-the-ground political and other practical activities [Collins 1991]). These previously unpublished questions included: "Why have women been considered the emotional gender?" "Why has emotion generally been pathologized, and pathology emotionalized, and normality masculinized?" "Why have men's moods and hormonal levels not been examined?" (Gottlieb 1990) "How have black and working-class women felt about their assigned place in society?" "What are the emotional defenses white and wealthy women have employed in their relations with less privileged women?" (Spelman 1991) "Why is anger an emotion considered relatively more inappropriate for women than for men by most in the US?" "How cross-culturally does a different gender division of labor influence women's prestige and self esteem?" "How would different social structures and a different allocation of social respect between women and men influence the likelihood of women fearing rape or other violence against their persons throughout their lives?" (Sanday 1990) "Where does the emotional force for male sexual violence come from?" "Why have so many men found childcare and housework so distasteful?" (Perin 1988). "What are the consequences of a political discourse in the US that is centered on questions of proper masculinity and emotional states in leaders?" "What are the emotional contexts of frequent male resistance to contraception?"

The questions feminists have asked are rarely inquiries into what most would consider basic or universal aspects of emotion. In emotion study, the call for basic research and the terms of its definition can seem orthogonal to women's concerns or even hostile to them. The fact is that for many scientists the most fundamental, basic, or important knowledge one can have about emotions concerns the psychobiological, not the psychosocial, processes. When the psychobiological both defines the emotions and sets a national research agenda as it does, the social world and a critique of it shrinks to insignificance or invisibility. Feminist analysis of emotion points out the power or interests served by normative work on emotions, and demonstrates just how partial it is in the two senses of that term (see also Scheper-Hughes, chapter 2).

Varieties of feminist emotion work

Feminist work is comprised of a large and diverse set of voices. What I do here is to summarize the varieties of feminist work on emotion I am most familiar with, which is mainly American academic work in or primarily drawing on psychology, anthropology, sociology, history, and philosophy. Feminist film and literary theory has also been concerned with the nature of the female subject, and has drawn extensively on psychoanalytic theory, but in a more limited number of cases with emotions *per se* (Cvetkovich 1992; Miller 1991; Silver 1991; Tompkins 1985). These have tended to focus on the questions of sentimentalism or melodrama in literature and film and on how affect in consumers and producers of that material is evaluated by critics. There is also a large and growing literature in history and cultural studies on this subject (Brumberg 1997; Cancian 1987; Ehrenreich 1983; Pfister and Schnog 1997; Rotundo 1989; Stearns 1992), although it is focused almost entirely on the US and Europe.

Feminist rereadings of developmental emotion dynamics

One of the earliest kinds of feminist retheorization of the self, this theme in feminism is psychoanalytic and has worked to reanalyze the emotional dynamics of gender. These approaches have treated emotional life as a central feature of gender identity and of gender relations. Unlike traditional psychoanalytic approaches, however, they foreground the potentially variable social power of women and men, and they treat the parent–child relationship less as a timeless crucible of gender identity and more as a social and historical institution (Benjamin 1988; Chodorow 1978). This work has been involved not just in rereading the family dynamic itself, but in analyzing its correlates in the emotional aspects of popular and literary culture. It has included explorations of the psychodynamic underpinnings of the demonization of women in Hollywood films like *Working Girl* and *Cocktail* (Traube 1992), explained Peewee Herman's gender ambivalence (Modleski 1991), and traced the historical and cultural contexts of the associations between women, mass culture, and sentimentality (Cvetkovich 1992; Modleski 1991).

The key feminist work in emotional development has been Jessica Benjamin's (1988), who takes as her central problem the question of how women can come to feel pleasure from being dominated by others or, in other words, how emotional life is deformed so as to allow women to participate in their own subordination. She treats cultural myths of women (as essentially masochistic, as natural, etc.) as important but insufficient sources of women's feelings about themselves, desire, and power. Social learning of feminine ideals of the self and affect cannot account for what she sees as a result, not the cause, of the propensity of women to experience "pleasurable fantasies of erotic submission" (1988:81). This perspective runs parallel to Mageo's and Knauft's introductory insight about how both (patriarchal) power and the self as culturally constituted by domination "can each produce distortive knowledge about the world." In contrast to MacKinnon and Griffin, Benjamin sees the problem not as the imposition of a male pornographic, sadomasochistic imagination and practice, but as the repression of women's sociability and social agency through the course of development in any family in which the mother does not assert "her own separate selfhood." Like Chodorow, Benjamin sees defensive male fantasies of omnipotence or denial of the other as the outcome of the attempt of boy children to break free of the mother. Girls' developmental "progress," however, is toward self-abnegation. The feelings associated with this system include female fear of independence, women's attempts to control anxiety about separation through service, and their "longing for recognition" in the midst of a gender-polarized world in which men are subjects, women objects.

The emotional life of women and men becomes central in this paradigm to understanding how feminist transformation will occur. Benjamin suggests marshaling the "longings" for interpersonal recognition in loving relationships as a device for instilling hope for both personal and social change. Her approach remains fundamentally a liberal one, however, in which feelings remain the property of individuals even as she traces, often poetically, the dialectic of feelings between self and other. Her utopian notions about intersubjective recognition notwithstanding, she leaves to others the task of linking the self–other dualism – the splitting of feelings of mastery and submission – to historical and social contexts and specific changes in those which would accompany such interpersonal changes. This is what Alison, Mageo, and Ewing put into practice eloquently in this volume.

Emotion as authentic femininity

An early and still culturally very popular feminist idea about emotion claims it as one of the centers of a revalorized femininity. In this view the dualism of emotion and rationality is not rejected, and the association of women with nature is extolled. Emotion *qua* natural capacity then becomes simultaneously something men fail to have and the sign of women's superiority. Women are advised to resist the repression of emotion that is seen as a form of male dominance (Griffin 1978; Showalter 1977). The classic statement of this view is Griffin's (1978): she sees the domination of women as related or equivalent to the repression of nature, rejects technocratic rationality, and lauds the identification of women with emotion and other aspects of what she associates with untamed nature. Emotion is seen as inherently transgressive.

Where Griffin makes a universal and essential argument, other feminists have focused on feeling as something that becomes female through social learning, but that ought to be reclaimed as a virtue. This is particularly so when the focus is on women's capacity for empathy and other feelings that motivate their caretaking for others (Noddings 1984; Ruddick 1989). Although currently rejected by what is perhaps most academic feminists who have written on the subject, many still draw at least tacitly on the idea of emotion as positive capacity (Haraway 1988; Hochschild 1983; Jaggar 1989; Scheman 1980). Feminist discussions of anger, in particular, seem to be particularly prone to a naturalized and hydraulic view of emotion, as when feminist pedagogues ask how they can "help students [in feminist classrooms] channel their anger in healthy and productive ways" (Lee 1993: 15). Anthropological study of the cross-cultural variation in attributions of emotionality to women and men problematizes the cultural assumption of female emotionality that much Western feminist work draws on. Dalton (chapter 6) gives the example of the Rawa of New Guinea, who generally expect emotion expressiveness from both women and men. Those ethnographic cases also demonstrate how the confession of something like feminist anger might also be see as a social process of simultaneous repression and hyper-surveillance and production of non-angry states.

Emotion as epistemic resource

Many feminist philosophers came to an analysis of emotion through a critique of traditional philosophy of science which heightened the cultural dualism of rationality and emotion and claimed that good science required its practitioner to be "dispassionate."[1] This claim's implicit gender and race politics were brought forward, its roots in the masculinist dreams of Bacon and others identified (e.g., Bordo 1987). Jagger states the case succinctly: the

function [of the myth of the dispassionate investigator], obviously, is to bolster the epistemic authority of the currently dominant groups, composed largely of white men, and to discredit the observations and claims of the currently subordinate groups. . . . The more forcefully and vehemently the latter groups express their observations and claims, the more emotional they appear and so the more easily they are discredited (Jaggar 1989:20).

An alternative feminist epistemology developed (Jagger 1989, Morgan 1983, Nussbaum 1995, Scheman 1990). In doing a sociology of the science of primatology, for example, Haraway (1989) writes about 'love' and 'knowledge' as the two things that those studying primates want from their scientific practice. She uses the notion of 'love' in place of other possibilities, such as desire or motive, and does so to avoid at least two problems from this new feminist epistemological perspective. Her first attempt is to reorient the sociology of science away from presenting all 'non-rationalistic' scientific motives in a negative light (hence 'love' rather than 'projection'). The second goal is to center analysis on a social relation (hence love rather than anxiety) between scientist and primate subject that helps to construct the story told. This method avoids an individualistic portrait in which male desire constitutes scientific practice.

Alison Jagger has coined the phrase "epistemic resource" to characterize emotion's potential role in women's lives. Learning rather than being born to feel as they do, women most often do so in ways that support existing social arrangements (for example when women, including feminists, often feel disgust for their own bodies). Emotions can be "outlaw," however (as when someone feels angry with a sexist joke), or feminist (as when they entail feminist perceptions and ideas). A dialectic between emotion and feminist theory is posited such that critical reflection on emotion becomes a necessary part of a developing feminist theory and feminist practice (not, as Jagger says, just a preliminary "clearing of the decks") : "outlaw emotions . . . are necessary to the development of a critical perspective on the world, but they also presuppose at least the beginnings of such a perspective" (1989:23).

Like Griffin, Jagger edges toward a view that women's emotionality constitutes their strength when she speaks of feelings as part of women's "epistemic advantage." Reflection on emotion is seen as a kind of political theory and practice at which women are generally more adept than men because of their social responsibility for caretaking (a connection which some socio- or psychobiology [e.g., Babchuck, Hames, and Thompson 1985] makes and reduces to genetic code). That is, women, people of color, and other subordinate groups are more likely to experience what she and others have called "outlaw emotions." Women's culturally glorified emotional empathy is radically reconceptualized as a "skill in political analysis" rather than a sign of their intuitive and nurturant virtue.

While the possibilities for emotional self-deception in the subordinate are acknowledged, it is left to Benjamin and others to describe how this occurs.[2] Spelman shows how the language of moral emotions can and has been used self-deceptively when she analyzes how white feminists have used the language of guilt, shame, or regret to focus on their own feelings more than on the harm done to women of color via their race privilege. If, as she claims, emotions are "powerful clues of the ways in which we take ourselves to be implicated in the lives of others and they in ours" (1991:220), then assumptions about one's importance as a white and well-off woman will be reflected in those emotions as well. While theorists vary in the degree to which they focus on the "misrecognition" or ideological distortion of emotion, each makes the claim that emotions can be remade through renaming and might constitute empowering forms of knowledge for feminist purposes.

Emotion as cultural-historical discourses on power

In all of these last three perspectives (rereading emotional development, emotion as authentic femininity, and emotion as epistemic resource), emotions are viewed as tools for collective social change, but in only some are they seen as central to the reproduction of patriarchal social relations. Others have taken on questions of power in a more direct and/or socially and historically contextualized way.

Feminist anthropologists and historians have drawn on the former discipline's standard notion of culture, as well as on the Foucaultian notion of discourses, to expand the questions asked about women and emotionality. The emphasis here shifts to describing and theorizing the connections between emotional life and relations of power (of gender but also and simultaneously of class and race) described in their historical and cultural variations (Abu-Lughod 1986, 1990; Kondo 1990; Lutz 1988, 1990b; Mageo 1996; Maher 1984, Martin 1987, Rosaldo 1984, Scheper-Hughes 1992, Seremetakis 1991, Shields, Steinke, and Koster 1995). Like the theorists just mentioned, they see emotion talk as political, but are more attuned to social structures and political economies. They trace the place of emotion discourse in societies with different configurations of power and different kinds of gender politics emerging from such things as matrilineal descent (Lutz 1988), an ethos of honor in a pastoral, patrilineal segmentary lineage system (Abu-Lughod 1986), and child-bearing and rearing under conditions of extreme privation in a class-stratified society (Scheper-Hughes 1992). Mageo opens new directions in the study of emotion, power, and history by suggesting that the emotional suffering articulated by possessed women in Samoa and elsewhere (e.g. Boddy 1989) be seen not as hysteric symptom but as creative contributions that seek "the resolution of cultural-historical paradoxes suffered by the individual" (1996:61). Such insight on emotional talk as history suffered and its meaning remade could be applied to other work that details the contexts of shifts in emotional norms for women and men in the US over the last several centuries (Cancian 1987; Rotundo 1989; Stearns 1992). This includes important work on how global economic restructuring has entailed historical shifts in the affective requirements of work assigned on the basis of gender (Bulan, Erickson, and Wharton 1997, Hochschild 1983, Ong 1987).

Abu-Lughod, for example, has detailed the deterioration of Awlad Ali Bedouin patrilineal authority with sedentarism and with the advance of the Egyptian state into their community (1990). Key to the erosion of power has been the strategic and often rebellious deployment of love poetry by younger women and men. That emotion is a relatively direct affront to elders for whom control of sexuality via codes of invulnerability and honor is key to maintaining strong bonds among the men of the lineage. Seremetakis (1991) takes a similar aesthetic phenomena – Greek women's funeral laments – and treats them as commentaries on and recoveries of cultural notice of women's labor. The unrecognized work includes agricultural fieldwork as well as women's traditional labor of mourning at funerals. The dynamic of recognition and rebellion is evident in the screaming body of the women during death rituals. The woman is literally made more socially visible and hence powerful, even as she metaphorically leaves society by ripping at her clothes and breaking through other constraints. Finally, Wiss (1994) notes that though racist ideologies led to the scientific dissection of a !Kung woman infamously brought to Europe in the early nineteenth century, the close attention paid to her feelings did not entail interest in her voice.

The cultural concerns of contemporary middle-class feminists are reflected not only in the question of how women can theoretically feel about their young children (see below), but also in a growing historical literature on love, and particularly heterosexual love (Cancian 1987, Ehrenreich 1983, Lewis 1989). While much of this work focuses on norms of behavior, it also generally attends to the social contexts producing such shifts as the narrowing gap in expectations about the ideal emotional profiles of men and women. From a peak of emotional differentiation in the sexes during the Victorian period, increased contacts between women and men outside the family, and the growing labor force participation rates of women, particularly in the 1920s and onward, led to a decline in normative sex differences in anger, fear, and jealousy. It was replaced with concern over socializing both boys and girls for the workplace through such things as an equivalent control of anger (Stearns 1992).

There has also been much work in this vein on depression. This emotional syndrome predominates in women both in the West (Brown and Harris 1978, Nolen-Hoeksema 1990) and cross-culturally (Jenkins, Kleinman, and Good 1991, Strickland 1992). It is associated with situational factors of powerlessness rather than constitutional factors in the most detailed contextualized studies (Brown and Harris 1978), which show poor women are most vulnerable.

Some of the most challenging work on gender, affect, and politics is found in the study of German fascism. The problem is to explain human participation in institutionalized and quotidian evil on a grand scale, and what is relevant to us here is the fact that Nazism and the Holocaust were highly gendered in ways that require attention if we are to understand how gender identities and the emotional investment in them are malleable in changing social circumstances, and how one resists. Koonz' (1987) work takes on the question of how women emotionally responded to Nazi demands that women both leave paid employment as well as collaborate in their anti-Semitic and cultural change projects. Theweleit (1987) examines the problem of German fascist mentality, and draws a picture of men whose fear of women was conflated with and fueled their anti-communism and their attempts to control those whom they considered the "masses."

The widespread use of gendered forms of torture in warfare has also been documented, in conjunction with the emotional discourses it violently shapes (Bunster-Burotto 1994). The horrors of counter-insurgencies, wedded to patriarchy in crisis, have made emotion unspeakable through the shame that attaches to rape and the retraumatizing character of memory itself (see also Jenkins 1995).

Bringing the analysis of militarism and gender home, Krasniewicz' (1992) vivid study of American militarism gives a detailed ethnographic sense of the rage that greeted the feminist peace activists at the Seneca Falls Army Depot. She convincingly suggests that it was their violations of expectations of proper femininity and (hetero)sexuality more than their opposition to nuclear weapons per se that so angered the surrounding community. In this ethnography, emotional response is indexical of the politics of militarist masculinity as well as the conflicts between women within the camp and between camp and village women.[3]

In paying attention to relations of power enacted through emotion discourse, feminist ethnographers have used reflexive analysis to examine how their own fieldwork and writing can unwittingly reproduce, even as they resist, gender relations as they are. Morgan (1983) re-examined her work in a feminist health collective in New England for its tacit acceptance of the epistemology which dichotomizes rationality and emotion. This led her to neglect to take seriously feelings expressed by clinic workers. Reflexive analysis has also been used to highlight differences between the culture under study and the researcher's cultural background of thought and feeling about gender and affect (Kondo 1990,

Lavie 1990, Lutz 1988). Lavie presents a particularly poignant example of the value of this kind of analysis in her description of such a contrast of feelings about circumcision among a Sinai Desert group of Bedouins. Describing the ceremony, her "participant observation," and the operation's aftermath, she tells of the young girls running "panic-stricken" into the sea to stop the bleeding, and her own escape to the edge of the settled area. There she begins vomiting and crying, vomiting and crying, all the while wondering

whether I cry because of pleasures never known and already lost by the girls, or because of their mothers' firm belief in the power the circumcision gives a woman over a man by removing lust, or perhaps because my own sexuality seems diminished as I carefully walk the thin rope stretching between the worlds of Mzeina men and women (1990:146).

The rhetoric and force of Lavie's feelings in this excerpt provide a political analysis that is all the more nuanced and effective in the ambivalence it faces. The political analysis, in other words, is neither simple, reductive, nor Manichean because it (emotionally/cognitively) recognizes the difficulty of feminist evaluation and action in this context, the multiple critical perspectives that merit attention.

Emotion as a form of social labor

Connecting questions of a gendered division of labor with questions of emotional meaning, feminist historians of the West have elaborated on the correspondence between the separation of the workplace and the home under capitalism, the allocation of women to the domestic sphere of unpaid labor, and the ideological split between notions of emotion and interest, expressive and instrumental roles and personalities, and association of women more intensively with the affective side of those dualisms. Over time, the family was reconceptualized as primarily an emotional unit. Women were thereby more firmly associated with both domesticity and affect as they came to stand as the heart of a heartless world. The effects of this include the preservation of women as a reserve pool of labor for business, the reproduction of labor power without cost to the corporate world, and so on. The cultural equation of woman, family, and affect is also reproduced in part through the pursuit of commercial interests, for example the greeting-card and floral industries and the therapeutic industries.

The idea that emotion is a requisite for social life leads to seeing emotion as a form of labor required of women, at least in the modern industrial world. This formulation involves materialist rereadings of cultural feminism's (and to a lesser degree discourse approaches') tendency to focus on representation and to underplay connections between ideologies of gender and emotion and the allocation of resources. Hochschild (1983) has the first and most elaborate discussion of this in her work on airline stewardesses and bank repossession agents. She takes the Marxist notion of exploitation into the psychological realm and allows connections to be made between women's and men's feelings and the division of labor, labor costs, and the reproduction of the labor force and of profit. Her focus is on stewardesses, whose emotional labor consists of smiling pleasantly throughout a flight and making each passenger feel she (standing in for the airline) is happy to serve them. Most service occupations, dominated by women employees, have these emotional requirements. Hochschild also researched repossessors as an occupational group whose emotional requirements are for angry toughness. One of a set of predominately male occupations, its recruitment practices follow from the gender exceptionalism of anger.

Emotional labor is usually unrecognized as such, a mystification that is key to its commercial exploitation (Hochschild 1983). The exploitation process occurs in the household as well, as di Leonardo (1987) demonstrates in describing "the work of kinship" done by Italian-American women. This work involves planning and executing the yearly cycle of greeting cards, buying gifts, and family rituals, particularly as organized between households. These important practices are virtually defined by their evocation and reproduction of affective ties, but are ignored or trivialized as a form of labor. If, moreover, emotion is defined as a natural expression and if women's feelings toward kin are assumed to be naturally positive or maternal, then even more powerful is the ideological incentive to see women's kin work as pleasant or as leisure.

With this same emphasis on emotion as labor, Hochschild (1989) has provocatively described the complex "economy of gratitude" within married middle-class heterosexual couples and its role in sustaining an unequal division of household labor, as that is traditionally defined. This research addresses the problem of some feminist work on women and nurturance that fails to show that " 'altruism' (read compassion) and 'self-interest' (read rationality) are cultural constructions that are not necessarily mutually exclusive" (di Leonardo 1987:452; see also Medick and Sabean 1984). Altruism's association with emotion (such as compassion, love, and fear for others' safety) and self-interest's with cold rationality are another reason to see these redefinitions of the nature of women's labor as key to unmasking the damage done by the dualism of affect and reason.

In political-economic frameworks, emotion is also seen as a resource that – like the commodity under capitalism – can be redistributed (out of the nuclear family, for example) or fetishized. Cvetkovich (1993) shows how this is so in her complex and telling reading of the historical development of sensational literature and its critique in the nineteenth century (and its corollary in mass culture criticism in the twentieth). She shows that the emergence of the middle class in the 1860s and 1870s in Britain is linked to the growth of a large market of readers and writers of so-called sensational literature. What defined the latter for critics was the evocation of emotion in readers, an "unnatural excitement" elicited by reading about predominately female characters engaged in unnatural (often criminal or sexual) acts. Critical focus at the time was less on the social relations indexed (between sexes and classes) than on the emotion itself, which was defined as a problem. The canon was established, then, in part through an opposition between base instinctual, emotional responses to reading and high aesthetic responses, although it was gender and class conflict rather than an autonomous cultural ideology of affect opposed to rationality that fired the critics' behavior and canon formation.

Whether they expressed it or restrained it, the middle classes, like women themselves, were being defined by their relationship to feeling in this way. And, like the increasingly domesticated and privatized middle-class woman's life, affect was defined as a hidden phenomenon. For both women and affect, liberation then seemed to require that the hidden pain or problem be made visible or even a spectacle (something not logically necessary); conservative critics clearly then had to respond negatively to sensational literature. Going beyond literature, Cvetkovich astutely points to the dilemma of drawing attention to concrete instances of emotional suffering in women's lives: doing so "can both call attention to and obscure complex social relations and can both inspire and displace social action" (Cvetkovich 1993:5).

Feelings associated with motherhood in different societies and time periods have often been the center of feminist analysis tacitly using this definition of emotion as labor and resource (e.g., Maher 1984, Scheper-Hughes 1992, Shields, Steinke, and Koster 1995). Scheper-Hughes (1992) contested the normative view of a natural intense attachment between mother and child in her ethnography of Brazilian shantytown women. She traces the emotional injuries of class and race for these women, noting the competition with and indifference towards children that sometimes develops under conditions of privation and racism. Her analysis struggles not to (but sometimes does) reproduce the injunction on women to have that surplus of emotional resource to give to their children, something these Brazilians demonstrably do not have.

Emotion as life on the social margins

Women's life on the social margins can provoke an emotional response or even constitute the idea of the emotional itself by establishing a contrast with those whose mainstream or central place is (mis)taken for rationality. Some theorists have generalized about the emotions/marginality of women as a class, while others have focused on the violence of women's emotions in madness, and the truth or protest in those mad emotions (Chesler 1972, Lavie 1990; points given additional insight by Lachicotte and Scheper-Hughes in this volume in relationship to other disvalued persons, especially those institutionalized on account of it). Chesler (1972) gave a forceful early statement of this perspective, noting that the denial of full human status to women drives some mad. Such madness is essentially an intense experience of female biological, sexual, and cultural castration, and a doomed search for potency. The search often involves "delusions" or displays of physical aggression, grandeur, sexuality, and emotionality. Such traits in women are feared and punished in patriarchal mental asylums (1972:117).

One case of the play between emotions and marginality has been taken up by Seremetakis (1991), who speaks eloquently about Greek peasant women's lives as fragmented ones. Like Chesler, she explores the emotional contexts of the denial to them of the status of full person. She argues for the benefits or uses of the social margins, saying that the fragment "may be marginal, but it is not necessarily dependent, for it is capable of denying recognition to any center" (1991:1). These women's emotions are construed as "transformative," not merely expressive: as a materially powerful body practice, emotional pain or lament can reconstitute the fragmented self into at least "provisional, empowering wholes." The materiality of their emotions, bodies, and pollution is what gives women power. This is especially so given that they are on the margin of the modern Greek state, and so have not experienced the split of the public from the private, affective exchange from economic exchange: they can deploy their tears, as they have noted their urban counterparts cannot, as a sign of those connections between themselves and others. Fragments of "the self [i.e. one's tears] disappear with the absent other" (1991:216) at the funeral, and assert that something has been sundered, including relations between the living and the dead and between women's agricultural work and socially recognized work.

Not surprisingly, these theorists in several instances have been people who have focused on questions of doubled marginality as when Trawick (1990) studies an untouchable woman in South India and Butler (1991) the (Western) lesbian. Both analysts consider the category of the "abject," construed both as a socially excluded person and as a feeling. Both women also make major innovations in discussing the subversive pleasures as well as the pain of being denied full subject status. Butler's writing about the ambivalence or the impossibility of being "comfortably" identified as a lesbian is very suggestive of the problems with precise definitions and identifications of emotions and with standing under marginalized identity categories such as "a woman" or "the emotional." Her argument could be used to contest the idea that a positive project for women and for feminist science should be emotional transparency, that is, a clear sense of and singular quality to one's feelings and politics. Her notion of "gender trouble" can be extended and applied to what can be called "emotion trouble." This latter would highlight the performative aspect of emotion and its ontologically unstable character. Any emotion would be seen as a performance rather than an expression of a determinate underlying psychological or psychosocial phenomenon. Like gender itself in Butler's view, emotion would then be seen as shadowed by the notion of the biologically original feeling for which any instance of emotion becomes then simply a poor imitation.

Definitions and national research agendas: normative center and feminist margin

In the larger scheme of things, the vast majority of research on emotions is conducted within the framework of psychobiological and non-feminist definitions. Social definitions of emotion remain marginal in relationship to the centers of federally funded research, such as the National Institute of Mental Health, an institution ever more fundamentally organized around the brain and hence around the individual as the unit of analysis. Moreover, data on emotion produced in experimental work with (nationality, race, and class-specific) college students are still not treated as non-generalizable, while data on emotion collected ethnographically among African-American women are seen as particularistic and therefore as relatively unfundable. The upshot is that science continues asking some questions and not others about emotion, particularly those having to do with pressing problems facing the social groups most often associated with emotionality.

Even where social definitions of the emotions are taken seriously, the role of feminism in their development and the role of gender in the social are marginalized. It can be no coincidence that intense interest in emotion *per se* in the academy developed in the 1980s with the maturation of the women's movement, and the influx of women and, to a lesser extent, racial minorities into research positions. While these social changes have helped to create the feminist literature just reviewed, normative science has also revalorized emotion as an object worthy of scientific study in this same period. This latter work may be at least partially motivated by the attempt to coopt and evacuate the emotional of association with the female and irrationality. Feminist efforts are marginalized, if not in certain parts of the academy, then certainly in relation to the centers of emotion science in psychology labs. Modleski (1991) analyzes the 1980s in popular culture, which she characterizes sardonically as having deployed a "feminism without women." This general cultural backlash might have its academic corollary in emotion studies without women. It can also be said, however, that the emergence of much feminist literature on emotion from the white middle class has meant that it has often used definitions of emotion that tacitly erase race and class distinctions between women by allowing a conflation of affect, protest, and femininity.

It is the normative science of emotions, however, that is highly influential beyond the academic community, being disseminated through newspaper accounts, women's magazines, and television discussion shows. The effect funnels from the scientists out to the community and back again, something I was struck by again recently in conversation with an academic psychologist. We were together on a panel reviewing federal grant proposals, and she began to tell me about the differences between her two children, her son being much more aggressive than her daughter. She said this initially made her quite anxious and she made great efforts to redirect his behavior in more pacific ways. After she read a bestseller a friend recommended to her entitled *Brain Sex* (Moir and Jessel 1991), however, she has been much less troubled. The book argues from psychological research for the sex-specific hormonal and other biological factors in brain development and behavior. Boys are naturally more aggressive and angry, she and others can conclude, and there is nothing to be done.

On the day I finished the first draft of this chapter, a woman three blocks from my office was shot to death as she tried to escape from an attempted rape. Two decades of feminist work in redefining emotions allows us to ask new questions about the fear and anger, among other things, that made up this event and its largest contexts. It allows new answers, even if the first one is the double negative insight that "There is not nothing to be done," and it allows us to remake emotion definitions and research questions in service to new social relations.

NOTES

Notes to preface

1. But this statement is relative, see Lutz 1990a.

1. Feminist legal theorists have come to some similar conclusions based on their attempts to deconstruct the rationalist legal tactics that have had androcentric outcomes in the courts. They have proposed alternative emotional argumentative modes and reasoning strategies (Watson 1996).
2. Although I treat her work in a separate section below, Arlie Hochschild takes a related perspective when she defines emotions as a straightforward, indisputable "signal from the self." The implication is that women might learn their true feelings through careful reflection and sorting through of the culturally induced noise of a sexist world and its learned secondary emotions (Hochschild 1983).
3. As in other aspects of the field of gender study, however, not all work on the emotions of the twentieth century's militarized masculinity has been feminist in orientation (e.g. Costigliola 1997).

REFERENCES

Abu-Lughod, Lila. 1986. *Veiled Sentiments: Honor and Poetry in a Bedouin Society.* Berkeley: University of California Press.
1990. The Romance of Resistance. In *Beyond the Second Sex: New Directions in the Anthropology of Gender* (P. Sanday and R. Goodenough, eds.). Philadelphia: University of Pennsylvania Press.

Amos, V. and Prathiba Parmar. 1984. Challenging Imperial Feminism. *Feminist Review* 17.

Babchuck, Wayne, Raymond Hames, and Ross Thompson. 1985. Sex Differences in the Recognition of Infant Facial Expressions of Emotion: The Primary Caretaker Hypothesis. *Ethology and Sociobiology* 6:89–101.

Behar, Ruth. 1990. Rage and Redemption: Reading the Life Story of a Mexican Marketing Woman. *Feminist Studies* 16:223–258.

Benjamin, Jessica. 1988. *The Bonds of Love: Psychoanalysis, Feminism, and the Problem of Domination.* New York: Pantheon Books.

Boddy, Janice. 1989. *Wombs and Alien Spirits: Women, Men, and Zar Cult in Northern Sudan.* Madison: University of Wisconsin Press.

Bordo, Susan. 1987. *The Flight to Objectivity: Essays on Cartesianism and Culture.* Albany: State University of New York Press.

Bourdieu, Pierre. 1988. *Homo Academicus* (Peter Collier, trans.). Cambridge: Polity Press in association with Blackwell.

Broverman, I.K., D. M. Broverman, and F.E. Clarkson. 1970. Sex Role Stereotypes and Clinical Judgements of Mental Health. *Journal of Consulting and Clinical Psychology* 34:1–7.

Brown, George and Tirril Harris. 1978. *Social Origins of Depression: A Study of Psychiatric Disorder in Women.* New York: The Free Press.

Brumberg, Joan Jacobs. 1997. *The Body Project: An Intimate History of American Girls.* New York: Random House.

Bulan, Heather Ferguson, Rebecca J. Erickson, and Amy S. Wharton. 1997. Doing for Others on the Job: The Affective Requirements of Service Work, Gender, and Emotional Well-being. *Social Problems* 44(2):235–256.

Bunster-Burotto, Ximena. 1994. Surviving Beyond Fear: Women and Torture in Latin America. In *Women and Violence* (Miranda Davies, ed.). London: Zed Books.

Burack, Cynthia. 1994. *The Problem of the Passions: Feminism, Psychoanalysis, and Social Theory.* New York: New York University Press.

Butler, Judith. 1991. Imitation and Gender Insubordination. In *Inside/Out: Lesbian Theories, Gay Theories* (Diana Fuss, ed.). New York: Routledge.

Cancian, Francesca. 1987. *Love in America.* Cambridge: Cambridge University Press.

Chesler, Phyllis. 1972. *Women and Madness.* New York: Avon Books.

Chodorow, Nancy. 1978. *The Reproduction of Mothering: Psychoanalysis and the Sociology of Gender.* Berkeley: University of California Press.

Chun, Lin. 1995. Toward a Chinese Feminism. *Dissent*, Fall:477–485.

Collins, Patricia Hill. 1991. *Black Feminist Thought: Knowledge, Consciousness, and the Politics of Empowerment.* New York: Routledge.

Costigliola, Frank. 1997. Unceasing Pressure for Penetration: Gender, Pathology, and Emotion in George Kennan's Formation of the Cold War. *The Journal of American History* 83(4):1309–1339.

Cvetkovich, Ann. 1993. *Mixed Feelings: Feminism, Mass Culture, and Victorian Sensationalism.* New Brunswick, NJ: Rutgers University Press.

di Leonardo, Micaela. 1987. The Female World of Cards and Holidays: Women, Families and the Work of Kinship. *Signs* 12(3):440–453.

Ehrenreich, Barbara. 1983. *The Hearts of Men: American Dreams and the Flight from Commitment.* New York: Doubleday.

Ehrenreich, Barbara, and Deidre English. 1978. *For Her Own Good: 150 Years of the Experts' Advice to Women.* Garden City, NY: Anchor Press/Doubleday.

Ellis, Havelock. 1929. *Man and Woman.* Boston: Houghton-Mifflin.

Fine, Michelle, and S. M. Gordon. 1991. Effacing the Centre and the Margins: Life at the Intersection of Psychology and Feminism. *Feminism and Psychology* 1:19–27.

Frye, Marilyn. 1983. A Note on Anger. in *The Politics of Reality: Essays in Feminist Theory.* Trumansburg, NY: The Crossing Press.

Gilman, Sander. 1986. Black Bodies, White Bodies: Toward an Iconography of Female Sexuality in Late Nineteenth Century Art, Medicine, and Literature. In *Race, Writing and Difference* (H. Gates, ed.). Chicago: University of Chicago Press.

Gottlieb, Alma. 1988. American Premenstrual Syndrome: A Mute Voice. *Anthropology Today* 4(6):10–13.

Griffin, Susan. 1978. *Woman and Nature.* New York: Harper and Row.

Haraway, Donna. 1989. *Primate Visions: Gender, Race, and Nature in the World of Modern Science.* New York: Routledge.

Harding, Sandra. 1987. Introduction: Is There a Feminist Method? In *Feminism and Methodology* (S. Harding, ed.). Bloomington: Indiana University Press.

Hochschild, Arlie 1975. The Sociology of Feeling and Emotion: Selected Possibilities. In *Another Voice* (Marcia Millman and Rosabeth Kanter, eds.). New York: Anchor.

1983. *The Managed Heart: Commercialization of Human Feeling.* Berkeley: University of California Press.

1989. The Economy of Gratitude. In *The Sociology of Emotions* (D.D. Franks and E.D. McCarthy, eds.). Greenwich, CT: JAI Press.

Hull, Gloria, Patricia Bell Scott, and Barbara Smith. 1982. *All the Women are White, All the Blacks are Men, but Some of Us are Brave: Black Women's Studies.* Old Westbury, NY: Feminist Press.

Jaggar, Alison M. 1989. Love and Knowledge: Emotion In Feminist Epistemology. *Inquiry* 32:151–176.

Jenkins, Janis H. 1996. Women's Experience of Trauma and Political Violence. In *Gender and Health: An International Perspective* (Carolyn Sargent and Caroline Brettel, eds.). Upper Saddle, NJ: Prentice Hall.

Jenkins, Janis, Arthur Kleinman, and Byron Good. 1991. Cross-cultural Aspects of Depression. In *Advances in Affective Disorders: Theory and Research* (J. Becker and A. Kleinman, eds.). Volume 1. *Psychosocial Aspects.* Mahwah, NJ: Lawrence Erlbaum.

Kondo, Dorinne. 1990. *Crafting Selves: Power, Gender, and Discourses of Identity in a Japanese Workplace.* Chicago: University of Chicago Press.

Koonz, Claudia. 1987. *Mothers in the Fatherland: Women, the Family and Nazi Politics.* New York: St. Martin's Press.

Krasniewicz, Louise. 1992. *Nuclear Summer: The Clash of Communities at the Seneca Women's Peace Encampment.* Ithaca, NY: Cornell University Press.

Lam, Maivan Clech. 1995. Feeling Foreign in Feminism. *Signs* 19:865–93.

Lavie, Smadar. 1990. *The Poetics of Military Occupation: Mzeina Allegories of Bedouin Identity Under Israeli and Egyptian Rule.* Berkeley: University of California Press.

Leavitt, Stephen C. 1995. Political Domination and the Absent Oppressor: Images of Europeans in Bumbita Arapesh Narratives. *Ethnology* 34:177–189.

Lee, Janet. 1993. Teaching Feminism: Anger, Despair and Self Growth. *Feminist Teacher* 7(2):15–18.

Lewis, J. 1989. Mother's Love: The Construction of an Emotion In Nineteenth Century America. In *Social History and Issues in Human Consciousness: Some Interdisciplinary Connections* (A.E. Barnes and P.N. Stearns, eds.). New York: New York University Press.

Lutz, Catherine. 1988. *Unnatural Emotions: Everyday Sentiments on a Micronesian Atoll and Their Challenge to Western Theory.* Chicago: University of Chicago Press.

1990a. The Erasure of Women's Writing. In *Sociocultural Anthropology.* 17:611–627.

1990b. Engendered Emotion: Gender, Power and the Rhetoric of Emotional Control in American Discourse. In *Language and the Politics of Emotion* (C. Lutz and L. Abu-Lughod, eds.). Cambridge: Cambridge University Press.

Mageo, Jeannette Marie. 1996. Spirit Girls and Marines: Possession and Ethnopsychiatry as Historical Discourse in Samoa. *American Ethnologist* 23(1):61–82.

Maher, Virginia. 1984. Possession and Dispossession: Maternity and Mortality in Morocco. In *Interest and Emotion* (H. Medick and D.W. Sabean, eds.). Cambridge: Cambridge University Press.

Martin, Emily. 1987. *The Woman in the Body.* Boston: Beacon.

Miller, Nancy K. 1991. *Getting Personal: Feminist Occasions and Other Autobiographical Acts.* New York: Routledge.

Modleski, Tania. 1991. *Feminism Without Women: Culture and Criticism in a "Postfeminist" Age.* New York: Routledge.

Moir, Anne and David Jessel. 1991. *Brain Sex: The Real Difference Between Men and Women.* New York: Carol Publishing Group.

Morgan, Sandra. 1983. Towards a Politics of 'Feelings': Beyond the Dialectic of Thought and Action. *Women's Studies* 10:203–23.

Noddings, Nel. 1984. *Caring: A Feminine Approach to Ethics and Moral Education.* Berkeley: University of California Press.

Nolen-Hoeksema, S. 1990. *Sex Differences in Depression.* Stanford: Stanford University Press.

Nussbaum, Martha. 1995. *Women, Culture, and Development: A Study of Human Capabilities.* Oxford: Oxford University Press.

Ong, Aihwa. 1987. *Spirits of Resistance and Capitalist Discipline: Factory Women in Malaysia.* Albany: State University of New York Press.

Perin, Constance. 1988. *Belonging in America: Reading Between the Lines.* Madison: University of Wisconsin Press.

Pfister, Joel and Nancy Schnog, eds. 1997. *Inventing the Psychological: Toward a Cultural History of Emotional Life in America.* New Haven, CT: Yale University Press.

Rosaldo, Michele. 1984. Toward an Anthropology of Self and Feeling. In *Culture Theory: Essays on Mind, Self and Emotion* (R. A. Shweder and R. LeVine, eds.). Cambridge: Cambridge University Press.

Rotundo, E. A. 1989. Romantic Friendship: Male Intimacy and Middle Class Youth in the Northern United States, 1800–1900. *Journal of Social History* 23:1–26.

Ruddick, Sara. 1989. *Maternal Thinking: Towards a Politics of Peace.* Boston: Beacon.

Scheman, Naomi. 1980. Anger and the Politics of Naming. In *Women and Language in Literature and Society* (S. McConnell-Ginet, R. Borker and N. Furman, eds.). New York: Praeger.

Scheper-Hughes, Nancy. 1992. *Death Without Weeping: The Violence of Everyday Life in Brazil.* Berkeley: University of California Press.

Seremetakis, C. Nadia. 1991. *The Last Word: Women, Death and Divination in Inner Mani.* Chicago: University of Chicago Press.

Shields, Stephanie. 1987. Women, Men, and the Dilemma of Emotion. In *Sex and Gender* (P. Shaver and C. Hendrick, eds.). Newbury Park, CA: Sage Publications.

Shields, Stephanie, Pamela Steinke, and Beth Koster. 1995. The Doublebind of Caregiving: Representation of Gendered Emotion in American Advice Literature. *Sex Roles: A Journal of Research* 33:467–89.

Showalter, Elaine. 1977. *A Literature of Their Own.* Princeton: Princeton University Press.

Silver, Brenda R. 1991. The Authority of Anger: *Three Guineas* as a Case Study. *Signs* 16(2):340–70.

Smith-Rosenberg, Carroll. 1975. The Female World of Love and Ritual: Relations Between Women in 19th Century America. *Signs* 1:1–29.

Spelman, Elizabeth V. 1989. Anger and Insubordination. In *Women, Knowledge and Reality: Explorations in Feminist Philosophy* (Ann Garry and Marilyn Pearsall, eds.). Boston: Unwin Hyman.

1991. The Virtue of Feeling and the Feeling of Virtue. In *Feminist Ethics* (Claudia Card,ed.), pp. 213–232. Lawrence: University Press of Kansas.

Stearns, Peter. 1992. Gender and Emotion: A Twentieth Century Transition. *Social Perspectives on Emotion.* Vol. 1:127–60.

Strickland, Bonnie. 1992. Women and Depression. *Current Directions in Psychological Science* 1(4):132–35.

Theweleit, Klaus. 1987. *Male Fantasies. Vol. I: Women, Floods, Bodies, History.* Minneapolis: University of Minnesota Press.

Tompkins, Jane. 1985. *Sensational Designs: The Cultural Work of American Fiction.* New York: Oxford University Press.

Traube, Elizabeth G. 1992. *Dreaming Identities: Class, Gender, and Generation in 1980s Hollywood Movies.* Boulder, CO: Westview Press.

Trawick, Margaret. 1990. Untouchability and the Fear of Death in a Tamil Song. In *Language and the Politics of Emotion* (C. Lutz and L. Abu-Lughod, eds.). Cambridge: Cambridge University Press.

Watson, Barbara. 1996. The Psychosocial Courtroom: Towards a New Theory of Argumentation. *Canadian Journal of Law and Society* 11(1):99–123.

Wiss, Rosemary. 1994. Lipreading: Remembering Saartjie Baartman. *Australian Journal of Anthropology* 5(1–2):11–40.

Index

Abu-Lughod, Lila, 8, 20 n. 10, 166 nn. 11 & 14, 203–204
addressivity, 54
agency, 49, 122, 166 n. 13 & 15, 194, 199–200
  and identifications, 60–62, 65
  and power, 2, 4–13, 15, 17, 20 n. 8
  and self models, 141–143, 147–158, 160–164
Allison, Anne, x–xi, 11–12, 14, 16, 18, 19, 21 n. 17, 65 n. 13, 123, 141–142, 194
Althusser, Louis, 111 n. 3
architectonics (of expression), 61
authority
  and legal discourse, 94–99, 105, 109–111, 111 nn. 2 & 3
  and power, 177, 181–184, 188, 192, 202–204
  and orchestration, 55–56, 59–61, 65 n. 14
  figures, 32, 109
  state, 97, 105, 109–111, 111 n. 2, 122–223, 181
autonomy, 14, 48, 106, 108, 129, 145–146, 200

Bakhtin, Mikhail M, 6, 10–11, 48–62, 62 n. 1, 63 n. 7, 65 nn. 12, 13 & 14
Benjamin, Jessica, 21 n. 17, 81, 200, 203
Benjamin, Walter, 30, 33
bipolar affective disorder (manic-depression), 10, 50–51, 58, 61
bodies, 2–12, 14, 17, 21 n. 17, 60, 65 n. 12, 95, 112, 185, 196, 202, 209
  and play, 72, 79, 81–82, 83–88
  and violence, 29–30, 36, 39, 42–44
  in Papua New Guinea, 122, 125–127
  in Samoa, 144, 154–158, 164, 166 n. 16
borderline personality disorder, 10, 48, 51–54, 59–61, 64 nn. 10 & 11
Bourdieu, Pierre, 195
  and bodily hexis, 29
  and creative models, 147
  and praxis, 6–7
  and strategies, 49, 64 n. 12

and symbolic violence, 30–31, 34–35, 65 n. 14
Butler, Judith, 209–210

cargo cult, 12, 14, 16, 18, 117–123, 132–134, 136
changes, cultural, 205
Chatterjee, Partha, 147, 166 n. 13
Chesler, Phyllis, 208–209
children, 14–17, 31, 33–40, 71–89, 105, 142, 145, 148, 198, 204
  in Papua New Guinea, 117, 122–123
  in Samoa, 155–164, 166 n. 12, 167 n. 27
  of immigrants, 95–96
Seltaman, 184, 188
Christianity (Christianization), 132, 153–164, 167 n. 23, 186, 191
citizenship, 34, 40, 95
class, 20, 32–35, 38–41, 44, 57, 94, 97, 100, 148, 164, 178
  and emotion, 196–198, 203–204, 208–210
colonialism, 6, 12–14, 18–19, 117–136, 141–143, 147–150, 154–158, 162, 167 n. 25, 168 n. 46
compartmentalization, 93, 96–97, 103, 109–111
consciousness, 6, 21 n. 17, 49, 56, 61, 66, 134, 144
  and inner activity, 53–54
  legal, 96–97
  and double bind, 119, 132–136
  and metaphoric substitution, 120, 123–125, 134–135
  disorder, 135
counter-identity, 48
counter-memory, 48
creativity, x, xi, 14, 15, 19, 48, 55, 94, 147, 162–163, 194, 204
  and energy, 128
  creative models, 143, 147, 160–164, 165 n. 1
  potential for, 73
critical theory, 1, 4, 8